Welcoming Linguistic Diversity in
Early Childhood Classrooms

PARENTS' AND TEACHERS' GUIDES
Series Editor: Colin Baker, *Bangor University, UK*

This series provides immediate advice and practical help on topics where parents and teachers frequently seek answers. Each book is written by one or more experts in a style that is highly readable, non-technical and comprehensive. No prior knowledge is assumed: a thorough understanding of a topic is promised after reading the appropriate book.

Full details of all the books in this series and of all our other publications can be found on http://www.multilingual-matters.com, or by writing to Multilingual Matters, St Nicholas House, 31–34 High Street, Bristol BS1 2AW, UK.

PARENTS' AND TEACHERS' GUIDES
Series Editor: Colin Baker, *Bangor University, UK*

Welcoming Linguistic Diversity in Early Childhood Classrooms

Learning from International Schools

Edited by
Edna Murphy

MULTILINGUAL MATTERS
Bristol • Buffalo • Toronto

Library of Congress Cataloging in Publication Data
A catalog record for this book is available from the Library of Congress.
Welcoming Linguistic Diversity in Early Childhood Classrooms: Learning from International Schools/Edited by Edna Murphy.
Parents' and Teachers' Guides: 13
1. Language arts (Early childhood). 2. Early childhood education--Cross-cultural studies. 3. Child development--Cross-cultural studies. 4. Multicultural education. I. Murphy, Edna.
LB1139.5.L35W35 2011
372.6–dc22 2011000610

British Library Cataloguing in Publication Data
A catalogue entry for this book is available from the British Library.

ISBN-13: 978-1-84769-347-1 (hbk)
ISBN-13: 978-1-84769-346-4 (pbk)

Multilingual Matters
UK: St Nicholas House, 31–34 High Street, Bristol BS1 2AW, UK.
USA: UTP, 2250 Military Road, Tonawanda, NY 14150, USA.
Canada: UTP, 5201 Dufferin Street, North York, Ontario M3H 5T8, Canada.

The policy of Multilingual Matters/Channel View Publications is to use papers that are natural, renewable and recyclable products, made from wood grown in sustainable forests. In the manufacturing process of our books, and to further support our policy, preference is given to printers that have FSC and PEFC Chain of Custody certification. The FSC and/or PEFC logos will appear on those books where full certification has been granted to the printer concerned.

Typeset by Techset Composition Ltd, Salisbury, UK.
Printed and bound in Great Britain by the MPG Books Group.

Contents

Section 2

Section 3

Preface

JOURNEY'S END: WELCOMING YOUNG ENGLISH LANGUAGE LEARNERS TO THE CLASSROOM

One September day, many decades ago, when there were more American and British schools abroad than international ones, a small American school in London was suddenly faced with a large influx of Iranian students precipitated by the overthrow of the Shah. This was the first, but not the last time that 'foreign' students sought enrollment in this and many similar schools around the world. The trend continues to the present day, although now its cause is not usually related to a coup d'état, but rather to the increase of global trading and the widespread notion that the young are more apt to have a better career if they are able to speak and understand a widely used language such as English.

This increase in the number of non-English speakers accepted in American and British schools abroad was also made possible by the fall in numbers of English-speaking ex-pats looking for schools (and sometimes founding new ones) in which their children could continue their education. As the imbalance grew, most schools began to reassess their mission, many deciding to include the word 'international' in their name to reflect the change. What this shift in demographics signalled to schools early on was the need for specialists to teach English to children with little or no knowledge of the language so that they could begin to participate in the full educational program of the school. English as a second language (ESL) had arrived.

Most ESL training at that time was designed to meet the needs of businessmen working abroad, and the first ESL teachers working in schools had to learn on the job. It took a few years for the appropriate training to become available, and, even now, teachers must keep on learning as the field continues to grow. The way to deliver an ESL program seems not to have changed very much over the years; what has changed is everything else that should go along with it for those who arrive at the school with no knowledge of the language of instruction. The emphasis in the beginning was, and in a large number of schools still is, simply on the teaching of English. Teachers were not expected to concern themselves with native languages. As a Head might say to the parent of an ESL student inquiring about keeping up the first language: 'As we have 20 (or 33 or 75) languages represented here, there is simply no way … .' This response seemed to have some merit at the time – at least it was an attempt to explain why the school did not undertake the teaching of first languages. It is, however, no longer an acceptable response.

THE FIRST-LANGUAGE CHALLENGE

We are often reminded that a child's first language is not fully established until the age of five (or three, four, six or seven, depending on the book you read) and that neglecting the native tongue carries the risk of anything from inadequate development in both native and additional languages, to stunted cognitive growth, or both. We can no longer discharge our obligation to children simply by telling parents that it is up to them to keep up the child's home language, especially when many parents harbour the misconception that this would interfere with their child's acquisition of English. We must begin to look more deeply into what effect first-language deprivation has on children's development. We must listen to those calling for change before we allow these thousands of children to pay the price of our ignorance. We must acknowledge the importance of all first languages in the classroom and see that the conversation between school and parents continues.

Several years ago I was one of the 15 ESL and mainstream educators who were invited to Bath University to discuss possible lines of research in international education. Each of us was asked to bring a research question for the group to discuss. Many years later, the only one that has remained fixed in my memory is the following from a then Kindergarten teacher: 'How can I teach a class of 18 five-year-olds, when only two of them are native English speakers, and among the other 16 there are few instances of a shared language?' And, she could have added, 'with many of them in a state of shock because of their recent move to yet another "foreign" country'.

My first thought was to try to imagine the first day of school for those children, bursting into the room speaking a variety of languages and filled with a sense of adventure. Then, the inevitable silence. No one, they would soon come to realize, could understand a word they were saying, including the teacher. They would begin to see that the world they had entered was an alien one. Children instinctively want to fit in and they would soon conclude that to do so they would have to remain silent, keeping their language to themselves, perhaps even hiding the packed lunch they brought from home because it did not resemble the food that other children were eating.

My second thought was of a Learning Disabilities teacher who once told me how puzzling it was that a few children who had done reasonably well in their early years at school and had apparently mastered social banter in two and sometimes three languages, regularly fetched up in the fifth or sixth grade as learning disabled. The common handicap identified in these children was their inability to think abstractly. Today, we have come to realize that such a condition might not have been an inborn learning disability, but rather that it was more likely to have been precipitated by the loss of their first language in pursuit of the second.

There are remedies for the first-language challenge. Schools have different capacities and different populations. Some, whose intake is usually confined to children from three or four language backgrounds, could, should and often do offer bilingual programs in those languages. For the majority of international schools that regularly take in a far wider and ever-changing linguistic mix, serious thought must be given to dealing with first-language development in other ways. This is the most recent challenge presented to teachers, both ESL and mainstream, and many have already taken steps to meet it.

THE ROLE OF TEACHERS AND ADMINISTRATORS

Once schools acknowledge the importance of bringing the whole child into the classroom, cultivating the first language and culture of every student, it will inevitably fall to classroom and specialist teachers to lead the way. Teachers, however, cannot assure its continuity in the school. Inevitably they retire or move on to other schools; or enrolment grows, forcing the hiring of new staff. Any number of things might happen to precipitate the hiring of uninitiated teachers, who would then spend a long time catching up.

What is required is a whole-school reorientation, starting with the rethinking of the curriculum at a deeper level. Some schools have already begun to do this, and some indeed have completed the process. It is obvious that every teacher in the school must contribute to the task, by helping, for example, to create a school Language Policy which would recognize and support the many languages and cultures represented there. The school administration must obviously be active in support of such initiatives, making sure that the school's philosophy and mission statement underpin and support them. Such policy changes have implications for teacher training: experienced teachers could be enlisted to train newcomers, professional help could be brought in from outside the school, and selected teachers could benefit from relevant conference offerings. For new teachers, an introduction to the school's commitment to multilingualism and multiculturalism should be a regular feature of the first week of school.

THE BOOK'S PURPOSE

Promoting the spread of good practice in schools with young children from many different linguistic and cultural backgrounds is the main purpose of this book. It was written by teachers for teachers, especially for those new to this kind of inclusive education. Many of the chapters describe in detail the different successful strategies used for teaching children English while at the same time keeping alive and in the classroom their first languages and as many aspects of their cultures as teachers can work into the program.

The book is divided into three sections. After an introductory chapter by Professor Fred Genesee debunking some prevalent misconceptions, Section 1 consists of descriptions by veteran teachers of first- and second-language programs as they are found today in particular schools and used throughout the school year. Section 2 consists of chapters dealing with first- and second-language teaching through an association with other subject areas such as PE and mathematics; or in a particular way, such as teaching children with learning disabilities, teaching through sign language and so on. Section 3 includes important related topics such as the role of Mother Tongue Coordinator, writing a Language Policy and talking to and listening to parents.

CONCLUSIONS

Teachers wanting to improve their teaching of young English language learners (ELLs) will find in this book the various ways that experienced teachers over the years have responded to the challenge of teaching English while encouraging children to share some of their own language and culture with their classmates and teacher. They are offered here in the belief that the hard-won knowledge they have accumulated must not be confined to their classrooms alone, but shared with the community of teachers all over the world who face the same challenges.

It is not a book to be read from beginning to end in one sitting. Some chapters overlap in a few content areas, endorsing the view that some things cannot be said often enough. Most chapters, however, have a particular emphasis or address a particular issue, and readers will find them a good resource for solving a host of different problems.

The willingness of so many busy educators to take the time to contribute to this book did not surprise me: I have worked with them long enough to know that they would volunteer gladly. Their experience, accumulated over years of thoughtful practice, will enable readers to employ successful methods of communicating with, and teaching and learning from their young ELLs from the start. And it must be said that the other beneficiaries of the successful teaching in such multilingual classes are the native English speakers themselves, who, through these children, will be introduced to the languages and cultures of parts of the world they might otherwise have never known about.

I would like to thank my brother James Golden, a computer wiz who guided me through the final stages of putting the book together, and finally to pay tribute to the very many researchers working out of universities the world over whose names and works are listed after each chapter. Not least among these is Professor Fred Genesee who has kindly taken the time to read the final copy of the book and to contribute an introductory chapter. They have made it possible for those on the front line to realize and fulfil their obligation to the ELLs in their schools. It is to them and to the thousands of teachers, working their magic around the world to produce the next generation of truly multilingual children, that this book is respectfully dedicated.

Edna Murphy
March 2011

Introduction

FRED GENESEE

THE LANGUAGE DEVELOPMENT OF ENGLISH LANGUAGE LEARNERS: DEBUNKING SOME COMMON BELIEFS

Educators are increasingly faced with the challenge of educating young students who are not proficient in the language of schooling – the subject of this book. Historically, these challenges have been faced primarily in school contexts with immigrant students or children of immigrant parents who have not yet mastered the language of the community in which they live. For a variety of reasons, not the least of which is globalization, the challenges of educating second-language students are present in an ever-growing number of school contexts. For example, in Canada, where I work and live, there has been a strong demand on the part of English-speaking parents for their children to learn French through immersion programs where all or most instruction during the primary grades is delivered in French. Also in Canada and in other 'new world' settings (like the United States, Australia and New Zealand), there has been a longstanding challenge of how best to educate children from aboriginal backgrounds who come to school speaking an indigenous language that differs from the societally dominant language used by teachers in their schools; for example, students who live in Northern Canada and speak Inuktitut at home but are educated in French or English.

International schools are likewise welcoming a growing number of second-language learners into their classrooms. Many of these students are members of the community in which the school is located thus speak the language, for example, German-speaking students attending the Frankfurt International School or

Italian-speaking children attending Marymount International School in Rome. Many are the children of foreign or international families from around the world who are residing temporarily in a foreign country for business or personal reasons and have decided to enrol their children in an English-speaking international school.

Thinking about how best to educate ELLs has often been shaped by a number of beliefs about young children's language-learning abilities, in particular their ability to learn a second language (L2). In this brief preface, I would like to review a number of these beliefs and how they often shape educational practices and policies for ELLs. I also want to review current research findings that address these beliefs. The ones I have selected to review are, in my experience, widespread and quite influential – many classroom teachers as well as school administrators subscribe to these assumptions and make important programmatic and instructional decisions based on them. It is important, therefore, to determine whether current scientific evidence supports these beliefs or whether, in contrast, alternative practices should be considered that align with the evidence. The beliefs that I review are: (1) younger is better when it comes to learning a second language; (2) young learners can learn an L2 'naturally' and, therefore, need minimal direct or systematic support to acquire it for schooling and (3) the use of ELLs' L1s is not necessary for the effective learning of English as a second language (ESL) and, in fact, use of the L1 can impede mastery of the L2 because it takes away time that could be devoted to learning the language of the school. These interrelated beliefs have important implications for planning and delivery of language and academic instruction for ELLs, such as how early in their schooling they should be immersed in English; whether they should be given instructional support in their L1 while they learn English; how much and what kind of instruction they should be given in English to ensure that they acquire the high levels of proficiency they need to master increasingly demanding academic objectives; and, finally, whether their academic achievement should be assessed in the same ways and to the same standards as native English-speaking students.

The research that is reviewed in the next sections concerns students who acquire an additional language after their first language has already been established – sometime after three or four years of age. Research on children who acquire two languages simultaneously (i.e. simultaneous bilinguals) is not considered here (see Genesee, 2010, for a review of that research).

YOUNGER IS BETTER

It is widely believed that young children are effective second-language learners and, therefore, that L2 acquisition will proceed more quickly and effectively the younger the learners. This assumption is associated with the widespread practice of submersing ELLs in L2-programs with minimal instructional support for acquiring the L2. Indeed, many parents of ELLs, especially immigrant parents from minority language backgrounds, believe that the best way to support their children's education is to use English at home and discourage their children from using the home language; in this way it is thought that the children will have a head start learning the school language.

Indeed, there is research evidence that, other things being equal, children are more likely to attain native-like levels of oral proficiency, or at least higher levels of proficiency, in an L2 in the long run than learners who begin to learn an L2 when older. Twelve to 15 years of age is often thought to be the critical period before which L2 learning is easy and most effective (Long, 1990). However, there is no consensus on how early is early enough for the advantages of an early start to learning the L2 to be realized. Moreover, people's views of the advantages of an early start to L2 learning are based largely on comparisons between child L2-learners and adolescent or adult L2-learners – that is learners who begin learning another language before the critical period versus learners who begin after the critical period. The picture is different when findings from research that compares younger versus older school-age children are examined. In an early review of research on age and L2 learning, Krashen *et al.* (1979) found, contrary to common belief, that older learners actually make faster initial progress in learning an L2 than younger school-age learners. My own research on Canadian students in L2 immersion programs has shown that students in late immersion programs in Grades 7 and 8 sometimes achieve the same levels of proficiency in an L2 as students who begin immersion in Kindergarten, despite the fact that early immersion students have two to three times more exposure to the new language. The impressive performance of the late immersion students in these programs attests to their effectiveness as L2 learners. The advantage that older students have when it comes to L2 learning in school is not limited to immersion-type programs since this has also been reported in evaluations of less intensive forms of second-language instruction (e.g. Burstall *et al.*, 1974, in Britain).

There are a number of reasons why older students can make such rapid initial progress in acquiring L2 in school. First, older students have the benefit of a well-developed L1 and, in particular, often have fully developed, or well developed, L1 literacy skills. Literacy skills acquired in one language can facilitate literacy development in another (Genesee & Geva, 2006; Riches & Genesee, 2006), especially if the languages are typologically similar and/or have similar orthographies (French, Spanish and English, for example). Furthermore, older students may be faster L2 learners than younger students because language teaching and learning in school settings are generally abstract and context reduced, to use Cummins' terminology (Cummins, 1981), and thus probably call on learning strategies that are better developed in older learners. In any case, younger is not always better when it comes to L2 learning in school and, in fact, delaying ESL instruction until after the primary grades can result in language-learning outcomes that are just as good as those for students who begin learning the new language at the start of school (see Lindholm-Leary & Borsato, 2006, for a review of studies on bilingual programs for ELLs in the United States). In light of these findings, educators and parents should be encouraged to help ELLs continue to develop their home language because there is no evidence that this will detract from their acquisition of English and, as we will see shortly, it could in fact facilitate it. Many of the chapters in this book make a similar point.

YOUNG STUDENTS ARE NATURALLY EFFECTIVE L2 LEARNERS

According to a related belief, young second-language learners are effective because they have innate natural language-learning abilities that they can apply to acquiring another language in school. Thus, it is believed, they can not only acquire the language quickly but also effortlessly with minimal direct or systematic instruction, much as children acquire their first language. Older students, in contrast, lose these natural language-learning abilities and, as a result, it is thought they are less efficient and less effective. Is it because of these beliefs that educators usually stress the importance of early immersion and education in the dominant language of the community? What does the research evidence say?

Despite widely held beliefs about the efficiency of young second-language learners, evidence indicates that the acquisition of an L2 in school-age students is a complex process that takes considerable time, time during which they are also expected to cope with academic instruction delivered through the new language. It takes elementary school students much longer to acquire full competence in a new language than most people imagine. Saunders and O'Brien (2006) carried on a detailed and thorough review of research conducted since 1980 on the oral language development of ELLs in the United States.

They concluded that evidence indicates that ELLs seldom achieve ratings of 'generally proficient' (but not native-like) even by grade 3 and, in fact, none of the studies they reviewed reported average ratings of 'native-like' until Grade 5. In a longitudinal study of 24 ELLs in Edmonton, Canada, Paradis (2006) found that even after 21 months of exposure to English in all-English schools, only 40% of the students performed within the same range as native speakers on a test of grammatical competence, 65% on receptive vocabulary and 90% on story grammar. Yet, other studies indicate that it can take ELLs between five and seven years to achieve native-like proficiency in aspects of English that are linked to the academic curriculum (August & Hakuta, 1997; Cummins, 1981; Lindholm-Leary & Borsato, 2006; Thomas & Collier, 2002). In a review of research on child L2 learners, Paradis concluded that attaining 'oral language proficiency in the L2 at par with native speakers can take most of the elementary school years' (2006: 401). Moreover, there is considerable variation in the rate of L2 development among ELLs, so that some take even longer than these average times. The estimates of the time required to achieve native-like proficiency in an L2 are sobering when viewed in the context of the other challenges that ELLs face – including the mastering of academic subject matter and skills, adaptation to a new culture and acquisition of the social skills they need to get along with and integrate with mainstream students in the school. These results should not be interpreted to mean that ELLs cannot do well in all-English programs until they acquire full native-like proficiency; or that they should not be taught grade-appropriate challenging academic material. Rather, they indicate that ELLs could benefit from systematic and sustained instruction in English that is tailored to their particular language-learning needs in order to accelerate their acquisition of English for academic purposes.

Increasingly educators and educational researchers recognize the distinction between language for social communication and language for academic purposes. Language for social communication is the kind of language that ELLs learn from their peers – at school or outside school. Language for academic purposes is 'the language that is used by teachers and students for the purposes of acquiring new knowledge and skills … imparting new information, describing abstract ideas, and developing students' conceptual understanding' (Chamot & O'Malley, 1994: 40). To expand on Chamot and O'Malley's definition, academic language refers to the specialized vocabulary, grammar, discourse/textual and functional skills associated with academic instruction. It is the language skills that are necessary to master academic subject matter. Academic language includes both oral and written forms of language. It is support in acquiring language for academic purposes that ELLs need, but often do not get because school administrators and classroom teachers believe that they will 'naturally' absorb the language they need in the classroom.

How best to provide the kind of instruction in oral English that ELLs need to optimize their English language and academic development is an ongoing debate. But available evidence suggests that a two-pronged approach is probably necessary and most effective. One prong clearly involves systematic ESL instruction that aims to promote the oral language proficiency of ELLs. This instruction might be provided in separate dedicated periods of instruction in English as a second language by ESL specialists (the so-called pull-out ESL) or instructional support for ELLs that is provided by classroom teachers with assistance from ESL specialists (the so-called 'push-in' ESL). In either case, ESL instruction is planned and delivered by or with the support of an ESL specialist.

The other prong involves systematic integration of English oral language instruction with academic instruction by classroom teachers; this is often referred to as sheltered instruction. Sheltered Instruction for Oral Proficiency (SIOP) is an example of such an approach, one that enjoys empirical support (Echevarria & Graves, 2007). The SIOP Model is a framework for teaching the academic curriculum to ELLs using strategies and techniques that make the content of the curriculum comprehensible and, at the same time, promote the development of their language skills for academic purposes. In effect, SIOP is a set of pedagogical strategies that seek to circumvent or reduce the linguistic barriers that ELLs face during academic instruction in English and, at the same time to enhance their proficiency in English for academic purposes, using the academic curriculum as a vehicle for planning and promoting language development (see Echevarria et al., 2010, for more detailed rationales and empirical justifications for this approach).

Clearly, a comprehensive plan for educating second-language learners should include long-term plans for ways to promote their English oral language skills. These plans should include both ESL specialists and classroom teachers since, after all, ELLs spend most of their time with their classroom teachers. In effect, classroom teachers also need to be ESL specialists if they are to serve their ELLs effectively.

ENGLISH-ONLY FOR ESL STUDENTS

The final belief I would like to discuss is the notion that ELLs acquire English more quickly and effectively the more they are immersed in the second language and the less they use or rely on their first language skills and knowledge. This belief is based on two assumptions. According to the time-on-task assumption, the more time spent learning and using English, the better their English will be. According to the second assumption, use of the L1 to learn the L2 interferes with and slows down L2 learning. Indeed, educators and others often interpret intrusions of the L1 into the L2 as errors and evidence that the L1 has a negative impact on L2 learning, as, for example, when a Spanish-speaking student pronounces the letter 'j' like an 'h' because that is how it is pronounced in Spanish.

However, and once again in contrast with these commonsense beliefs, systematic scientific studies of second-language learners indicate clearly that ELLs who use their first language to support the acquisition of their second make faster and better progress learning English than ELLs who do not (Genesee & Geva, 2006; Lindholm-Leary & Borsato, 2006; Riches & Genesee, 2006). The benefits that ELLs derive from the support provided by their home language is most evident when it comes to reading, writing and oral language for academic purposes (August & Shanahan, 2006; Genesee *et al.*, 2006). For example, primary grade ELLs with emergent or initial literacy skills in their first language make relatively faster progress in acquiring literacy skills in English than those who lack these L1 literacy skills (August & Shanahan, 2006; Riches & Genesee, 2006). In a particularly useful study, Jimenez *et al.* (1996) found that second-language-learning children in Grades 6 and 7 who were successful learning to read and write in English used a number of bilingual strategies, such as translating, looking for cognates and using knowledge acquired in the L1, to read in English. In contrast, ELLs who were struggling with reading and writing in English viewed reading in the L1 and L2 as separate abilities and saw the L1 as a source of confusion. The unsuccessful ESL readers clearly had less well-developed metalinguistic awareness of their two languages than the successful students, a point I return to shortly. In brief, ELLs' use of their first language should not be seen as an impediment to learning a second, but rather as a learning resource that can actually facilitate their acquisition of literacy skills in English.

When ELLs use knowledge of their home language in these ways, they are actively filling in gaps in their English by drawing on corresponding skills and knowledge from their L1; this is what researchers call bootstrapping or scaffolding (Genesee *et al.*, 2006). When they use their knowledge of letters and sounds from the L1 to decode in English, for example, they are showing us that they know that there is a correspondence between written letters and sounds in language – a critical fundamental skill in learning to read and write in any language. They do not have to be retaught letter–sound relationships, although they may need to learn the sounds and letters of English. By encouraging students to use the L1 to scaffold their acquisition of literacy skills in English–L2, classroom teachers can encourage them to become more engaged in literacy activities in the classroom than they would otherwise be.

For ELLs to transfer knowledge from their L1 to reading and writing in English they must have metalinguistic awareness of the two languages; that is, they must understand how the two languages represent sound and meaning, and the similarities and differences in the ways they do this. Urging ELLs to focus explicitly on the structure of their two languages by encouraging them to draw comparisons between them, classroom teachers promote the development of metalinguistic awareness (Bialystok, 2001; Cummins, 2000); for example, when they point out that to a Spanish–English student the letter 'j' is pronounced /h/ in Spanish but /j/ in English or that English sentences always need a subject, but in some languages, like Spanish and Italian, the subject can sometimes be omitted. Metalinguistic awareness is essential for the acquisition of reading and writing skills because good readers and writers have explicit insights about how written language works (Helman, 2004). Focusing on similarities and differences between languages can be a great tool for teaching all students, not just ELLs. Making native English-speaking students aware of how other languages are the same as, and different from, English and how they represent oral language in written form, are ways of showing monolingual English-speaking students the richness of language diversity and, in this way, developing their metalinguistic awareness at the same time. To better understand how their ELLs are using their L1 to bootstrap into English, teachers should get to know how the various home languages of their ELLs compare to English with respect to sound, word formation rules, grammar and conventions for conveying meaning (see e.g. Comrie *et al.*, 1996; Nakanishi, 1990).

Many of the chapters in this volume provide excellent practical examples of how to make use of ELLs' knowledge of their L1 during classroom activities, even in the case of teachers who do not know or speak other languages (see also Cloud *et al.*, 2008, for other tips).

LAST WORDS

Many commonly held beliefs about young learners' ability to acquire language fail to acknowledge the complexities of L2 acquisition for academic purposes and the extended effort that is needed to support ELLs in meeting these challenges. This brief preface has sought to clarify some of these beliefs. During the last two decades, a great deal of research has been carried out that can be used to validate these beliefs, or not, and help us better understand the challenges faced by ELLs and how we can support them in meeting those challenges. Fortunately, ELLs are extremely resourceful learners – they use all of the resources at their disposal to succeed in school, and one of the most important is their L1. Educators who ignore or diminish the value of a student's L1 skills risk ignoring an extremely valuable learning resource that they can use to promote the acquisition of English and, ultimately, academic success.

This introductory chapter has focused on the ELLs' L1 as a resource for learning English. However, it is also a resource in its own right since maintenance of the home language along with the acquisition of English as a L2 gives these students a repertoire of language skills that will give them personal and professional advantages. As the world continues on its path of globalization, all students will benefit from knowing additional languages. ELLs make our task as educators easier because they already come to school knowing another language. We should not squander this resource.

REFERENCES

August, D. and Shanahan, T. (eds) (2006) Developing literacy in second language learners. In *Report of the National Literacy Panel on Minority-Language Children and Youth*. Mahwah, NJ: Lawrence Erlbaum.

Bialystok, E. (2001) *Bilingualism in Development: Language, Literacy and Cognition.* New York: Cambridge University Press.

Burstall, C., Jamieson, M., Cohen, S. and Hargreaves, M. (1974) *Primary French in the Balance.* Slough: NFER Publishing.

Chamot, A.U. and O'Malley, J.M. (1994) *The CALLA Handbook: Implementing the Cognitive Academic Language Learning Approach.* White Plains, NY: Addison Wesley Longman.

Comrie, B., Matthew, S. and Polinsky, M. (1996) *The Atlas of Languages: The Origin and Development of Languages Throughout the World.* London: Quatro Publishing Plc.

Cummins, J. (1981) The role of primary language development in promoting educational success for language minority students. In *Schooling and Language Minority Students: A Theoretical Framework* (pp. 1–50). Los Angeles, CA: Evaluation, Dissemination, and Assessment Center.

Cummins, J. (2000) *Language, Power and Pedagogy: Bilingual Children in the Crossfire.* Clevedon: Multilingual Matters.

Echevarria, J. and Graves, A. (2007) *Sheltered Content Instruction: Teaching English Language Learners with Diverse Abilities* (3rd edn). Boston: Allyn & Bacon.

Echevarria, J., Vogt, M.E. and Short, D. (2010) *The SIOP Model: Making Content Comprehensible for Elementary English Learners.* Boston: Allyn and Bacon.

Genesee, F. (2010) Dual language acquisition in preschool children. In E. Garcia and E. Frede (eds) *Young English Language Learners* (pp. 59–79). New York: Teachers College Press.

Genesee, F. and Geva, E. (2006) Cross-linguistic relationships in working memory, phonological processes, and oral language. In D. August and T. Shanahan (eds) *Developing Literacy in Second Language Learners*. Chapter 7. *Report of the National Literacy Panel on Minority-Language Children and Youth* (pp. 175–184). Mahwah, NJ: Lawrence Erlbaum.

Genesee, F., Lindholm-Leary, K.J., Saunders, W. and Christian, D. (2006) *Educating English Language Learners.* New York: Cambridge University Press.

Helman, L. (2004) Building on the sound system of Spanish: Insights from the alphabetic spellings of English language learners. *Reading Teacher* 57, 59–67.

Jimenez, R., Garcia, G.E. and Pearson, P.D. (1996) The reading strategies of bilingual Latina/o students who are successful English readers: Opportunities and obstacles. *Reading Research Quarterly* 31, 90–112.

Krashen, S.D., Long, M.A. and Scarcella, R.C. (1976) Age, rate and attainment in second language acquisition. *TESOL Quartley* 13, 573–582.

Lindholm-Leary, K.J. and Borsato, G. (2006) Academic achievement. In F. Genesee, K. Lindholm-Leary, W. Saunders and D. Christian (eds) *Educating English Language Learners* (pp. 176–222). New York: Cambridge University Press.

Long, M. (1990) Maturational constraints on language development. *Studies in Second Language Acquisition* 12 (3), 251–286.

Nakanishi, A. (1990) *Writing Systems of the World: Alphabets, Syllabaries, and Pictograms*. Tokyo & Rutland, VT: Charles E. Tuttle.

Paradis, J. (2006) Second language acquisition in childhood. In E. Hoff and M. Shatz (eds) *Handbook of Language Development* (pp. 387–405). Oxford: Blackwell.

Riches, C. and Genesee, F. (2006) Cross-linguistic and cross-modal aspects of literacy development. In F. Genesee, K. Lindholm-Leary, W. Saunders and D. Christian (eds) *Educating English Language Learners: A Synthesis of Research Evidence* (pp. 64–108). New York: Cambridge University Press.

Saunders, W. and O'Brien, G. (2006) Oral language. In F. Genesee, K. Lindholm-Leary, W. Saunders and D. Christian (eds) *Educating English Language Learners: A Synthesis of Research Evidence* (pp. 14–63). New York: Cambridge University Press.

About the author

Fred Genesee is Professor in the Psychology Department at McGill University, Montreal. He has conducted extensive research on alternative forms of bilingual and immersion education for language minority and language majority students. His current research interests include language acquisition in pre-school bilingual children, internationally adopted children, second language reading acquisition, and the language and academic development of students at risk in bilingual programs. He is the recipient of the Canadian Psychological Associate Award for Distinguished Contributions to Community or Public Service and the 2-Way CABE Promoting Bilingualism Award.

Section 1

Chapter 1

Young Children Have Stories to Share

EITHNE GALLAGHER

Early Childhood programmes in international and indeed national schools around the world are opening their doors to very young children who have no knowledge of the language of instruction. And unfortunately all too often the language they know best is not allowed to come with them. The author has spent many years devising, teaching, collecting and writing about ways that school administrators and teachers could do better by encouraging first language development in mainstream classrooms, and this chapter is her latest effort to spread the word.

INTRODUCTION

We know that young children try to make sense of their world from the moment of birth or even before. Halliday (1978) points out that 'We learn how to behave linguistically from the auditory processing that occurs before birth and continues through life.' By the age of two and a half, most young children develop a sense of persona: they can use the words I, me and mine. This identity needs to flourish. But when these young children arrive at school to participate in Early Childhood programs they often find themselves for extended periods of time in settings where none of the sounds around them are familiar and all of the well-known faces have disappeared. This can be very traumatic for young children and may even put their fledgling identity at risk. Their parents, often busy professionals, leave them in this alien environment for up to eight hours a day unaware of the stress they may be putting their children under; babysitters may pick them up after school and when their parents return from work there may not be time for a bedtime story in their own familiar language (Gallagher, 2001).

In this chapter we will look at what research says about involving parents as partners in Early Childhood education and in particular why this is particularly important when the language of instruction is different from the child's home language. We will also consider the importance of additive bilingualism and view what research has to say about the negative effects on young children of being plunged into another language environment without the support of their mother tongue. A new concept for international education is proposed: 'Interlingual Classrooms' (Gallagher, 2008); ways of promoting other languages with young children are outlined so that *all* children will be able to tell their stories.

Parents as partners in Early Childhood education

We now know that parental empowerment is the key to success for bilingual and multilingual children. It used to be that parents were not normally invited to participate in the everyday life of the school but this has changed with the coming of the Parent–Teacher Association. There is still a legacy in many schools, however, of a dominant Anglo-centric culture that pervades the Parent–Teacher Association. Parents who do not speak English well or at all might thus hesitate to participate in their activities, thinking that they would have little to offer, or would be too embarrassed to participate. Some, according to the custom of their countries, would not think it their place to tell the school what to do. However, parents can form one of the most important decision-making groups in a school. Without their input, the issues concerning their children might not be fairly addressed.

One example of this is the practice in many international schools of charging parents for ESL lessons over and above the cost of tuition fees. This certainly implies that such lessons are outside what the school considers to be its mission. Can a school that calls itself 'international' really consider the education of ESL children to be outside its mission? Schools, especially those that call themselves international, have a duty to ensure that all parents and their children, regardless of the language they speak, are valued and feel included in the life of the school. 'International' does not mean monolingual and monocultural; it should mean the acceptance of the many languages and cultures of the school community.

There is an increasing number of schools that strive to involve *all* their parents in the life of the school. This involvement starts at the admissions stage where a language profile should be drawn up on each new child. Parents can be asked questions about language usage, for example with whom and for how long has the child been speaking particular languages. It is not unusual for children to speak one language with their mother, another language with their father and a different language with their siblings. For older children it is important for us to establish whether they read and write in their first and subsequent languages. Then there is direction: does the script run from left to right as in English, from right to left as in Arabic or from top to bottom as in Chinese? We also need to find out about cultural and religious practices. For example, children may need to be absent from school to fulfil religious obligations; they may have dietary needs that are not met by the traditional cuisine offered in the school cafeteria. Schools tend to be well informed on the latter but it is being informed about *all* differences and showing understanding that leads to a school's being truly international in outlook.

School personnel and the mission to educate

When we speak of resources in schools we often tend to forget the valuable contribution that the nonteaching employees working in our schools can make. A language survey of, the entire community, including teachers, librarians, admissions officers, secretaries, nurse and so on, would be a good place to start. The number of people working in our schools who are proficient and knowledgeable about other languages and cultures and who can be of great value to the school can be quite surprising. I can recall using a Danish nurse, a Croatian computer expert, a high-school science teacher who spoke Urdu, a middle-school P.E. teacher who spoke Japanese – to name but a few – who have helped me in the early days of working with a new arrival. Often it is the ESL teacher who spends her time running around looking for help. But a language survey done every couple of years of all the adults working or volunteering in the school and then shared with the community would save valuable time and highlight how international the school is. It is up to the community to value and take advantage of the tremendous potential for internationalism that often goes untapped in schools. When a school community is informed about all the cultures and languages at work in the school, a powerful message is sent to all stakeholders that it values multilingualism and multiculturalism.

Educating teachers

An effective school will educate and inform. It can organize professional development for its teachers on aspects of the different cultures and traditions that are present in its community. It can offer in-service sessions that inform teachers of differences and similarities amongst the school's cultures. It can offer a workshop on the different writing systems used in the community. Teachers can learn much about a child's development in the English language if they have some idea of the way the child writes in her first language. If teachers know, for example, that the writing systems of Punjabi and Gujarati, where the basic units or graphemes correspond to syllables – usually a sequence of consonant and vowel *(ba, bi, bu, ga* and *gi)* or that Arabic and Hebrew writing systems use only consonants, no vowels – they will realize when they read a text such as 'sm lnggs cn b wrttn nd rd wth lttl prblms' that the writer is not dyslexic but simply transferring knowledge from another script. (For a fuller discussion of writing systems see Edwards, 2004.) International schools should surely strive to develop all their students' languages. It is not a choice between English and other languages but more a question of achieving balanced multilingualism.

Balanced multilingualism in the Early Years

Balanced multilingualism requires a pedagogical approach that is open to other languages and cultures. And teachers and administrators should from the outset convey to parents the importance of the part they can play in helping the school educate their children. Parents should be made to feel welcome in the school. Baker says 'Parent–teacher relationships must be sealed with understanding and cooperation to avoid antagonism and alienation' (Baker, 2000: 82). Where parents cannot speak the language of the teachers then help should be sought from other parents or embassies. 'When parents are included in the learning process, their cultures are valued and celebrated' (Baker, 2000: 85). It is important that we incorporate these social, cultural and intellectual resources as essential elements in our international curricula.

International schools that admit two-year-old children, and then can only speak to them in a language that they do not understand, must involve the children's parents. Children, and very young children in particular, should not be left in an environment where they understand nothing for extended periods of time. The ideal situation would be for children to have exposure to the language of instruction and their own language in equal measure. This seems to be possible in schools located in large, cosmopolitan cities such as London, where there are large populations of speakers of the languages represented in schools. Where it is not possible to find teachers then – at least in the early years – available, willing parents might be apprenticed in teaching roles that guide and explain to children the basics of the curriculum. This can be done through an organized mother-tongue programme. It is now very common to find a large number of host country children in the Early Years in international schools. It is not difficult to find teachers of the host country language and to establish a bilingual programme, but it has to be said that, unfortunately, this solution is too often avoided. Many international schools only begin instruction in the host country language in Grade 1 though the majority of their children come from host country homes. Administrators, teachers and parents in such schools appear to have failed to realize the benefits that would accrue to their young children if a mother-tongue programme had been implemented in the early years.

In January 2008, I gave the keynote lecture at the Association of German International Schools Conference (AGIS). There were many fledgling international schools from East Germany present. After my talk, a young woman from one such school came up to me and said

> I hear what you are saying and I agree but in our schools we follow an English only policy. No use of German is allowed except during mandatory German language classes. When I come into the Grade 1 class to teach German, the children are so happy to see me! This is the part of the day when they can say what they want; they can share their stories with me and I understand them.

How very sad that young children are kept from talking, kept from sharing their tales and woes, which sounds like something out of a Dickens story. Can education really be about stopping children from talking?

The positive effects of additive bilingualism

Cummins (2004) cites more than 150 empirical studies carried out during the past 30 years that have reported a positive association between additive bilingualism and students' linguistic, cognitive or academic growth. The most consistent findings among these research studies are that bilinguals have a more developed awareness of the structure and functions of language itself (metalinguistic abilities) and that they have advantages in learning additional languages. The term additive bilingualism refers to the form of bilingualism that results from students adding a second language to their intellectual repertoire while continuing to develop conceptually and academically in their first language.

The findings suggest that the proficiency attained by bilingual students in their two languages may exert important influences on their academic and intellectual development. Cummins maintains that continued development of both languages in literate domains is a precondition for enhanced cognitive, linguistic and academic growth. In his book, *Negotiating Identities*, Cummins describes several studies where bilingual children perform better than children who were proficient only in English. In one of the studies, Riccadelli (1992, 1993) compared 57 Italian–English bilinguals and 55 monolingual English five- and six-year-olds in Australia using the Torrance Fluency and Imagination Measures. (This test measures creative thinking, metalinguistic awareness such as correct word order and verbal and non verbal activities.) The children who were proficient in both Italian and English performed significantly better than the children in the English monolingual group. For a fuller discussion on this and other comparative studies on bilingual/monolingual children, see Cummins (2004).

It seems more than obvious that children who master two languages have a linguistic advantage over monolingual children. Studies conducted in Canada reveal that when a bilingual child's first language is developed and maintained academically it has a positive influence on the learning of additional languages. However, when bilingual children are not given the educational support needed for the development of literacy they develop a subtractive form of bilingualism. Subtractive bilingualism can result when a second language is learned to the point where it gradually replaces the first language.

Loss of mother tongue: The norm among language minority children

Lily Wong Fillmore's (1991) research suggests that loss or lack of continued development of the mother tongue is the norm amongst most US language minority children. Her studies revealed that these children have difficulty communicating with their families, and alienation of children from parents can occur as development progresses. Teachers in international schools can also affirm that this happens when the mother tongue has not been fully developed and nurtured alongside the second language. Certain children may become 'wannabe' Americans or Brits to the detriment of their own culture, and end up disadvantaged upon their return. International schools have a duty to promote both additive biculturalism (being able to identify with the culture of two different language groups) as well as additive bilingualism. As International school educators we should not have bilingual children entering our schools and leaving as monolinguals with a monolingual outlook. It is rare among children who speak the host country language but more common among children from other language backgrounds. Parental involvement is the key to this. Many parents are unaware of what research says about the importance of L1, nor that it is widely agreed among experts that maintaining and developing mother-tongue literacy is the way to academic success for second-language learners. (For a fuller discussion of this see Gallagher, 2008.) Effective schools talk to parents about such issues at the admissions stage and hold information evenings for the benefit of parents, thus helping them to become partners with the school in educating their children.

A NEW CONCEPT FOR INTERNATIONAL CLASSROOMS

The word bilingual can define the speaking of two languages or a text written in two languages. The term bilingual classroom suggests the use of two languages and, in the context of international education, is often associated with the majority language and the host country language. The term 'multilingual' is commonly understood to mean the speaking of many languages, but in some international schools it can mean 'too many' – too many languages to deal with! In the international school context many students are multilingual. However, often these many languages are used passively and sometimes not used at all. Children should have opportunities to learn something of the less familiar languages of our world as well as the majority ones, and to hear them in the classroom. A new concept is needed for international education; one that will promote plurilingualism in international school classrooms. Students and teachers alike should begin to consider their classes *interlingual.* The *inter* stands for international mindedness, that is, the notion that everyone should be open and responsive to learning about other languages. But it also stands for all the languages of the classroom having a part to play in extending children's knowledge of language.

Effective International Schools often strive to prepare children ultimately to function in two languages, each at a high level. Few as yet have managed to exploit the great language learning and awareness potential readily available in classrooms that contain children from many different language backgrounds. Teachers should try to work collaboratively with parents and students to learn more about the home languages of the children in their classes, the better to understand the child in front of them. Language surveys and profiles (mentioned earlier) can help to establish the range of languages used by their children and the circumstances in which they are used.

Mainstream teachers need to familiarize themselves with such surveys so as to better understand the language diversity in the school. But they should also know the extent to which each child in the class has developed his first language and the amount of time he has had to practise it. In interlingual classrooms, teachers encourage children to make use of all their languages to help them become aware of the differences and similarities of languages. There is normally one language of instruction but all the languages in the classroom can be used to help children access it and feel they have a part in it. This does not mean that the teacher needs to be a polyglot but she does need to have a mind that is open to other languages and cultures, and to be interested in learning from both her students and their families. This opportunity and mindset would of course also be passed on to those children in the class who speak only English.

Simple interlingual strategies

Enlightened language teachers have been using interlingual teaching and learning strategies for years, most commonly in small withdrawal teaching situations. The time has come for these strategies to assume a major role in mainstream classrooms.

It is not difficult or time consuming to promote other languages and it can be done from early childhood through to upper secondary. By simply asking students 'How do you say that in Urdu, Japanese, Italian?', etc., the teacher shows she values all the languages of her class. Children are more than happy to write key vocabulary words for display in their home languages. For young learners content-based language learning happens quite naturally because the school's curriculum for young learners is by its very nature concrete. For Grade 1 and Kindergarten children the content of the school curriculum is not very different from the language curriculum. The topics covered are things like families, homes, communities, subjects which easily lend themselves to parental involvement. Children learn to count; they learn the names of colours, days of the week, and so on. It is easier here than anywhere else in the school curriculum to involve and inform parents about what is going on. If they are told to reinforce the idea of counting at home in L1 we can be sure that the concept will be more meaningful to the child. The concept of time is a little more abstract, but if parents also talk to their children about day, week and season, as it is being studied, the child will make associations with what she knows in her L1 and the new words being taught for this in English.

It is quite common in primary classrooms to study traditional tales that come from the children's home countries. When doing such a study the teacher can point out that stories begin and end in the same way in many languages. The children can make a poster of how they say 'Once upon a time' and 'They all lived happily ever after' in all the languages of the classroom. Children are generally thrilled to have their language on display in the classroom; it gives them a sense of belonging and it makes the classroom walls come to life with the wonderful variety that such activity offers. In interlingual classrooms children have time to reflect on their learning as well as time to relax. If they choose to relax by reading a book in their home language, that is fine. One of the things that mainstream teachers need to build into working with children whose home language is different from the language of instruction, is making them feel proud of what they can do in their own language. A great way of doing this is having them create what Jim Cummins calls 'identity texts' (for more information on identity texts see The Dual-Language Showcase at <thornwood.peelschools.org>). These are dual-language texts about things that are meaningful and relevant to children, and that affirm their identity. By doing such things teachers show the class just how much those whose language is different from the language of instruction can actually do. In Moll *et al.*'s words 'We affirm their funds of knowledge' (Moll *et al.*, 1992: 21). (For a fuller discussion on interlingual teaching/learning strategies see Gallagher, 2008.)

Translanguaging and transliteracy

Cen Williams introduced the term 'translanguaging' in 1994. As the word suggests, translanguaging gives children the freedom to move in and out of languages while working. The teacher introduces the topic in a majority language but the tasks are carried out in the student's preferred language. In other words, the children receive input in reading or listening in one language and they produce output speaking or writing in another language. Baker (2006) says that 'translanguaging and transliteracy may promote a deeper and fuller understanding of the subject matter: if the students have understood in two languages they have *really* understood' (p. 297). Translanguaging therefore attempts to develop academic language levels in both the child's languages. Teachers may feel uncomfortable at first not knowing what exactly a child with little or no knowledge of English has written when they produce a text in a different language or script. But this is something they can overcome. The focus here is on self-expression and allowing the child to do this in the mode she feels more comfortable working in. In some cases it will be possible to use other children with the same language background who are also proficient in English to translate the child's text. Alternatively, a note to parents asking them to read over or check the child's work is also a good way of overseeing the work while further involving parents. Failing this, the teacher should rely on one-to-one communication with the child through drawings and gestures or online translation facilities such as Babelfish to help her in understanding what the child has written. All this becomes easier with practice and both children and parents appreciate the efforts made by teachers who do their best to honour and imbed the child's home language into her learning.

An example of translanguaging

In early November, my Grade 4 children were busy learning about government, colonies, slaves, elections and democracy as part of their studies on Ancient Greece. As their ESL teacher I was helping my students comprehend these concepts and their relevance for today's world and also to help them do well on their social studies tests.

As I was driving to school on November 5th listening to the news of Barack Obama's election victory, I wondered how I was going to bring this historical moment alive for my children. Well, in Grade 4 it proved to be no problem; they were already familiar with many of the concepts and vocabulary that ensued when I brought up the topic of the election of Barack Obama as the first African American to become president and also one of the youngest.

During the month of October, Grade 4 had been learning about hunger in our world and in November they were in the midst of writing letters to Ban Ki Moon to share their ideas for stopping it. So the idea of writing to President Elect Obama came quite naturally to us. The children, Akari, Kang-In, Nam–Wan, Makiho and Marios wrote beautiful dual-language letters to the new president to congratulate him and ask him to give Ban Ki Moon a helping hand. Their parents were enthusiastic for the project and became involved proofreading the children's mother-tongue letters. This project was based on the notion that children making use of all their languages is a good idea.

As mentioned previously translanguaging gives children the freedom to move in and out of languages while working. I introduced the topic in English but the tasks were carried out in the student's first language. In other words, the children receive input in reading or listening in one language and they produce output speaking or writing in another language. I spoke with my Grade 4 children about the election in the United States, linking it to their studies on Ancient Greece. I elicited ideas in English from them for their letter to the President. They then wrote their first draft of the letter in their mother tongues (Greek, Korean, Japanese and Thai) and they then wrote a translation of this in English. Baker (2006) says that 'translanguaging and transliteracy may promote a deeper and fuller understanding of the subject matter' (p. 297): 'if the students have understood in two languages they have really understood it'.

Translanguaging therefore attempts to develop academic language in both spoken by the child languages. This is something we should be striving for across all levels of schooling. Baker also points out that translanguaging and transliteracy can facilitate home/school cooperation where parents become partners in their children's education by becoming involved, for example, in research and proofreading in the home language.

Ofelia Garcia, one of the keynote speakers at the European Council of International Schools' ESL/MT conference in Geneva in 2008, suggests that 'the facility to speak and write bilingually is seldom recognized by educational systems throughout the world'. ESL teachers have been using translanguaging and transliteracy strategies for years; the challenge now is to make them common practice in the mainstream. This kind of instruction communicates respect for students' languages and cultures and allows them to invest their full identity in the learning process.

Genuine experiences

To sum up, interlingual teaching and learning takes as its starting point the practices of bilingualism, which include translanguaging and transliteracy in the individual, and expands them for the benefit of the individual and the community. Through genuine experiences with other languages in the formative years of schooling we can avoid any possible ill effects of the suppression of a child's first language. Furthermore, they can set a trend of international mindedness that will be a step towards our world becoming more genuinely pluricultural and plurilingual.

Multilingual competencies

Currently in many international school classrooms there is little focus on how we can build on students' multilingual competencies. Teachers may know the range of the languages of students in their classrooms but, in practice, little use is made of this knowledge. In some schools students are discouraged from using their L1 in certain classroom and school contexts. In others, they are encouraged to learn their L1 out of school rather than in it. By contrast, in an interlingual classroom students will learn through their own mother tongue and learn from all the other mother-tongue languages in the classroom. There will be a focus on different languages as well as English. In his book, *Language Maid Plane* (sic), Anthony Burgess (1964) suggests that schools need to teach children *about* languages rather than simply teaching languages. In other words, before we teach children specific foreign languages, students should engage in an awareness study of language as such. Such a study introduced in the early years eventually helps children to choose languages they have learned about earlier and are interested in studying further. Interlingual classrooms promote other languages rather than denying they exist.

A whole-school language awareness and appreciation programme could include the following:

- The origins of language: where it originated and how it has evolved.
- The study of different language families Afro/Asiatic, Attaic, Dravidian, Indo-European, Sino-Tibetan, and so on.
- The study of where in the world a language is spoken (geography).
- The study of the main religions associated with a language (social studies).
- The number of speakers of the language (math-related activities).
- The language *per se* (children can study the different writing systems present in their classrooms and schools).

As we can see from the above, a language appreciation and awareness programme can stretch across many subject areas of the curriculum. It can help international school children to develop a truly interlingual and international perspective on language. Children can see their own language and culture highlighted while at the same time extending their knowledge of other cultures.

The potential here for actively teaching international understanding and respect for cultural diversity is evident. A Language Appreciation and Awareness Programme is something that can easily be built into the school curriculum.

In an interlingual classroom:

- All students' cultural knowledge experiences and mother tongue languages are viewed as precious resources for academic growth.
- All students participate actively in all academic areas because the teacher and the instruction affirm their identity.
- All parents are welcome in the classroom and are considered a valuable resource in helping to develop literacy in both the language of instruction and the home language.

There is now ample research (Bransford *et al.*, 2000) suggesting that prior knowledge and experience should be used as a foundation for all learning. Schools that ask children to leave their languages and cultures at the school gate should be aware of the shaky foundation they are trying to build on.

Affirming students' identities

When students' identities are affirmed and extended, they make more effort to participate and have a better chance of going on to succeed. An approach which inherently affirms students' identities belongs to an interlingual classroom where the teacher understands the importance of prior knowledge and experience and sees them as a valuable resource for learning and transferring skills across languages. This kind of instruction communicates respect for students' languages and cultures and allows them to invest their full identity in the learning process.

A supportive environment that respects children's talents

The more students learn, the more their self-confidence grows. But for this to happen we need to show that we respect them and their many experiences and talents, including what they are able to do in their first language. A majority-language-only environment does not fully recognize the intellectual and personal talents of children who are learning in a foreign language. Cognitive psychologists (Bransford *et al.*, 2000) say that we learn by integrating new input into our existing cognitive structures or schemata. By activating prior knowledge and background knowledge, we increase students' cognitive engagement and enable them to function at a linguistically and intellectually higher level. We also show our students that we value the cultural and linguistic knowledge they bring to the classroom. The single-language world that many of us grew up in is fast disappearing.

Tolerance and respect

We need to develop (and also encourage in the children we teach) a mindset that is open to knowing more about the many languages on our planet. International education has the opportunity to play a leading role in this effort by promoting an inclusive education for all. This will happen when we stop viewing the other languages in school as a difficulty to be overcome. The learning about mother-tongue languages should become an integral part of the curriculum in an international school. Interlingual classrooms should become a common feature of international education. They are very supportive of multiliteracy development, which should be the goal. Such classes should be places where educators use teaching as a vehicle to transfer skills and concepts from the L1 to the language of instruction.

Schools that promote interlingual teaching and learning will have the following features:

- A website with 'welcome' written in all the languages of the community.
- Information signs displayed in community languages.
- Letters and forms sent home in community languages.
- A Parent–Teacher Organization that goes out of its way to recruit members for committees from all language backgrounds.
- A language policy produced by all stakeholders in collaboration stating the shared vision that all languages are equally valuable, and one which includes a plan of action to make its statements a reality.
- Classrooms, corridors and playground where many different languages are heard and used.
- All parents viewed as valuable resources.
- Theatrical performances in different languages.
- Administrators and teachers from diverse cultural backgrounds, speaking other languages.
- Parents and children open minded to other languages and cultures.

Interlingual classrooms will:

- Have illustrated vocabulary lists exhibiting the many languages of the class-room linked to different areas of the curriculum.
- Display translations of students' favourite stories and work.
- Contain a classroom library made up of books in many different languages as well as dual-language books.
- Have resource books & bilingual dictionaries in all school languages.
- Instill a genuine ethos of international learning, because everyone – teacher, student, parent and administrator – has something to learn in a truly international school.

Interlingual classrooms can be places where, through cultural awareness and respect for other languages, the ideas and responsibilities of 'world citizenship' can be nurtured and developed. Interlingual classrooms are places where international-mindedness is seen in action, internationalism is directly felt, and interlingual children learn who they are in the context of the classroom and the broader society, and learn to work within a framework of tolerance and respect.

REFERENCES

Baker, C. (2000) *The Care and Education of Young Bilinguals: An Introduction for Professionals.* Clevedon: Multilingual Matters.

Baker, C. (2006) *Foundations of Bilingual Education and Bilingualism* (4th edn). Clevedon: Multilingual Matters.

Bransford, J.D., Brown, A.L. and Cocking, R.R. (2000) *How People Learn: Brain, Mind Experience, and School.* Washington, DC: National Academic Press.

Burgess, A. (1964) *Language Maid Plane.* London: Hodder and Stoughton.

Cummins, J. (2004) *Language, Power and Pedagogy.* Clevedon: Multilingual Matters.

Cummins, J. (1996) *Negotiating Identities: Education for Empowerment in a Diverse Society.* Los Angeles: California Association for Bilingual Education.

Edwards, V. (2004) *The Other Languages.* Reading, MA: National Centre for Language and Literacy.

Gallagher, E. (2001) Foreign language learning in early childhood. *International Schools Journal* 20, 54–56.

Gallagher, E. (2008) *Equal Rights to the Curriculum: Many Languages One Message.* Clevedon: Multilingual Matters.

Garcia, O. Education, multilingualism and translanguaging in the 21st century. In A. Mohanty, M. Panda, R. Phillipson and T. Skutnabb-Kangas (eds) *Multilingual Education: Challenges, Perspectives and Opportunities.* New Delhi: Orient.

Halliday, M.A.K. (1978) *Language as Social Semiotic.* London: Arnold.

Moll, L.C., Amanti, C., Neff, D. and Gonzales, N. (1992) Funds of knowledge using a qualitative approach to connect homes and classrooms. *Theory into Practice* 31, 132–141.

Riccadelli, L.A. (1992) Bilingualism and cognitive development in relation to threshold theory. *Journal of Psycholinguistic Research* 21, 301–316.

Riccadelli, L.A. (1993) An investigation of the cognitive development of Italian–English bilinguals and Italian monolinguals from Rome. *Journal of Multilingual and Multicultural Development* 14, 345–347.

Williams, C. (2000) Welsh medium and bilingual teaching in the further education sector. *International Journal of Bilingual Education and Bilingualism* 3, 129–148.

Wong Fillmore, L. (1991) When learning a second language means losing the first. *Early Childhood Research Quarterly* 6, 323–344.

About the author

Eithne Gallagher is a recognized authority in the field of ESL in international education, in which she has taught for 20 years. Presently working in the Elementary Department of Marymount International School, Rome, Eithne is a regular presenter at international school conferences and has given workshops and lectures for teachers and administrators across Europe. Her writings on ESL and Mother Tongue have been published in books and educational journals. Eithne is the mother of three bilingual children and lives with her family on a hilltop outside Rome.

Chapter 2
Using Multilingual Strategies in Monolingual Early Childhood Classrooms

DENISE SULLIVAN

The author is the product of an international school education, a 'TCK' (Third Culture kid) who has come full circle – she now teaches at the same international school she graduated from, and which her three sons currently attend. In this chapter she sets out what she sees as the most urgent refinement of international education, namely the development of mother-tongue languages alongside English in the classroom, and cites specific ways to achieve this goal.

INTRODUCTION

As a student in the late 1970s and 1980s, I felt fortunate to have friends from many different countries. I enjoyed the different perspectives they brought to our friendships, and I learned so much about the world from them. What I remember most about the 'ESL' (English as a second language) students back then was that those who learned English the fastest and who managed to acquire an 'American' accent seemed to fit in best. I doubt there was a conscious assimilation effort on the part of the school, but there were definitely underlying, unspoken assumptions. One of my best friends in school managed to adopt an American accent at lightning speed, and received frequent praise as a result. When I went to visit her several years later, I was surprised to hear her speaking English in a totally different (and non-American) accent! Having moved to another country, she had rapidly adapted to the cultural expectations of her new surroundings – a true linguistic chameleon.

My hope is now, more than 20 years later that our schools' orientation towards other languages and cultures has become more inclusive, and so the chameleons are not the only survivors. However when I read a journal entry like the one written a few years ago by one of our second-grade ESL students, I have to wonder how far we have truly come:

> *When I Came to School*
>
> *One day I came from Japan to (this school). That day I liked school very much. The second day I didn't like school because I didn't know English so I didn't say anything. Third day I knew English a little because my mom told me some things . . . . Fourth day, I went to ESL. I sang a song, did a calendar and many things to learn English. I came back to the classroom, went to snack and to P.E. My favorite work was P.E. We didn't need to talk English and I liked P.E. too. I did Math in the class and then I went to the lunchroom. I ate lunch and everybody was looking at my lunch because my lunch was Japanese food. Everybody's food was hot dogs or potato chips so that day I didn't eat my lunch. I did a lot of work and went back to my house. My mom said, 'Why you didn't ate your lunch?' I told my mom about (what happened) so I said, 'Never, ever make Japanese food except at home or in Japan, Okay?' And my mom said, 'Okay.'*

What can international schools do to truly 'embrace the diversity that enriches life', as our school mission statement proclaims? Before we answer that question, we need to take a brief look at how young children acquire language.

Background

A child's first five years are critical for language development. During these years, children develop linguistic skills to express their needs and feelings and communicate with others. Language development supports a young child's thinking and problem-solving processes, as well as the ability to develop and maintain relationships with others. Learning to understand, use and enjoy language is the critical first step in literacy, and the basis for learning to read and write. All of this develops quite naturally when a child is immersed in the rich linguistic context provided by parents, caregivers, Early Childhood teachers and peers.

We are justifiably proud of the quality of instruction and language-rich environments we provide in our Early Childhood programs in international schools. These types of classrooms offer the best possible conditions for nurturing budding language and literacy skills in our youngest learners. We feel confident that children gain the literacy foundations needed to become proficient readers and writers as they move through the grades.

The question is, do international school classrooms provide the best possible learning environment for *all* students, including second-language learners? Research shows that first-language acquisition does not stop after the first five years. Children continue to acquire complex grammatical features and vocabulary of their first language well into the elementary school years (Ballantyne, 2008). Few educators are aware of how fragile young children's mother tongues can be, and how quickly they can lose their ability to communicate in the home language if it is neglected. Within just two to three years of being immersed in a second language, children can lose their ability to communicate in their mother tongue. This is especially true for children who do not have a strong representation from their linguistic group in the school and community. To minimize home language loss, parents need to have a strong commitment to use the native language at home. They can also try to expand the contexts in which it is used, such as play dates, social or religious groups, extended visits to the home country, and so on (Jim Cummins *et al.* 2005).

As Ofelia Garcia points out:

> Even though young children are capable of learning more than one language, it is imperative that their mother tongue be well developed at the same time. Bilingual education is possible with good attention to both languages. Immersion in a language other than the child's language is not a good idea ... all children's home language needs to be developed, and it is the teachers' responsibility to do so, even in English-only immersion contexts. This is especially important in early childhood. (Personal communication, October 2008)

The message is clear: International schools need to be actively engaged in promoting mother-tongue development from the very beginning in order to avoid the negative consequences that may come from a failure to do so. Are we doing everything we can to ensure all students have an opportunity to do so? In the large PreK-12 international school where I work as an Elementary ESL teacher, we serve students from over 60 countries. Approximately 50% of our students have a mother tongue other than English, and more than 45 different languages are represented. Our school mission is to '... ensure that each student achieves his or her educational and personal potential'.

While we accept students in Pre-K and Kindergarten classes who do not speak English, our ESL program does not begin until grade one. The rationale for not offering ESL in the early years is that children are all learning the 'basics' in a language rich, developmental Pre-K and KG program. Yet, research shows learning to read is not the same for native and nonnative speakers. Native speakers have the advantage of an oral language foundation in English. When they begin to learn letters and sounds, they have something to 'hook' it onto – a framework for understanding. They also have a large vocabulary base, as well as syntactic knowledge of the language. They are learning to read in a language they understand.

Our multilingual students have oral language development too, but in their own mother tongue. However, more often than not in international schools, they are not learning to read in those languages. Research tells us that students who do not develop native language and literacy can take longer to catch up to their native speaking peers in the second language (English). There can be long-term negative cognitive, academic and social consequences for these children. With this in mind, how can we enable these students to meet their academic and personal potentials?

How can we foster first- and second-language development in an additive context? To address these issues, administrators, policy makers and/or school board members, teachers and parents must work together to provide an optimal learning experience for all students.

DEVELOPING A SCHOOL-WIDE LANGUAGE POLICY

International schools need to have clearly articulated language policies that are understood and adhered to by all constituents (Hamayan & Freeman, 2006). The language policy should serve as a touchstone to drive all decisions concerning multilingual students. One factor that must be considered in a language policy is the school's position on mother-tongue development and use of the native language in school. It is not enough just to celebrate and encourage linguistic diversity; we must also make use of students' mother tongues as a tool for learning both English and academic content. In a school with a clearly articulated language policy, we would not have one classroom that welcomes native language use, and the next with a posted sign saying, 'English-only spoken here'. Having a language policy will help to guard against the potential inconsistencies that may come with frequent teacher and administrator turnover in international schools.

Educating parents

International schools have a responsibility to educate parents about the implications of enrolling their young children in our schools. This responsibility begins at the admissions office. Parents need to know that by choosing to send their children to our school, they agree to enter into a bilingual partnership with the school. This should not be presented as a penalty or punishment, but rather as a privilege and an opportunity to be involved in their children's education.

The next step is for schools to make information and resources available to all multilingual parents through parent presentations, handouts, websites and so on, keeping in mind that personal communication is most effective with multilingual parents. Ideally, whenever possible, important communications should be translated into the native languages of those who will receive them. It is impossible for parents to receive a message if they do not understand it. It is encouraging to see that many international schools already have multilingual websites in place.

Currently, our school provides education on language issues only to parents of officially designated ESL students (10–15% of our student population). Since over 50% of our students have mother tongues other than English, we are missing a large segment of our potential target audience. Recognizing this discrepancy, we have plans to include parents of all multilingual students in our future programs and communications.

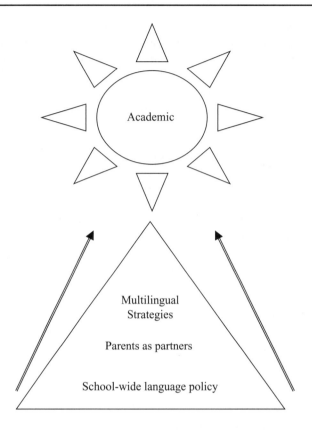

The teacher's role

What can individual teachers do to promote mother-tongue development? First of all, we cannot wait for our schools' administrators and policy makers to come on board. Many international schools do not have language policies and it may be many years before they do. The multilingual children in our classrooms deserve a chance *right now* to reach their personal and academic potentials. As educators we have a choice to make. We can choose to treat all students like native speakers, or we can do our best to develop the home languages and cultures of all our students using the resources available to us. To me, it is a moral and ethical decision as well as an educational one.

Establishing a partnership

Even with the best of intentions and ideals, classroom teachers cannot accomplish this task alone. We must get and keep parents on board as active members of the bilingual partnership. Parents want what is best for their children, but most do not have the background in language acquisition or bilingual education on which to base their decisions. I often hear well-intentioned parents of young children say they want to wait to develop the home language until the child has a firm grasp on English. They do not want to 'confuse' or overburden their children. Some parents do not read to their children in their native language because they believe it might hinder their learning in English (Ballantyne, 2008: 10). Naturally, they want their children to be successful in the language of the school, for both social and academic reasons. Parents often find it counter-intuitive when we tell them how important it is to develop native language and literacy first, or at least simultaneously with the second language. As teachers, we must provide parents with formal and informal research-based information on these and other important language issues, in a way they can understand. We cannot wait for several years until the child begins having difficulties in school, and then backtrack to find out what went wrong. More often than not, the problem comes from having under developed or nonexistent L1 literacy. The time to get this information to parents is when they first walk through our school doors. Providing accurate information to parents can be done with the help and support of your school's ESL specialists, but must be clearly communicated and reinforced by Early Childhood educators.

Telling parents about the importance of using their native language and developing L1 literacy, however, is not enough. We need to provide tangible resources and support to encourage the realization of their good intentions. The ideas listed in this chapter will offer some practical suggestions on how to do that.

Strategies to create inclusive classrooms, nurture emerging multilingual identities and develop bilingual partnerships with parents:

The classroom environment

Always talk in positive terms about languages and cultures, language learning and the benefits of bilingualism. Language should never be seen as a problem to be overcome, but as a resource to be developed.

Learn as much as you can about your students' languages and cultures. Even learning a few basic greetings in each language goes a long way towards fostering respect and appreciation for diverse languages. Your students will see that learning goes both ways and will appreciate your efforts.

Let signs and labels in your classroom reflect the linguistic diversity of your class (ask parents to help) so that students will know their languages are welcome in our schools.

Encourage parents to find books, songs, poems and rhymes in their languages related to your classroom themes and invite them to share them with the whole class. This is a great way to show students that we value everyone's language.

Enlist older L1 reading buddies. It is empowering for kids to hear someone besides their parents using their native language.

For students who are learning to read, set aside some time in school for silent reading in their language. It is not enough to tell students to read in their language at home; we need to give 'air time' to what we say is important.

Make multilingual books part of your classroom library display. Children need to see books in their languages displayed prominently alongside English language books. If your school does not have a multilingual library, ask parents to share books from home. Better yet, enlist volunteers to begin a multilingual library for your school.

Utilize bilingual teaching assistants. Many international schools hire teacher aides and assistants who are host country nationals; likewise, there are usually several children in each classroom who speak the host country language. We need to make the best use of this invaluable resource by reassuring our assistants that not only is it 'okay' to use the native language, it is desirable to do so.

Read simple pattern books in English and ask children to retell the story in their own language:

> I listen amazed as one by one the students retell the story in Urdu, Turkish, Vietnamese, Chinese, Gujarati, Tamil, Korean and Arabic. The other students in the class appear to be equally entranced, although neither I nor they understand most of the languages being used. It is captivating to hear the same story repeated in different languages with new or sometimes the same gestures to express a change in action. (Excerpt from *Educational Leadership*, September 2005)

Use bilingual writing projects for students in grade one and up to help students develop literacy in both languages. Students can create bilingual expository or fiction books on topics of their choice. Normally students at this level are more comfortable writing first in English, and then taking their books home to get parental help with the native language translation. Wordless picture books work very well for bilingual writing projects. My colleagues and I start with student-generated joint construction of the English text, followed by a native language translation by each student. Some students who share the same native language may choose to collaborate in constructing their translations, which is an excellent way to encourage native language use at school. It is fun to watch students debating and negotiating over how to translate certain words and phrases into their language. At this level, having students create repeating pattern books or books with only a few words per page is more manageable than attempting extended discourse texts, and will allow students to experience success in both languages.

Support for parents

Never miss an opportunity to talk to parents about the importance of using their native language at home. Reading native language books together should be a daily habit. If L1 books are not available, parents and children can talk about the pictures in English books or retell stories together in their native language.

If your school has a multilingual library, make sure parents know where it is and how to use it. Do not leave it to chance that they will discover this invaluable resource for themselves. Also, guide students to check out native language books during your regularly scheduled library time.

Encourage parents to form same-language playgroups for their children. I some-times hear teachers advising parents to develop friendships with English-speaking children, so that their children will have more chances to practise speaking English. This is not a bad idea; we obviously want children to have friends from a variety of cultural backgrounds who speak many different languages. In such contexts, the children are almost inevitably going to speak their common language, usually English. However, children also need time to interact with children who speak the same native language they do. By playing together, children have a chance to hear and practice language in ways they rarely do with parents or other adults. It is also important for their emerging cultural identities to have some friends who are 'like' them. I think parents need to hear teachers validate this idea.

Send home wordless picture books that can be 'read' in any language.

In your newsletters to parents share information about topics or themes being studied at school. Parents can reinforce concepts and vocabulary in their L1. This will build background and allow transfer across languages – and ultimately lead to more language learned and retained in both languages.

Here is a sample from one of our Pre-K newsletters:

Today we brainstormed words associated with water, and I am sending you the list just to show how much is going on in their brains, and also for those who want to explore and expand on these words in their home language. The chil-dren's learning about objects that sink or float has been made more interesting with the objects from home. The children tested their hypothesis. Many thought that if something was heavy, it would sink – then we tried another object that weighed the same but floated … The thinking continues ….

We have begun learning fish poems and rhymes, and making ocean scenes. The children are enjoying the water table, and I will now be adding or taking away different containers to see how water works! I will also add different substances to the water to keep the children thinking – what will happen to the bar of soap? How long will it take to dissolve? Will the water look the same? Will it make any difference if we handle the soap?

In math we have focused more on numbers, and we have been reading number books about water creatures – adding one more, taking one away, and recogniz-ing numerals.

Words Related to Water

Rain	Clouds	Drink
Sea	Bathwater	Cooking water
Ice	Snow	Pool
Puddle	River	Lake
Waves	Sink	Drown
Wash	Dry	Float
Wet	Sink (verb)	Ocean
Cold water	Warm water	Hot water
Spray	Swim	Tap
Sprinkler	Hose	

While sending home thematic word lists is a good first step, it may be hard for busy, well-intentioned parents to follow through in their native language without further support. Some suggestions of tangible ways are given below.

Use technology to support multilingual learning

Websites such as www.echantedlearning.com have excellent resources that can be adapted for any language (full access is for site members only, but much is available without a subscription). Continuing the water theme example, there is a printable book about ocean animals that can be sent home and translated into the home language (lines for writing are provided). There are ocean animal printouts that can be labelled in any language, rebus nursery rhymes related to the water theme, and many other activities suited for young learners up to Grade 3.

Teachers can use sites such as Google 'images' to introduce thematic vocabulary (it is better if you use an LCD projector for larger groups). My son's kindergarten teacher recently did this to introduce vocabulary and concepts related to their unit on the moon (phases of the moon, features of the moon's surface, etc.). My child, who normally shares very little unsolicited information about his school day, came home bursting with excitement about the pictures he had seen of the moon. His wise veteran teacher also used this topic as an opportunity to integrate culture and talk about how Ramadan is linked to the phases of the moon.

Internet images can also be used to make your own thematic books, which can be sent home and translated. Use Google images or surf the net to find free printable resources such as http://www.english-4kids.com/flashcards.html or http://bogglesworldesl.com/cards.htm. Any supports such as these that we can send home will encourage busy parents to follow through with home language and literacy development.

There are a number of websites that have multilingual or dual-language books such as http://thornwood.peelschools.org/dual/index.htm. The Dual Language Showcase, with student created texts in 17 languages (http://www.childrenslibrary. org/). International Children's Digital Library with online books in 39 languages. You can search for books by age and language (http://www.childrensbooksonline. org/library.htm). Children's Books Online: The Rosetta Project has a variety of downloadable books in multiple languages, but parents might need help to navigate this site.

For students who are developing literacy skills, use online bilingual dictionaries such as Little Explorers Picture Dictionary in several languages (http://www. enchantedlearning.com/Dictionary.html) and/or translation tools like Babel Fish (http://babelfish.yahoo.com/) or Google Translate (http://translate.google.com/ translate_t#). While the translations are not perfect, it is powerful for kids to see their writing translated from English into their home language or vice versa. I also use these tools for beginners in English who are literate in their native language. It helps to bridge the communication gap and establish a connection with my students. They are thrilled when I try to pronounce words or phrases in their language, and enjoy teaching me how to 'say it right'.

Use iPods to record parent volunteers or older students reading books in different languages as part of your listening center.

Do not forget about your digital cameras! These can be used to document a multitude of language experience activities and create dual-language books. The English text can be jointly constructed in school, while the native language text may be added with the help of parents at home. Children will enjoy reading books about their own lives and experiences. These books can also be used to inspire oral practice in the native language at home, since children will have a lot to say about activities they were part of.

And finally

Celebrate International Mother Language Day (February 21), proclaimed by UNESCO in November 1999, and observed every year since February 2000 to promote linguistic and cultural diversity and multilingualism. Launch a school-wide effort to highlight this important day. A bilingual project showcase can be part of this celebration. The following is a list of suggestions given to our teachers last year:

Suggestions for teachers for International Mother Language Day on February 21
(Some ideas are more appropriate for upper elementary)

- Ask each of your bilingual students, to say 'Hello' or 'Yes' or some other word or phrase in their own language.
- Ask each nonnative speaker to bring a book from home in their mother language to share with classmates.
- Provide a poster or chart on which each student could write 'Hello' or some other word or phrase in their mother language. During our school-wide 'year of

the reader', students wrote 'I love reading' in multiple languages; in the 'year of the writer', we wrote 'I can write in _____ (name of language)'.

- These charts were put on display at the entrance to our school, and students enjoyed seeing how many languages they could read.
- Take the entire class to the school library to look at the multilingual book collection. Students show the teacher and other students some of the books in their language.
- Check out some books from the multilingual book collection to display in the room, making them available to students to read during silent reading time.
- If there is a birthday this week, sing the 'Happy Birthday' song in each language represented in the classroom.
- Students start a multilingual picture dictionary of the most important school words a new student might need to learn.
- Students read aloud a Mother Tongue picture book while others listen and discuss what they think the book is about according to the pictures.
- Read aloud one of the multilingual books that is bilingual with English, reading it in both languages.
- Create a world map and add the languages the students know to the countries where the languages are spoken.
- Get a wordless book for the entire class to write about in their mother tongue.
- Learn to count in the languages represented in your class. Record parents or older students saying the numbers slowly and clearly to use as a model. Ask a parent to come share information about a different culture/language.
- Ask a parent to tell the class an interesting story about language use in their country (e.g. a student may come from a country where there was a period in history when their language was banned).
- Discuss why it is valuable to maintain many different languages in the world.
- Write about what your language means to you. How would you feel if you were forced to use a language you do not know?
- Create a project that would benefit other students from their home country or language group (e.g. a dual-language manual or voice recording about the school or host country, recordings of books on MP3, etc.).

CONCLUSION

In international schools with children from many different language backgrounds, we can still foster mother-tongue development even though it may not be feasible to have a bilingual program. As Cummins points out, 'an additive orientation does not require the actual teaching of the minority language' (Cummins, 1986).

Research clearly shows that having a strong foundation and literacy background in the first-language promotes second-language acquisition. As we move beyond 'English Only' practices and policies, we have a responsibility not just to tolerate the use of L1, but to create classroom environments where our students' native languages may flourish; where multilingual and multicultural identities are valued; where the native language is seen as a resource rather than a liability; where English is learned in an additive, rather than a subtractive context and where all children are enabled to meet their personal and academic potentials. Using multilingual strategies to promote home language development is a choice we as educators can make, regardless of our educational context.

REFERENCES

Ballantyne, K.G. (2008) Learning a second language while you are still working on the first. *AccELLerate!* The quarterly newsletter of the National Clearinghouse for English Language Acquisition 1, 9–11. On WWW at http://www.ncela.gwu.edu/accellerate/AccELLerate1.1.pdf. Accessed 17.1.09.

Cummins, J., Bismilla, V., Chow, P., Cohen, S., Giampapa, F., Leoni, L., Sandhu, P. and Sastri, P. (2005) Affirming identity in multilingual classrooms. *Educational Leadership* 63, 38–43.

Cummins, J. (1986) Empowering minority students: A framework for intervention. *Harvard Educational Review* 56, 18–36.

Cummins, J. *Bilingual Children's Mother Tongue: Why Is It Important for Education?* On WWW at http://www.iteachilearn.com/cummins/mother.htm. Accessed 25.1.09.

García, O. (2008) Personal communication to author.

Hamayan, E. and Freeman, R. (eds) (2006) *English Language Learners at School: A Guide for Administrators.* Philadelphia: Calson Publishing.

Irujo, S. Promoting native language and culture in English-only programs. *The ELL Outlook.* On WWW at http://www.coursecrafters.com/ELL-outlook/2005/may_jun/ELLOutlook ITIArticle3.htm. Accessed 3.2.09.

About the author

Denise Sullivan is an elementary ESL teacher at Cairo American College in Cairo, Egypt. She has an MA in Teaching English as a Foreign Language from the American University in Cairo (1994). She has presented papers regularly at conferences (TESOL, NESA, ECIS, ESL/MT) on a variety of topics relating to ESL and Mother Tongue teaching. Denise has previously published 'Celebrate Me: Writing an Autobiography'. In *New Ways in Teaching Secondary ESL*. Deborah Short, ed. (1999).

Chapter 3

A Year with Five Beginners: Excerpts from the Journal of a First-Grade Teacher

PATRICIA PARKER

This chapter is a collection of excerpts from the reflection journal of a first-grade teacher. It charts the process of settling in for five non-English-speaking students, and describes how they gradually became involved in classroom activities through art and projects linked to the units of study.

INTRODUCTION

In the week of preparation which preceded the start of the school year, I was informed by the head that amongst my new students, there would be five total beginners in English: three Israelis, an Icelandic and a Korean boy and also a girl with learning difficulties. As is the case in many international schools, my school was witnessing the rapid growth of its ESL population, most of whom have two or more languages. However, I had never had so many complete beginners before and was aware of the challenges that this would present.

Tuesday 28th August 2007

I enjoyed meeting all children with their families at our 'Meet the Teacher' session the day before the start of school. The sun poured into my classroom, high up on the second floor surrounded by trees. The children explored their new surroundings. We talked about the animal posters which covered the wall as I explained that learning about animals would be our first unit of study.

This was a wonderful opportunity for me to get to know the families, answer questions and to talk about our first-grade program. The parents of my 'Beginners' acted as translators for their children – 'Do you like animals?' I asked and the children nodded and beamed their approval. Through these meetings I was able to build up a picture of my future class. Along with the five beginners, there were also 10 students with multiple languages. They had parents with different nationalities and some of them had already done their preschool education at a Belgian school, either in Flemish or in French. I realized that I would only have five native English speakers in my class, who had both parents speaking English as their mother tongue. My final meeting was with Bethan and her parents. Her father is Welsh and her mother is Dutch. Bethan already has been diagnosed with learning difficulties. She has a low IQ and will need lots of extra support. The children were all delightful but I realized that the composition of the class was complex and that I had many interesting challenges.

Wednesday 29th August

Today, my beginners were faced with the reality of starting school in a totally new language. I went out to collect my class and as they lined up on the playground, I noted the varied expressions on their faces – happiness, excitement and anticipation; but for some there was acute anxiety. I looked at the three Israeli children. Netta, blonde and curly haired, clung to her father, weeping silently. Daniella nestled close to her mother, while giving me a reproachful look. Yair stood stiffly as he tried to be brave. Hendrik, the tall fair-haired Icelandic boy also sobbed loudly, as his parents held his hands. Sang Il, the Korean, was the only one of my beginners who appeared to be feeling positive about this new experience – perhaps because he had lived in Belgium for a while, although, because he had been to a French-speaking maternelle, learning in English would also be a new language for him.

I took the children upstairs, accompanied by some of the parents, for our first day together. I had set up the classroom with lots of interesting learning centres, but first the children found their cubbies, hung up their bags and then tentatively made a circle on the rug. 'Let's introduce ourselves', I said 'We can say Hello in our own language' – which they obligingly did. There were greetings in French, Greek, Spanish, Japanese, Hindi, Urdu, Korean, Icelandic, Dutch, English and even Welsh. But my two Israeli girls refused to comply. Netta sobbed loudly and Daniella joined in too, clinging to her mother's legs as she sat behind. What could I do to alleviate their anguish? I suddenly thought of the first-grade guinea pigs and remembered how a couple of years before our furry friends had given comfort to little Cecilia from Sweden. I took Emily and Chocolate Chip from their cage and these Beatrix Potter-type creatures blinked their eyes, twitched their noses and obligingly squeaked at the class. Netta suddenly smiled, as I placed Emily in her lap and gave Chocolate Chip to Daniella. The guinea pigs had helped save the day!

With our introductions over, the children moved off to play. This would be a good opportunity for me to observe and for them to make new friends. I took Netta, Daniella and Yair over to the painting table. Reluctantly they had let their parents leave, but they naturally wanted to stay together, talking urgently in Hebrew. They were joined by Tako, a Japanese boy, Bethan, half Dutch and half Welsh and Maria, the daughter of our school music teacher. 'Let's paint our favourite animals' I said. Maria offered to help and I could tell that she was going to be my right hand girl! 'What colour paper would you like?' she said to Netta, 'There's blue, yellow, green and pink.' 'Pink', said Netta, pointing to the pink. It was her first word in English and she had learned it from a peer! Netta painted a beautiful white rabbit with pink nose and blue whiskers – 'I like your rabbit', said Maria. Daniella painted a brown bear with a purple bow and Yair painted a whale spouting water. I asked him if he had seen a whale. He looked at me blankly. 'You see whale?' said Tako, pointing to his eyes. Yair nodded. I observed how my Beginners were beginning to learn English from their peers, and how much Maria, Bethan and Tako were enjoying their role. After the paintings were finished, we made labels. I remembered I had some animal picture cards with names in different languages on the back. Bethan helped Netta find the rabbit picture card. I wrote Rabbit on the label for Netta's picture and then copied the word in Hebrew. The Israelis watched with delight as I struggled with the letters of their alphabet and then repeated this process for Maria, Bethan and Tako in their languages. I realized how important it was for them to see their own language in this strange English environment.

Next I took them out to the open area adjoining the classroom where other children were playing. The girls went to the dress-up clothes and Yair and Tako went over to the building blocks to join Hendrik, the Icelander. Hendrik had already embarked on a huge, well-balanced construction, aided by some new friends. In the months to come, Hendrik made some amazing things that often became the centre of group play. Today, his first day in school, he was already standing on a chair to add more and more blocks. 'Higher' said his assistants in awe waiting for his construction to topple. 'I like your tall building' I said. 'Hengingsbor' said Hendrik. Not having a word of Icelandic, I could only nod in approval. 'It's very high' I said. 'High', repeated Hendrik. I got my digital camera to photograph Hendrik's masterpiece, much to his delight. I reflected that my beginners seemed to be happy, but what about Sang Il? I found him at one of the classroom laptops playing number shark with Sushant, a boy from India, who had immaculate English. As Sang Il solved the addition problems on the computer he yelled out the answers in English. His wise mother had already taught him to count to 20. Sushant was impressed and Sang Il, a very congenial boy seemed happy. I wondered why change and separation were so much easier for some children than others.

Somehow we got to the end of the first day despite the tears. The school councillor called in to see how things had gone. I told her that I could do with some interpreters. She offered the help of some Israeli sixth graders and Hendrik's brother for the following morning, to make things easier. It was almost time to go home. The strain was evident on little Netta's face and she was overjoyed when her father walked into the classroom to collect her and showed him her rabbit painting. Hendrik's father admired his son's building. 'What is Hengingsbor?' I asked. Hendrik's dad explained that it was the biggest church in Iceland. We decided to keep Hendrik's block construction and I made another label – 'Hengingsbor, the biggest church in Iceland!' Hendrik went off with his Dad, obviously feeling very proud.

As I drove home from school I reflected on the events of our first day and the phenomenon of culture shock. During the summer vacation I had read *Third Culture Kids* by Pollock and Van Reken) which offered an amazing insight into the problems and confusion that children experience who travel the world with their parents. My five beginners were prime examples of Third Culture Kids or TCKs as they are now known. Netta's mother is a diplomat and the family had recently spent three years in Korea. After this assignment they had returned to Israel for a long vacation where the children enjoyed continuous sunny weather, outdoor neighbourhood play with large groups of friends and the loving support of their extended families. Now they were living in an apartment in Brussels, with no family support and frequent grey skies. Yair's parents are also diplomats and had been relocated to Bolivia for just two months before moving on to Brussels because there was no room for their children in the local international school. Hendrik's family had moved from Iceland to Belgium because of his mother's job with the Icelandic embassy. In Iceland, he had been used to a kindergarten, with lots of freedom, outside play and not too much emphasis on academics. I tried to understand the sense of alienation and dislocation that these children must all be feeling, probably not unlike what I myself had suffered when moving from England to Belgium, many years ago.

Thursday 30th August: The second day of school

Netta, Daniella and Hendrik were again very tearful when I went to collect the class, but we were accompanied upstairs by the two sixth graders, Jonathan and Jenia, and by Hendrik's brother. What a difference it made to have interpreters!

After our 'Good Morning' ritual, I explained that we would be drawing pictures and writing about something exciting we had done in the summer vacation. This writing assignment would be for the whole class and would serve as an assessment piece to discover what the children knew about writing. Originally we had planned, as a first-grade team, that the Beginners should not participate. Then on second thought we decided it was important for them to feel part of the process and the class. They could tell about their vacation by drawing pictures and dictate their comments to our sixth-grade translators – perhaps some of them could write a caption in their own language. The children's pictures were wonderful and definitely evoked the events of the summer. Daniella drew herself wearing armbands with her friends at the swimming pool. Netta had been on a big rollercoaster and drew herself clinging on. Yair drew himself and his pet dog at his grandmother's in Israel. The sixth graders wrote captions in Hebrew and translated them into English. Hendrik drew a picture of himself at the biggest church in Iceland and surprised us by writing about it himself in Icelandic; his brother translated it into English. Sang Il enjoyed drawing a large plane. We established, in French, that it was a drawing of him coming back from vacation in Korea. Afterwards, I noted the pride of the beginners as their pictures and writing were shared along with the rest of the class. I thanked our interpreters and this was the first of many visits. It was decided that this work with first-grade children should be part of their sixth-grade community service project.

That evening I reflected on how comforting it had been for the Beginners to hear their mother tongue in their new and bewildering environment. I also thought about the power of the children's drawings and how it would have been possible to understand their vacation stories, even without the writing. As a teacher in first-grade, I value the role of drawing and art to help young children express what they feel, think and understand. A few years before, as part of my professional development, I had been lucky enough to go with a group of colleagues to visit the schools of Reggio Emilia in northern Italy. These had been founded by Loris Malaguzzi, a local teacher, after the destruction of World War II. Malaguzzi saw art as a powerful tool for children to show what they know without using written language and the value of art is integral in the Reggio philosophy. An article in *Time Magazine*, made the schools of Reggio Emilia world famous and their practices were adopted by many Early Childhood institutions. After my visit, I realized that art would also be a powerful tool for my first graders, especially those who were just beginning to learn English. As I planned my units of study, I thought of the many ways in which art could be integrated.

Tuesday, 25th September: Our visit to the Antwerp Zoo

It was with great excitement that the whole first-grade boarded two buses bound for Antwerp Zoo. Some parents were invited to join us as chaperones. Our class was accompanied by Yair's mom, Sophia's mom and Hendrik's dad. For a whole month we had been learning about animals. We had enjoyed many books, both fiction and nonfiction. We had looked at DVDs and found information on the internet. We had done lots of drawing and painting and made animal masks. The main purpose of this unit of study was for the children to understand how an animal's body is adapted for survival in its habitat. We took clip boards with us to the zoo so that the children could draw some of the animals, and they went off in small groups with the parents. In the schools of Reggio Emilia, high importance is attached to observational drawing; by spending time and looking carefully, children can better understand the true essence of what is in front of them. Yair went with his mom, accompanied by Netta and Daniella. I thought it would be good for them to be able to converse in Hebrew. She also had Maria and Sushant in her group and so English was very much part of the language experience too. When I caught up with them, they were busy drawing the giraffes, including Yair's mom who was obviously quite an artist. 'Why do giraffes have such long necks?' I asked and Yair's mom translated into Hebrew. Yair answered 'to reach the leaves' and I repeated his answer in English. I continued to question the children. 'Why do they have such a beautiful patterned skin?' Maria said she thought it was for camouflage as the grass in Africa is yellow. 'Why do giraffes need camouflage?' I continued. 'Because of enemies ... lions, cheetahs and hyenas', said Sushant.

And so, as the drawings were completed the discussion had evolved. The English speakers had been able to explain their understanding of camouflage and the food chain in the African savannah. The Israeli children had been able to participate because Yair's mom acted as an interpreter, but they were also learning new vocabulary in English such as the names of the animals and the parts of their body. 'Giraffes have long tongues', I said, sticking my tongue out and pointing to the giraffe, curling its tongue around the leaves at the top of the tree. 'Yes, to get the leaves' said Maria and Netta laughed as we all stuck out our tongues!

Throughout the day we continued to draw and had many conversations about the different animals we had seen. We enjoyed a picnic and I took lots of digital photographs to record our visit. I find digital photography one of the most important tools in teaching, as it captures the moment, can be immediately printed and serves as a great stimulus for writing the following day. Finally before leaving, we visited the zoo shop. The children had brought spending money and were able to choose a souvenir. Feeling tired and happy, they played with their new purchases on the bus. 'What have you got?' I said to Netta. She thought ... 'Tiger', she said clutching her fluffy stripy toy. 'Beeeer' said Daniella showing me her white polar bear. Yair had a seal and was playing with Sushant who had a seal too. These new acquisitions were to prove very precious and were brought into school for many weeks to come.

Wednesday 26th September

What a busy day! The school photographer came and we also started our books about the zoo. Each child had his own book of brightly coloured pages to be filled with the drawings that we had done at the zoo, along with the digital photos, writing and a map of the zoo so that the children could retrace their footsteps on the visit. I had made a power point of the photos I had taken, which I posted on the school internet for all the parents to see. I showed it to the children. They were delighted to relive the visit and lots of conversations accompanied our viewing. Our sixth-grade interpreters were there too and enjoyed hearing about our day at the zoo. The children then chose their own photo to write about. The Beginners started with a simple 'This is' formula which they would use many times – 'This is me and my mom at the zoo. We are drawing the giraffes', wrote Yair.

It was at this time that I gave the Beginners their first reading book 'At the Zoo'. We sat together and read as a group. It had a simple formula, repeated on every page . . . .

'I went to the zoo and saw a lion',

'I went to the zoo and saw a monkey', etc.

Later in the day I went down with the children to their art class. The art teacher had been to Reggio Emilia too and we both shared the same enthusiasm for working in the Reggio way. The children were split into two groups and changed activities halfway through the lesson. Some of them used pastels to draw their favourite animals, thinking of pattern of skin and body parts. Other children worked on a zoo mural. There was a huge canvas stretched on the floor and about 10 children ready for painting. We discussed the rules, which were to respect each other's work and gradually the animals appeared side by side. Sang Il, forever the transport enthusiast, painted our bus. Every detail was included, not only the animals, but fences, the picnic area, the shop, the seal show, and so on. I observed the Beginners starting to communicate in English, 'Give me the grey', said Hendrik about to paint a huge elephant. As the children painted I heard many interesting conversations.

On my journey home I thought about the ways my Beginners were starting to use English, to talk and write about the zoo visit and to interact with their classmates while painting the mural.

Wednesday, 21st November: The Bake Sale

We continued to work on our animal unit, with lots of different activities to stimulate thinking and the use of language. We decided to have a pets' week. I had brought in my new puppy called Gloria, and Maria brought in her Chihuahua. The children also brought in photographs of their pets to write about. Yair brought a picture of his dog, Sufa, who was back in Israel being cared for by his grandmother. We also had a visit from a local vet.

As a team, my colleagues and I thought it was important to discuss the problem of endangered species with the children as we wanted to foster a sense of responsibility among the children for the animal life on our planet. We decided to have a Bake Sale to support WWF. My class wanted to support the orangutans of Indonesia, who are threatened by loss of habitat.

We found a website showing sanctuaries where orphaned orangutans are cared for and trained to return to the wild. We did some 'persuasive' writing, describing the plight of the orangutans and used this and some appealing photos for our posters. Our sixth-grade interpreters explained the project to the Beginners who learned some new vocabulary, such as 'Please come and help the Orangutans.' Our parents helped by baking cakes and cookies and we had lots of international specialties. The children made price tags and this was a good opportunity to look at the euro and the cent pieces. We invited the whole of the Early Childhood Center and the Elementary school to come and buy. Parents helped the first graders to serve up the goodies. Afterwards we counted up our takings, another good opportunity for math, as we piled the euros into tens. We were delighted to have made almost 300 euros for a very good cause.

Wednesday 30th November: Animal habitats

Our animal unit was drawing to a close and we decided that each child should make his own animal habitat, as a form of assessment. Written language was not required for this and so we felt this would be a good way of assessing what the children had learned, whatever their level in English. I started collecting empty boxes from the photocopy room and in art class, the children made their favourite animal out of clay. The box would become the habitat, showing appropriate vegetation, shelter, sources of food and possible enemies or danger. We began by painting our boxes and talked about appropriate colours – warm or cold depending on the location of the habitat. Hendrik made a white polar habitat, complete with polar bear, and seals and fish to eat. His brother came to view his work at the end of the day and we talked about dangers for the polar bear. We decided that global warming and melting ice was a big threat. Hendrik discussed this with his brother and added a large orange sun to his arctic habitat. Daniella made a panda. We had lots of bamboo growing in our school grounds and she stuck this into play dough for her panda's habitat. 'What is the panda's enemy?' I asked. Jenia her sixth-grade friend took Daniella to the library to do some research and discovered it was a mountain leopard. Netta made a brown bear and painted a river in her box, full of fish. 'It's like baby bear', she said, referring to a book she had read called Baby Bear goes Fishing. Maria commented that bears also like berries and drew a tree to show Netta what she meant. Sang Il made an African elephant and used guinea pig straw for the savannah. Yair made a whale in an underwater ocean scene. 'Be careful of the hunters', said Sushant and he and Yair drew a whaling ship which was stuck at the top of the ocean habitat. And so the children learned from each other. As the class completed their boxes, we displayed them on the window ledges around the room. Then we made a short video clip of each child talking about his animal habitat. The Beginners were able to say a couple of simple sentences too and we posted the clips on our class website for the parents to see.

Friday, 8th December

At the end of the first term, we decided to give the children a spelling test to see how they were doing. We, the first-grade team, felt that the Beginners could participate as they had been doing lots of work on words and phonics as part of their special intensive English class which they attended for an hour a day, although they would only do the first few words. The test was taken from the *Words Their Way* spelling scheme and would help us ascertain knowledge of beginning and final consonants, short and long vowels, consonant digraphs and blends and inflected endings. I showed pictures of the words and pronounced them slowly to help the beginners. They wrote the words cautiously. Netta was very serious and unsure of herself, but by comparison, Hendrik was very happy and enthusiastic. I was very pleased that they all knew some beginning and final consonants and some short vowels. Hendrik was the most successful, I presume because Icelandic is a Nordic language with some letter pronunciation like ours. Daniella and Yair had also made good attempts. Netta had found it more difficult perhaps because of her unwillingness to have a go. Sung Il did the test with enthusiasm but was less successful in relating the sounds he heard to the correct letter. Did his Korean mother tongue impede his ability to differentiate sounds in English?

We have ended the term and the year with numerous activities. We went to the Grand'Place as part of our Belgian Studies programme, designed to give our children an insight into the history and culture of Belgium. The Grand'Place was decked out in all its Christmas finery with a huge decorated Christmas tree. We admired the nativity scene with its live sheep and we enjoyed looking in the shops at all the Belgian specialities – beautiful crystal, lace, tapestries and delicious chocolates. Sung Il's mom came to help as a chaperone and so did Netta's dad. Netta was delighted and was also excited because her parents are coming to school again later this week to help us celebrate Hannuka. We celebrated Hannuka and also Santa Lucia with our Swedish parents. I marvelled at how lucky our children are to learn so much about each other's cultures through festivals and celebrations.

SPRING TERM, JANUARY 2008

We started back to school with cold frosty weather and a little bit of snow. Hendrik was delighted. 'It's like in Iceland', he told me. Netta and Daniella shivered. 'Do you have snow in Israel?', I asked Yair. He smiled but did not reply. I noticed how little he was willing to communicate and I talked to our school psychologist. We were beginning to suspect that the diagnosis of autism, which had already been suggested after Yair had been tested in Israel, was true. He is an interesting boy – verbal communication and emotional responses are difficult for him, but he is obviously a very intelligent boy, particularly gifted in math. Yair's mom is worried about him and I have frequently tried to reassure her. He has suffered from frequent moves in his short life, and since autistic children do not handle change well, he might have been particularly affected by them.

Monday, 15th January

We have started our new unit of study called The Human Body. I brought in a full-size skeleton and we talked about bones and joints. The ESL teacher is covering the same unit in her classes and my Beginners are learning words like ankle, wrist, elbow, and so on. We are now making body maps. The children have been working in partners and drawing round each other. They have painted around their own outline in pink. Netta and Daniella love this and have spent a long time painting their hair too! Then the children used white paint for their skeletons, observing the full-size skeleton to get the bones in the correct place. When the paint was dry the children cut out their body maps. Then we looked at a chart showing all the main organs. Using different coloured paper, the children drew and cut out their main organs and stuck them on. We used blue crepe paper for our small intestine and the children could not believe how long it is! During this whole process, I photographed the class at work and noted down the Beginners conversations. 'Tako made me too fat', complained Sung Il, while Hendrik proclaimed he was very tall!

Friday 20th January

Today was 'Share in our Learning Day' and the parents came to observe their children at work. We showed our knowledge of the skeleton. Each child had a chance to name and point to a part of the body. Then we looked at a power point presentation of the children making their body maps. After this the Beginners went off to their intensive English class, while the rest of the class did 'procedure writing' describing how they had made their body maps. I had printed for each one a photo of themselves at work as a prompt. The children also had a vocabulary list with the names of body parts to refer to. Then I gave them a skeleton to cut out and assemble. When the Beginners came back they also did the writing assignment. They are now writing introductory phrases and beginning to write independently using developmental spelling. Daniella wrote 'This is my body map. Netta dro mi. I pated mi pinc wiv a wit scetan'. (This is my body map. Netta draw me. I painted me pink with a white skeleton). I was delighted that she was having a go!

Friday 2nd February: Making a family book

We started another writing project last week. The children are making a book about themselves and their families. I have asked the parents to send in or email photos of the children starting from babyhood, and photos of the family, including grandparents, pets and family holidays, and so on. This is now the second week and everyone is very excited! Netta and Daniella have lots of photos of their families back in Israel and their school and a dancing class that they both went to. Hendrik has photos of a visit to Legoland. Yair has photos of his dog back in Israel. Sung Il has photos of his visit to see his grandparents back in Korea. He is especially excited about the journey there as he loves airports and aeroplanes. Luckily, from time to time, the sixth graders have been able to come over to help with explanations, but the children are doing a wonderful job orally and beginning to speak and write with much more confidence, especially Hendrik. Written Icelandic does have some similarities to written English.

20th February: Owl pellets

About this time every year we do an owl pellet investigation. A few years ago, a colleague and I went to a science conference in St Louis, Missouri (USA), where we had the privilege of hearing Buzz Aldrin speak about his adventures in space. We had a good look at what the publishers and educational suppliers had to offer, and decided that owl pellets would be a great addition to our study of animals. We have done lots of preliminary work about owls in the classroom and enjoyed some excellent nonfiction books from the library and some wonderful owl stories, the favourite of which was *Owl Babies* by Martin Waddell and *The Owl Who was Afraid of the Dark* by Jill Thomlinson. We talked about how owls regurgitate fur and bones in pellet form after eating their prey. Each child was given his own owl pellet and worked with small wooden sticks to take the wrapped parcel apart. I paired the Beginners with a fluent English speaker and the children had a bone chart to help them identify the various bones and check them off. 'My owl ate a rat', said Hendrik decisively. 'My owl ate a bird' said Netta. It was wonderful to hear the children expressing themselves so confidently.

14th March: Portfolio Conference Day

The children have been looking forward to this occasion for days and were excited to show their parents all their hard work. They had been busy decorating their huge portfolio envelopes and making choices of their best work to put in.

The conferences took place, four at a time. It was wonderful to hear the children discussing their work with their parents in both their mother tongue and English. Daniella said 'This is my Body Book and I can write a lot!' Yair showed his parents his owl pellet investigation taking them to a chart on the wall which explained the food chain. Hendrik proudly shared his Star Wars story, reading it carefully in English. Sung Il showed all his math work to his mom, explaining how he had used links to measure the distance different cars rolled in his car-rolling experiment and how he had made a graph of the results. Netta read her journal to her parents, who were delighted to see how she was now able to write about her weekend activities in English.

My greatest feeling of satisfaction came from seeing how much the children had learned and from talking to the parents afterwards: hearing how happy their children are at school and how impressed the parents are with their progress!

SUMMER TERM: MAY 2008

Our new unit is called 'Communicating through the Arts' and the main event this term is our work with the Theatre in Education (TIE). People from this truly excellent organization work with teachers to put on a play with costumes and scenery. The plays are usually mimed to music to take away the burden of learning lines. We usually chose fairy tales as a basis for our plays. My class is going to perform Hansel and Gretel. Lynne and Steve, from TIE, are working with my class. Steve does various games with the class and then casts the children in their parts. He often encourages less confident children to take the more important parts. He has chosen the Beginners for many of the main parts: how wonderful for their confidence! Hendrik is going to be Hansel. Bethan, the girl with learning difficulties, is so happy to be Gretel. Sung Il will be the Father, Daniella is the wicked step mother. Netta is the little white cat and Yair is a candy monster guarding the witch's house.

21st May: The big production

After four twice-weekly sessions of rehearsal we were ready for our show. We painted a wonderful candy house on canvas as part of our scenery. The children excitedly put on their costumes, complete with makeup. Everyone had a part. Maria was the perfect witch. The girls were beautiful birds and animals of the forest, comforting Hansel and Gretel when they were lost. The boys were wicked candy monsters keeping Hansel and Gretel prisoner in the witch's house. The play was performed to the music from Humperdinck's beautiful opera.

CONCLUSION: JUNE, 2008

The end of the year is rapidly approaching and I look back with satisfaction at the progress made. My Beginners are beginners no more. They love school and are beginning to talk confidently in English. They have learned many basic English words which they use in their writing and they are building words themselves. Netta and Daniella are proud to have written their first story. They all enjoy books and are now reading simple texts. They have acquired good strategies such as using picture and meaning clues to figure out the text. They are beginning to blend sounds to decode words. Hendrik especially has made amazing progress, now reading almost on grade level. They have all enjoyed our math activities. Yair seems to be especially gifted in this area, although he still has difficulty socially. Sung Il has loved all our projects and I will miss his enthusiasm and warm personality next year. But as with all good mothers, I have to be content that they have progressed so far and that they are now ready to leave me and go to second-grade.

I think that the children's success in this first year must be attributed indirectly to some of the major influences on my professional development. A visit to the schools of Reggio Emelia was a formative experience and ever since I have incorporated art into all the children's units of study. The philosophical ideas of John Dewey has also been central to my thinking: I believe strongly that young children learn best from real experiences. A summer session at Harvard to study Howard Gardiner's theory of multiple intelligences has also been a strong influence in my work.

About the author

Patricia Parker obtained her teaching diploma at the University of London's Institute of Education. She began her teaching career among the diverse communities of Islington and Shoreditch. She has been a teacher at the International School of Brussels for many years, working with Kindergarten and First Grade children. She has served on the ECIS Early Childhood Committee and has enjoyed working as a presenter at conferences. At present she is completing her MA in International Education with the University of Bath, UK.

Chapter 4

Developing the Basic English Language Skills of Young Children in a Linguistically Diverse Classroom

CAROL BREEDLOVE

This chapter relates the concerns of an international school teacher when she accepted a position teaching 20 five- and six-year-olds, a mix of native English speakers and ESL learners, and the strategies she used to support the development of basic language skills in her young students are described.

INTRODUCTION

When I accepted the position teaching a Preparatory class, I did so with some reservations. This was the beginning of my 11th year teaching elementary-aged children, nine of which had been spent working in international schools. I had taught first- and second-grade English as a second language (ESL) and native English-speaking students on two continents but never before had I taught five- and six-year-olds. As I took a deep breath, put on my best smile and plunged in that first day, I had two nagging questions at the back of my mind: Should I be teaching these children to read and write in English when they had not begun learning to read and write in their mother tongue? What can I do to maximize the learning of literacy skills for my ESL students as well as for my native English-speaking children?

Before the first day of school, I spent some time reflecting on my basic beliefs about teaching literacy skills to children, since my words and actions in the classroom would stem from them. If a teacher believes students who are given time for reading books of their own choice become better readers because they are more motivated, that teacher will make time everyday for her students to read books of their choice. If a teacher believes students will spend more time on their work if they write about topics that interest them, that teacher will encourage students to share authentic stories from their personal experiences. Such reflecting was an important first step in pre-year planning: if I could identify what I believed in, I would know what to do and why I was doing it.

I also read professional literature to become more knowledgeable. I found no published research specifically addressing the effects of teaching *young* ESL students to read in their L2 before they had learned to read in their mother tongue. Clearly research is needed in this area. The best I could do was to take note of what experts in the field of ESL instruction were saying, and apply their knowledge or adapt their strategies to the teaching of literacy skills to my young students. When I found something that spoke to me, validated my beliefs or raised a red flag, I wrote it in my journal. Very often things get hectic during the school year or I become distracted by the daily housekeeping and administrative details of teaching, and so I began routinely reviewing my journal as I rode the train to work. This habit helped keep me focused and on track during the busy year. In this chapter, I will share some of the ideas that impacted my first year teaching Preparatory students.

RESEARCHING CHILDREN'S LITERACY BACKGROUNDS

> [It is] important ... for teachers to find out about the reading experiences and practices as well as the expectations which young emergent bilinguals and their families bring to school. (Gregory, 1996: 18)

In her book, *Making Sense of a New World: Learning to Read and Write in a Second Language,* Gregory (1996) illustrates through case studies that children come to school with many literacy experiences. She encourages teachers to find out about those experiences in order to build on them. It was a relief to be reminded that I was not at the beginning of the process. Actually, parents are the first teachers of important pre-literacy skills for their children (Baker, 2004; Gregory, 1996). My students had been acquiring literacy skills for the past five or six years through conversations with their parents, listening to bedtime stories, singing songs, reciting nursery rhymes and possibly even through direct reading and writing instruction. I returned to the question in my journal: Should I be teaching these children to read and write in English when they have not begun learning to read and write in their home language? It proved to be a mistake to assume that the young children in my class had not begun to learn to read and write in their home languages. I was now quite interested to discover what early literacy practices and expectations my students and their families had.

To begin with, I carefully read their files. From these I learned which languages were spoken at home and whether or not the children attended preschool, and if so for how long and what the language of instruction was. I read any comments written by previous teachers regarding language achievement and social and emotional development. Reading student files is the obvious place for teachers to start gathering information, although I found this source of limited usefulness. Not all the questions that needed answering were on the forms. Furthermore, some forms contained partial data or no data at all. I made a note to suggest a second look at what is asked in these forms. My next step then was to give the parents a questionnaire to complete. Through these completed forms I became acquainted with the children's interests and could thus use these as a way to motivate them to learn. I also asked the parents to describe their child's strengths, weaknesses and what they hoped their children would learn this year.

And finally, I briefly interviewed the parents before or after school. Several children in my class were bilingual, while others were multilingual or monolingual. I took this opportunity to discuss with parents the languages spoken at home, at what age their child first began speaking, which language was dominant, whether or not the children were learning to read and write in their home languages, who was teaching them and about their child's attitude towards reading and writing. All parents sincerely appreciated the opportunity to discuss their child's literacy experiences in such detail. Not only had I gathered important data to inform my teaching, I had established a positive, cooperative relationship with the parents.

Knowing the language backgrounds and early literacy experiences of my students proved to be valuable information. It enabled me to do more than just choose read-aloud books that reflected the diverse cultures in my class. It enabled me to help children make connections between what they knew about their language and what they were learning about English. If a child had begun learning letter sounds in their native language, I could help them discover similarities and differences between letter sounds in English and their language. If a Japanese child wrote vertically in his journal, I could compliment him for knowing the direction of writing in Japanese and remind him to write horizontally in English. For some activities, we pair students with the same mother tongue so that they can discuss their learning in their own language if they so choose. Thus, I could group my students with children from the other two Preparatory classes or when pairing them with their fourth-grade Book Buddies (more about this later). All young students come to school having been exposed to literacy skills. It is helpful for teachers to investigate these experiences and use that information to inform their teaching.

Building a sense of community while developing speaking and listening skills

> ... the classroom environment – how the teacher affects the socialization process, what the expectations are and how they are communicated, and the modelling

component – can significantly influence student motivation and attention. (Sprenger, 2005: 20)

Teachers who help their students feel good about learning through classroom success, friendships and celebrations are doing the very things the student brain craves. (Jensen, 2005: 77)

While becoming familiar with my students' early literacy experiences, I also considered what I could do to help them feel happy and safe in class. This was one of my efforts to answer the question, 'What can I do to maximize the learning of literacy skills in English for my ESL students?' If the children felt content, socially accepted and secure, they would be better able to learn to their full potential (Carder, 2007).

During our first Unit of Inquiry on games and play, I spent some time observing the students. I wanted them to feel part of a close-knit group, a group in which they were accepted and respected. I noticed, however, that many of the ESL children played alone or engaged in parallel play for much of the time. The two groups were not interacting or playing together. The children tended to group themselves by home language or language proficiency. I also noticed that disagreements often quickly turned physical. When one child wanted the materials another was using, he would simply snatch them away instead of asking for them. This resulted in the other child complaining loudly in protest. If that strategy did not garner the desired result, hitting, pushing and grabbing immediately followed. The inability to communicate effectively was of course a barrier to the children becoming the close-knit group I hoped for. Something needed to be done to develop their ability to communicate with one another, so that they could play together more easily and resolve their differences more peacefully. More time would be spent learning and playing and less time in isolation or fighting.

One day after mediating between two children an argument over Lego which had become physical, I gathered the whole class on the carpet for a talk. 'Many of us feel frustrated and lonely because we can not speak to one another' I began. 'If you feel this way, you are not alone. Did you know, we can still communicate even though we do not all speak the same language? Think about it. Babies and toddlers communicate and play with one another before they are able to speak! Give me a "thumbs up" if you have a baby brother or sister at home. How do you know when the baby is happy? How do you know when the baby is angry? Who would like to share? You are telling me that a baby communicates how it feels and what it wants with gestures, sounds and facial expressions'.

I explained that a gesture is a movement of the body. For example, when they wave their hand to say 'hello' or shake their head from side to side to mean 'no'. The students demonstrated other gestures that they knew such as nodding their head for 'yes', motioning with their hand to say 'come here' and clapping their hands to show pleasure or approval. We also talked about facial expressions. I made a happy face and asked the children to tell me how I was feeling. We noticed and described how my eyes, eyebrows and mouth looked when I was happy. Next I made a worried face. Again we noticed and described my eyes, eyebrows and mouth. Several children made facial expressions to express feelings and we took turns guessing how they felt. 'We can be clever like your babies; we can talk to one another using gestures and facial expressions! Let's brainstorm some gestures and facial expressions to communicate to others who do not speak our language. "What could you do with your body and face to show someone that they can sit next to you in the circle?" With a few suggestions from me to get them started, the children decided they could look at the person and smile, wave their hand towards themselves to say "come here" and pat the floor next to them to say "sit here"'.

'What gestures and facial expressions could you use to tell someone that you do not like what they are doing?' The students decided they could look at the other person, shake their head from side to side to say, 'no' and then back away from the person to indicate that they did not want to fight, and that they wanted the behaviour of the other person to stop. In subsequent lessons, we practised observing facial expressions and body language to understand how others were feeling and to understand their messages. A great book to explore facial expressions further with your students is *Walter Was Worried* by Laura Vaccaro Seeger.

We then discussed the importance of responding respectfully to others and stopping behaviours when asked to stop. We practised these skills through role play and with puppets. These lessons helped the children develop empathy and treat one another with kindness. The lessons also promoted listening skills because the children were taught to look at the person speaking to them and respond appropriately.

Throughout the year as new situations arose, we gathered together to brainstorm gestures and facial expressions to communicate with one another. With reminders and practice through role play, the children began to 'talk' to one another more and rely less on more aggressive ways of resolving their disputes. These lessons helped the children to feel physically safe and emotionally secure in the classroom. Furthermore, an expectation of being a communicator and developing friendships was established. The children were taught specific skills to achieve these goals.

As a result, the students felt empowered to take risks and communicate with one another and with me. They began using their speaking and listening skills. The English-speaking and ESL children began playing with one another more often. The ESL children were interacting more with the native English-speaking children and consequently hearing good models of English for a higher percentage of the time. In addition, when new students entered the class during the year, the children could immediately communicate with them. This reduced feelings of isolation and loneliness for new students. The children were naturally motivated to speak to one another about the games they were playing during the Unit of Inquiry on play and games, so that they practised conversational English more. It is important to find a topic that motivates children in this way. The games unit was perfect for it. Whether the sentences were simple such as, 'Your turn' or more complex, 'Would you like to go first?' I was pleased that the children were communicating with one another and becoming a group!

Incorporating students' languages and cultures into literacy learning

> Speaking, listening, reading or writing in the first or second language helps develop the child's whole cognitive system. (Gallagher, 2008: 38)

After researching the early literacy experiences of the children and helping them feel accepted and respected by their classmates, the next strategy I used to help develop their literacy skills was to incorporate the students' languages and cultures into the learning. I had discovered earlier that all my students had been exposed to pre-literacy skills in their mother tongues and some were indeed now learning to read and write. Eithne Gallagher's words further helped to assure me that my students were experiencing positive cognitive benefits even though the language of instruction was English. There was still reason to be wary, however. These children spend so much of their day in an English language environment at school that English might begin to replace their mother tongue. Furthermore, Carder (2007) made me aware that I would be teaching manners and social skills to my young charges in a language unknown to them before their own cultural identities were fully established. Clearly incorporating the students' languages and cultures into their learning of literacy skills was a crucial strategy to lessen any negative consequences that might occur if they were left out. Furthermore, the students would better understand the concepts and skills taught if they could access the information in their own languages.

It was not as easy as just encouraging or allowing students to read and write in their mother tongues in class. Although some of my ESL students were receiving reading and writing instruction in their first language from their mothers or through mother-tongue classes outside of school, my five- and six-year-old students did not yet possess the confidence to write or read independently in their first language in the classroom. Moreover, they were often shy or reluctant to use or display their mother-tongue skills. I noticed in the classroom environment young children preferred to be seen as being the same as their peers; they did not like attention being drawn to the ways in which they were different. But I wanted to support and encourage their skills in *both* languages, without causing them stress or embarrassment.

I considered ways to develop the children's language skills in English while supporting and encouraging mother-tongue use. We study six Units of Inquiry during the year. The concepts studied include games and play, the senses, systems, homes, magnetism and minibeasts. A good solution then presented itself. In June, parents of children entering the Preparatory class in August are given a list of the Units with a brief description of the inquiry points. With this information, parents of English language learners would be able to purchase resources for their children in their native language when they return to their home countries during the summer or school holidays. If the children already had books, games and other resources at home related to our Units of Inquiry in their home languages, I encouraged them to bring them to school.

During our first Unit of Inquiry on games and play, the children were invited to bring to school a game from their country that they could explain to the class. Since we could not read the instructions, we were dependent on the owner of the game to teach us how to play the game. If a child could not use words to explain the rules, they were encouraged to bring a game to school that could be taught through actions and gestures. This activity created a lot of excitement, interest and participation. Every child was eager to bring a game to school. Equally the children were fascinated to see the boxes with different languages on them and surprised when they realized they recognized the game from their own country. For example, the board game 'Aggravation' is known as 'Mensch ärgere Dich nicht' in Germany. This project helped every child to see that he or she had something in common with the others and could make a valuable contribution to the class.

Children often shared books from home during the other Units of Inquiry. This was a great opportunity to teach pre-reading skills. We learned to take 'picture walks' through books in languages we were not able to read. Just as we had learned to communicate even though we could not all speak the same language, we were now learning to enjoy books even though we could not always read the language of the book (Figure 4.1).

The first time a book in a language other than English is brought to school, I thank the student for sharing their language with us. I always model enthusiasm and interest when children share their languages or culture.

During circle time, I shared the book and posed some questions for consideration and discussion.

'Ki-woon has brought a book to class about homes to share with us. This book comes from Korea and is written in Korean. We are learning about homes, and this book is about homes. But I cannot read it to you because I can't read Korean. It has important information for us, but how can we learn something from a book in a language we can't read?' Many children immediately said 'We can't !' However, some children remembered previous 'picture walks' we had taken through books and said, 'Yes! We can look at the pictures.'

A 'picture walk' is simply examining and discussing the illustrations in a book. A good picture book can be 'read' from the action and details in the illustrations

Figure 4.1 Students' books to support our study of names

alone. We take many picture walks during the year; they increase interest in a story and get the children thinking about it by helping them become familiar with the story before they need to concentrate on the words to be read. Also, the children might recognize a familiar fairy tale or fable they have heard in their own language through the pictures. Instead of 'switching off' from English-language overload, they will often become quite excited and 'switch on' instead. The realization that we could 'read' the pictures of a book written in any language resulted in an avalanche of book sharing that lasted throughout the school year. The children enjoyed noticing which books are read from back to front and which from front to back. They also discovered that some languages are read horizontally from left to right, while other languages are read horizontally from right to left. They were particularly delighted to learn that some languages are read vertically from the top to the bottom of the page. The simple act of sharing books from home turned out to be a rich cultural exchange.

> If both languages are not working fully, perhaps because the school has an English-only policy for example, cognitive and academic performance may be hurt. (Gallagher, 2008: 39)

> Learning to read in one language facilitates reading in a second language. (Baker, 2004: 91)

I strive to support my students' learning and thinking in all of their languages. This does not mean that I teach my students in their home languages. I cannot speak or read all of them. Rather I actively promote mother-tongue language learning outside the classroom. I encourage parents to take advantage of the mother-tongue classes offered on our campus after school. I explain to them the importance of discussing in their home languages the work sent home each Friday with their children.

During the school day, I foster the students' language development by allowing and encouraging children to speak in their native languages in the classroom. This approach adds to the children's feelings of safety and of being valued and accepted. If a student does not understand an explanation or instruction, another child from the same background can repeat the information in their native language. Students can also help one another ask questions, share personal experiences or ease fears.

Book buddies

Sometimes it so happens that a child is the only one in the class who speaks a particular language. When this is the case, pairing this student with one who shares their language can be crucial to assuring the young child that there are people in the school who can understand them and communicate with them and for them. As alluded to earlier, Preparatory children are paired with a student from the upper elementary school (third, fourth or fifth grade) who speaks the same language. Within the first six weeks of school, the Preparatory students meet their Book Buddies and from then on they meet once in a nine-day cycle for 20–30 minutes.

The Book Buddy programme has academic, social and emotional objectives and benefit both the Prep students and the older ones. The older students read to the younger ones in both English and their native language to foster a love of literature and to be a reading role model for the younger ones. Furthermore, a friendly relationship is almost always developed between the two. Oftentimes the younger child will recognize their older buddy on the playground and give an excited wave and greeting. I have seen older elementary students look surprised and pleased by the enthusiastic manner in which the Prep students acknowledge and look up to them. Later if an older student notices that their Prep buddy looks lonely, scared or upset on the playground, he is much more likely to approach him or her to ask what is wrong and help out if possible. And finally, because young children with limited English language skills can feel isolated for most of the school day, the Prep students look forward to reading with their buddies because it allows them some time to talk to someone in their home language (Figure 4.2).

The older Book Buddies prove at times to be a valuable communication assistant as well. Once a bond of trust and respect has begun to form between the older elementary student and the younger one, I sometimes speak to the children through their Book Buddy if, for instance, a child becomes upset and I need to know what the cause is and how I can help.

Other times I might need to be sure that an explanation or behavioural expectation has been clearly understood or to check a child's understanding of a concept. On those occasions when I needed the older student's help, they were always happy to be of assistance and felt proud that they could use their home language skills to lend a hand.

Besides pairing the Prep students with a Book Buddy, we also group the children at times across the three Preparatory classes according to mother-tongue language. For example, for the culminating activity for the Play and Games Unit of Inquiry, the children played games with other Prep children who spoke their home language. We were surprised to find that groups of children who shared a home language other

Figure 4.2 Book buddies enjoying a book in Swedish

than English often chose to speak to one another in English, even when the game they brought from home was in their mother tongue! We found we had explicitly to tell the children that they could play the game and speak their home language with one another if they chose to. The students enjoyed this activity. It was a pleasure to see them become so animated as they experienced the freedom to express themselves to their friends with ease and competence.

Promoting parental involvement

> Parents [should be] informed of the importance of maintaining the mother tongue language and culture. Research shows that the student's level of language in his or her mother tongue has a direct impact on learning another language. (Carder, 2007: 42)

Involving parents in their child's learning means more to me than simply inviting parents into the classroom to help with a craft, chaperon a field trip, read a book or share a holiday or food from their culture. Although parents do all these things and more during the year, I try to include all parents in the teaching and learning of knowledge, concepts and skills when possible. When parents of ESL students ask me what they can do to help their children learn English, I tell them, 'Continue speaking to your child in your native language.' Some parents, anxious for their children to succeed in school, begin teaching them English at home when they should be focusing on developing their child's mother tongue. Zurer Pearson's *A Step-by-step Guide for Parents: Raising a Bilingual Child* (2008) and Baker's *A Parents' and Teachers' Guide to Bilingualism* (2004), are good resources for parents who want their children to learn two or more languages. Both authors explain the importance of maintaining the home language of the child and tell parents what they can do to achieve this end.

Long-term studies such as those of Thomas and Collier (1997) who have collected and processed data from tens of thousands of students over a 20-year period, show clearly that students who receive education in their mother tongue perform better academically and make faster progress in English, which in international schools is usually the target language. They also found that the main variable in students' achievement in English is whether or not they have kept up literacy in their mother tongue (Carder, 2007: 99). When I met parents at New Student Orientation during the first week of school, I advised them to read to their children every day and talk in their native language about the concepts and skills being taught in school. I also encouraged them to contact our ESL Department for information about the after-school mother-tongue classes being offered. I reiterated these recommendations at Back-to-School Night and when I interviewed parents individually. Developing home language proficiency is so crucial to children's' self-concept and academic success that parents should hear it repeatedly.

If parents are going to have meaningful conversations with their children about the concepts and skills being taught, they need detailed, timely information. Over the years, parents have told me again and again, 'I asked him what he learned today in school, and he said, "nothing".' Some children are happy to recount every minute of the school day to their parents during the drive home. Other children simply do not share. To help all parents, especially the latter, the curriculum information parents need is provided in a variety of ways. At the beginning of the year, parents are given a *Parent Student Handbook* that describes the curriculum and outlines the Units of Inquiry for each grade level. Curriculum documents are in the Elementary School library for parents to access at any time. The curriculum is discussed at Back to School Night and materials used are on display for examination by parents. Also a grade level newsletter is sent home every Friday that summarizes skills and concepts taught and those to be introduced the following week.

And perhaps most helpful of all, samples of completed work or work in progress are sent home periodically in a Friday Folder. To assist the parents in having a meaningful conversation with their child, I sometimes attach a 'Home School Connection' note to selected pieces of work. 'Home School Connection' notes clarify learning objectives and encourage parents to discuss their child's learning with them in their native language.

In every Home School Connection note I state the objective of the lesson, list new vocabulary if applicable, and offer suggestions of discussion points. Sometimes I briefly include information about the developmental expectations for five- and six-year-old children. For example, when I send home writing samples, I tell parents that invented spelling is developmentally appropriate and is encouraged to ease children's worries about misspelling words.

During a Unit of Inquiry on homes, the children designed a home by choosing rooms to include in it, as well as the furniture for each room. After completing the project, the students labelled the rooms and some of the items in the rooms. Vocabulary words such as bedroom, kitchen, playroom, living room and bathroom were used. Other words such as bed, sink, toy box, couch, window and door were also added. When the work went home on Friday, I asked parents to label the pictures with the corresponding word in their home language and talk about these words with their child. Throughout the next week, the students took turns sharing their pictures and telling us their native language words for 'bedroom', 'window' or 'sink'. This activity fostered pride in the children sharing their languages and generated great interest from the students in the audience. In addition, acceptance of all the languages and cultures was being modelled in the classroom.

A 'Home School Connection' note for a math investigation might read as follows:

Home School Connection

The objective of this math investigation is to develop language to describe and compare two-dimensional shapes and their attributes

Please discuss your child's picture with him or her. Your child has been introduced to the words: *shape, circle, square, triangle, rectangle, oval* and *rhombus (diamond)*. To support your child's mother-tongue academic skills, please talk about these shapes in your home language.

Encourage your child to describe their picture to you in their home language. For example, you could say: *Tell me what shapes you used in your picture. How did you decide which shapes to use? Which shape is the biggest? How many sides does the triangle have? What do you notice about the sides of the rectangle?*

If you have any comments or questions about this investigation, please write them on the back of this paper and return this work to school on Monday. Thank you!

Some Home School Connection notes are targeted specifically for ESL students, although most of the time these notes are sent home to all parents. Native English-speaking parents need to be informed of their child's learning too. It has been my experience that all children benefit when their parents are interested in their achievement and reinforce their learning at home.

CONCLUSION

My first year teaching Preparatory with both ESL and native English-speaking students was challenging and yet very rewarding. This chapter has aimed to explain how I prepared myself for teaching an unfamiliar grade level and to describe the strategies I used to get to know my students and to build an environment conducive to optimal social development and academic achievement. I hope that my examples of building a sense of community, incorporating the students' languages and cultures into the learning of literacy skills, and promoting parent involvement will help other teachers new to teaching young ESL students. Teachers should always strive to promote the learning of English within an environment which welcomes and encourages L1 growth.

REFERENCES

Baker, C. (2004) *A Parents' and Teachers' Guide to Bilingualism* (2nd edn). Clevedon: Multilingual Matters.

Carder, M. (2007) *Bilingualism in International School: A Model for Enriching Language Education*. Clevedon: Multilingual Matters.

Gallagher, E. (2008) *Equal Rights to the Curriculum: Many Languages, One Message*. Clevedon: Multilingual Matters.

Gregory, E. (1996) *Making Sense of a New World: Learning to Read in a Second Language*. London: Paul Chapman Publishing Ltd.

Jensen, E. (2005) *Teaching with the Brain in Mind* (2nd edn). Alexandria, VA: Association for Supervision and Curriculum Development.

Sprenger, M. (2005) *How to Teach so Students Remember*. Alexandria, VA: Association for Supervision and Curriculum Development.

Thomas, W.P. and Collier, V.P. (1997) *School Effectiveness for Language Minority Students*. Washington, DC: National Clearinghouse for English Language Acquisition. On WWW at http://www.ncela.gwu.edu/pubs/resource/effectiveness/index.html. Accessed 15.7.08.

Zurer Pearson, B. (2008) *A Step-by-Step Guide for Parents: Raising a Bilingual Child*. New York, NY: Living Language.

FURTHER READING

Center for Research on Education, Diversity and Excellence (2003) *A National Study of School Effectiveness for Language Minority Students' Long-Term Academic Achievement*. January. On WWW at http://www.cal.org/resources/digest/ResBrief10.html. Accessed 15.7.08.

Moats, L.C. (1999) *Teaching Reading is Rocket Science: What Expert Teachers of Reading Should Know and Be Able To Do*. On WWW at http://www.aft.org/pubs-reports/downloads/teachers/rocketsci.pdf. Retrieved 1.6.08.

Reid, J., Schultze, B. and Peterson, U. (2005) *What's Next for this Beginning Writer? Mini-lessons that take Writing from Scribbles to Script*. Markham, Ontario, Canada: Pembroke Publishers Ltd.

Virginia Department of Education (1998) *Ideas and Activities for Developing Phonological Awareness Skills: A Teacher Resource Supplement to the Virginia Early Intervention Reading Initiative*. On WWW at http://www.doe.virginia.gov/VDOE/Instruction/Reading/findings.pdf. Retrieved 12.10.08.

Warden, C. (2006) *Talking and Thinking Floorbooks: Using 'Big Book Planners' to Consult Children*. Auchterarder, Perthshire: Mind Stretchers.

About the author

Carol Breedlove earned her Bachelor of Science in Elementary Education from Mississippi State University, she went on to complete her Masters of Education in School Counselling at Valdosta State University. After two years teaching in Tallahassee, Florida, she left public school teaching to become an international school teacher. She has worked in international schools for the past eleven years. She has taught first grade students at Atlanta International School in the United States, and first and second grade students at the International School of Düsseldorf. She is currently teaching Preparatory students at the International School of Düsseldorf.

Chapter 5

An International School Celebrates its Diversity

NANCY STAUFT

International schools vary greatly in size, curriculum and student languages and cultures. This chapter looks at a well-established international school in the Middle East with particular reference to its Early Childhood and Lower Elementary sections.

INTRODUCTION

The school in which I work is a K-12 international school, which caters to the expatriate community in a Middle Eastern country. As the country's nationals require the approval of the Minister of Education to attend schools that do not follow their national curriculum, the population of our school is largely expatriate in nature.

The country has a population of 2.4 million, 24% of whom are expatriate workers (Oman Census Administration, 2003). Most are on nonaccompanied single work visas and work in the construction, farming and service industries. The balance of expatriate workers are employed in the business and education sectors and many of these arrive with families. Although Arabic is the official language of the country, English is the language used by the expatriate community in its day-to-day life. As a consequence, most of our students come from families who have at least one university-educated parent who speaks English.

There are many foreign language schools to choose from, but one of the main attractions of an international school is the opportunity for students to acquire English. Baker (2001) identifies three major reasons for learning a second or third language: ideological, international and individual. For many students attending

English-medium schools here the main reason for learning English is international. Their aim is that by attending an English-medium school they will be part of a wider, English-speaking community.

In an international school it is not unusual to have as many as 40 nationalities in the student population (Mathews, 1989). Our school has 950 students K-12, more than 60 different nationalities of students who speak 50 different languages, with a staff of 20 different nationalities. Our school is unique in that no one nationality predominates. We are truly international.

MISSION, VISION AND VALUES

The school has nearly doubled in size in the last 10 years and since we are an international school with an unusual amount of cultural and linguistic diversity, one thing that has unified staff and students is our Mission, Vision and Values. These focus on providing 'an international education of the highest quality to enable students to be confident, responsible, caring, lifelong learners' (Mission); nurturing students so they can 'achieve their maximum potential in an environment of inter-cultural understanding and respect, to meet the challenges of a rapidly changing world' (Vision) and valuing 'communication, diversity, inquiry, integrity, knowledge, openmindedness, reflection, thinking and willingness to take risks' (Values). All activities in and out of the classroom must be linked to one or more of these three categories. The school language philosophy which was first drafted in 2007 supports our Mission, Vision and Values and states in part that our school:

> ... Is an English-medium school and 'recognizes that language, our major means of thinking and communicating, is fundamental to learning, underpinning and permeating the whole curriculum' (IBO, 2007). Our students learn language but also learn about language and through language using authentic contexts and literature. The four communication strands of listening, speaking, writing and reading are learned and reinforced across and throughout all subject areas. In this context all our teachers are language teachers.

This statement of our teaching philosophy is largely inspired by the International Baccalaureate Organization (IBO) Primary Years Programme (PYP).

Celebrating our linguistic and cultural diversity

So, with a Mission, Vision and Values as well as a language philosophy solidly in place, all of which support and respect our school's linguistic and cultural heritage, it was a natural next step to look at how we celebrated our diversity both as a school and within the classrooms.

As a school, we have for many years hosted an annual *International Food Fair*, supported by the Parent Teacher Association (PTA). This evening of music and food from around the world has always been well attended by the school community. Groups of parents from different countries begin to prepare their country's food stall months in advance.

Another school tradition is the annual *United Nations (U.N.) Day* celebrations. For two evenings in November, students perform in the theatre around the annual United Nations theme. There is dance, music, comedy and art and all students are encouraged to participate in this production organized by the music and drama departments. The atmosphere of anticipation is palpable around the school. Most families attend UN evenings and are enthralled with the cultural diversity of the student performances.

In 2004, we added to our school-wide celebrations the UN's *International Mother Language Day* (21 February). This activity was initially a one-day event but quickly became a week-long celebration. During Mother Language Week, posters are prepared and can be seen around the school with tongue twisters, proverbs, poems and greetings in a variety of languages. The morning school TV bulletin features news in different languages as well as cultural vignettes from around the world. During break time, cartoons in different languages are projected in the school theatre or outside in a courtyard. It is the week where students take particular pride in speaking languages other than English.

Language is culturally specific (Garcia, 2005) and cultural background (sometimes referred to as ethnicity or nationality) has been linked to use and choice of language-learning strategies (Bedell & Oxford, 1996; Grainger, 2005; Politzer, 1983; Stauft, 2007). By knowing as much as possible about the languages and cultures of students we include and value all students within our classrooms as well as recognize their prior learning. As a school, with the help of the PTA, we also celebrate Diwali (Hindu, Festival of Light), Christmas (Christian, birth of Jesus), African Unity Day, Chinese New Year, Eid Al Fitr (Islam, end of the Holy month of Ramadan) and Eid Al Adha (Islam, Abraham's sacrifice) as well as all the local holidays.

These school-wide initiatives set the stage for numerous activities in the Elementary classrooms.

Elementary school celebrations

In the Elementary section, classroom teachers each have a resource book (prepared by the ESL specialist) of activities, puzzles, essays, fun facts and games related to language to inspire them. Many of these activities, although initially used only during Mother Language week, have become part of regular classroom activities throughout the year. These in the past have included the following:

- Every student wears a large badge on which others write the student's name in different scripts.
- Student-created bilingual story books – one page in English and the next page a translation in their mother language. A class collection is bound and put in the library.
- Teachers give lessons in their mother tongue.
- Students make hats from around the world.
- Students visit other classrooms acting as ambassador for their country and answer questions.
- Students speak only in their mother language (it's amazing how children manage to communicate!).

- Students bring in games from different cultures to play with their class.
- Stories in different languages are told by parents.
- Students graph their different languages and put them on a world map.
- Math students have fun with different numerical scripts.
- Elementary library students read stories in their mother language to the younger students.
- Music students learn songs in different languages.
- Elementary students come to school in their national dress or national colours (rather than school uniform).
- Students share work in their monthly Elementary assemblies.

This one-week celebration has, in turn, led to a greater awareness of the importance of mother languages for our families, staff and students.

Since our students come from around the world, student-specific home country celebrations are frequently highlighted within the classroom (Halloween, Girls Day (Japan), St Nikolas Day (Europe), National Day holidays, Valentines Day, etc.). In the classrooms of the youngest children, parents are invited to cook national dishes with the children in the Early Childhood Education (ECE) kitchen, and one of the Units of Inquiry in Grade 2 looks at celebrations around the world.

Maintaining the home culture is a goal of most international parents (Sears, 1998) and they often celebrate them at home. Bringing into the school and classrooms these home celebrations has enriched us all. It has validated to parents the importance of their home culture and language and helped reduce the cultural dissonance some families feel living in a foreign country.

Relevant research on second-language learning

There is research which suggests that children's cognitive skills grow with age and that the process lasts until young adulthood (Bialystok, 1991, 2001) and age is often mentioned as a key factor in influencing learning success (Ehrman & Oxford, 1989). Younger learners are likely to attain fluency through context-embedded language (Gallagher, 2008), talk and play (Halliwell, 2003). Older students, who have more developed abstract thinking capabilities, are able to use strategies that allow them to analyse the grammatical system and to apply their greater knowledge of the world to their language learning.

The different advantages language learners have at different ages can be attributed to one or more critical periods for language learning, prior experience in language learning, onset of formal operations, cognitive maturity, kind of input, affective factors and socio-cultural factors (Oxford & Ehrman, 1995). At our school we try to be aware of the whole child's development (linguistic and otherwise) and recognize and access whenever possible prior learning in another language. Teachers also ensure that language input is comprehensible and strive to create an environment where children's affective needs are recognized and supported.

There is evidence to indicate that children's meta-cognitive abilities develop fairly rapidly once they begin their formal schooling. In a series of experiments on whether preschool children knew (a) that they had been thinking and (b) what they had been thinking, Flavell *et al.* (1995) showed, not surprisingly, that 7–8-year-olds performed better than preschool children (3–5-year olds) on introspection tasks. Their study suggests that introspection skills undergo considerable improvement during the early school years.

In a separate study of immersion of French, Spanish and Japanese Elementary School students, Chamot and El-Dinary (1999) concluded that meta-cognitive aware-ness begins at quite an early stage. The results of a more recent study on children in an international school setting (Stauft, 2007) support these findings, as it appears that children as young as seven do indeed frequently use introspection in the form of cognitive and meta-cognitive learning strategies in addition to their known use of social strategies (Gunning, 1997; Lan & Oxford, 2003). We promote learning strategy instruction for all our students, as all PYP schools do. At the beginning of each school year, all Elementary students are introduced to learning styles and prompted to dis-cover how they learn best. Language-learning strategy instruction is included in the ESL programme throughout the school year.

Family support

When parents enrol their children in our school, the PTA arranges for a current family to act as a buddy. These buddies are frequently from similar linguistic and cultural backgrounds and support the new families during their transition to the new country and to the school. Often when children arrive for their first day of school they already know another student (maybe of the same age, maybe not) and are somewhat familiar with the school's support of cultural diversity. Since so many of our students speak languages other than English they easily empathize with stu-dents new to English and welcome them into the classroom with kindness and understanding. As parents and students arrive for their first day, they find outside every classroom, posters of the countries and languages of the students in that class, along with a class photo. Children in K1 to Grade 1 (3–6-year-olds) will meet their teacher as well as the local class teaching assistant. A buddy is also arranged for them if this has not already been organized through the PTA family buddy system. If the student has English as a second language, then the buddy will be one who speaks the same mother language. Sometimes a buddy cannot be found in the same classroom in which case someone in another class or grade level is found. Often secondary stu-dents help teachers and students in this regard as part of their Community Action and Service IB requirement.

In the classroom

For students who are new to English, teachers are always mindful to use compre-hensible language accompanied by visual cues; vocabulary consistent in its use of nouns and verbs (tidy-up, break-time, lunch-time, washroom, give, take …); and picture cards around the classroom. Parents are often informed of upcoming events and activities so that they can review the various activities in advance with their child in their mother language. Regular newsletters from the teachers about current and upcoming activities and work within the Unit of Inquiry allow parents the opportunity to pre-teach their children in their mother tongue. Newsletters include websites, photos of students in action and ideas to extend or consolidate learning at home. It is important for students new to English not to miss curriculum content simply because they are learning the language of instruction. Especially in those early days of English language acquisition, our students, with the support of parents, are frequently encouraged to produce work in their mother language.

Assessing young ESL students

For students new to the ESL program with little or no spoken English, we have found that a Likert scale evaluation is very useful and permits some communication between teacher and student. This semiquantitative probe is used with students when they start the ESL program to determine their perception of their proficiency/understanding of English in the various classroom situations they are presented with at school (PSE, Art, Music, Library, Math, Break-time, Assembly, ESL . . .). On the scale, a 'happy face' is at one end and a 'sad face' at the other end of a line. In the middle is a 'so-so face' (neither smile nor frown). Students indicate for each subject or activity how much English they understand. These surveys are conducted regularly throughout the year and help students to identify areas of difficulty as well as to celebrate their successes when previous evaluations are reviewed. Results are also shared with classroom teachers working with ESL students to show the degree to which a particular student perceives his or her own understanding in the class. Some teachers tend to speak too quickly and do not realize that the bobbing heads of the ESL students do not necessarily mean that they understand! Once the parameters of the scale have been explained in the mother language, the Likert scale can also be used by the classroom teacher to communicate with a student in those early days (like/dislike, understand/do not understand, etc.).

ESL and first-language support

For students K1–K3 (3–5-year olds) who are new to English, teachers provide language immersion learning within their classroom. Students in Grades 1–5 (6–10-year-olds) receive specialized instruction from the ESL teacher who also supports all primary school classroom teachers when needed. Cummins (1986) advocates the maintenance of the home language alongside the learning of the new language, and all students who enter the ESL programme are strongly encouraged by the school to continue with academic instruction in their mother language outside, school. At the beginning of the academic year, the ESL specialist makes a presentation to parents of children in the 3–6-year old group on the importance of maintaining age appropriate mother language proficiency throughout their child's academic life. The benefits would include true bilingualism, which is put in jeopardy if the first language is neglected. Parental support of English language learning through maintenance of their child's mother tongue can be counter-intuitive for many parents and the knowledgeable support of their child's class teacher adds strength to this message. The ESL specialist also meets regularly with individual families to discuss bilingualism and assists parents in finding mother language tutors if necessary. The school offers its facility after school for individual mother language instruction classes.

Maintenance of mother language proficiency is an issue faced by many international families with young children. Bilingualism, although desired by many parents for their children, can be difficult to achieve if instruction in the mother tongue of the child is not available at the school. Parents must therefore be encouraged to organize instruction either through private tutors (an endeavour that can be costly and difficult to organize) or through distance learning of national curricula at home (which can be stressful and time consuming). Even with the assistance of the school, families who are faced with the education of several children at home during evenings, on weekends and over school holidays find that this is a road they would rather not travel. The result is that some young ESL learners in international schools run the risk of ending up with a subtractive rather than an additive form of bilingualism (Baker, 2001). In short, their English replaces their first language, especially their academic language, since that is the language of instruction at school.

When mother language instruction is given along with instruction in the second language, cognitive and linguistic development continues, enabling students to transfer learning from one language to another. This is the message that teachers and the school give to parents in the hope that they will maintain their child's first-language proficiency, since we would find it impossible to teach properly the 50 different languages of our students.

CONCLUSION

A strong case has been made by Ehrman (1998) that language-learning aptitude is a complex nexus of cognition (both stylistic and strategic) and personality – especially tolerance of ambiguity, and of affect (motivation, self-efficacy and affective self-management). We have found that the best and easiest way to support children new to English in the Early Childhood and Elementary years is to create a school-wide environment which celebrates and supports the diversity of language and culture. The 'mother language buddies' of the PTA play an important role in transitioning students as they acquire and learn in English. Additionally, teachers recognize and celebrate students' prior learning in their mother language, ensure that their language is comprehensible and include languages other than English in their classes. All of this reduces cultural dissonance, and the message on the importance of maintenance of mother language proficiency, supported by research in second-language acquisition, is unambiguously conveyed to parents by the administration, teachers and ESL specialist of the school.

REFERENCES

Baker, C. (2001) *Foundations of Bilingual Education and Bilingualism*. Clevedon: Multilingual Matters.

Bedell, D. and Oxford, R. (1996) Cross-cultural comparisons of language learning strategies in the People's Republic of China and other countries. In *Language Learning Strategies Around the World: Cross-cultural Perspectives*. Honolulu HI: University of Hawai'i Press.

Bialystok, E. (1991) Metalinguistic dimensions of bilingual language proficiency. In *Language Processing in Bilingual Children*. Cambridge: Cambridge University Press.

Bialystok, E. (2001) *Bilingualism in Development: Language, Literacy and Cognition*. New York: Cambridge University Press.

Chamot, A.U. and El-Dinary, P.B. (1999) Children's learning strategies in language immersion classrooms. *The Modern Language Journal* 83, 319–338.

Cummins, J. (1986) *Bilingualism in Education*. New York: Longman.

Ehrman, M.E. (1998) The learning alliance: Conscious and unconscious aspects of the second language teacher's role. *System* 26, 93–106.

Ehrman, M.E. and Oxford, R. (1989) Effects of sex differences, career choice and psychological type on adult language learning strategies. *Modern Language Journal* 73, 1–13.

Flavell, J.H., Green, F.L. and Flavell, E.R. (1995) Young children's knowledge about thinking. *Monographs of the Society for Research in Child Development* 60 (1), 1–96.

Gallagher, E. (2008) *Equal Rights to the Curriculum: Many Languages, One Message*. Clevedon: Multilingual Matters.

Garcia, E.E. (2005) *Teaching and Learning in Two Languages: Bilingualism and Schooling in the United States*. New York: Teachers College Press.

Grainger, P. (2005) Second language learning strategies and Japanese: Does orthography make a difference? *System* 33, 327–339.

Gunning, P. (1997) The learning strategies of beginning ESL learners at the primary level. *Department of Applied Linguistics*. Montreal: Concordia University.

Halliwell, S. (2003) *Teaching English in the Primary Classroom*. New York: Longman.

International Baccalaureate Organization (2007) *Primary Years Programme*. Geneva: IBO.

Lan, R. and Oxford, R. (2003) Language learning strategy profiles of elementary school students in Taiwan. *International Review of Applied Linguistics* 41 (4), 339–379.

Mathews, M. (1989) The scale of international education, part 1. *The International Schools Journal*. 17, 7–17.

Oman Census Administration (2003) *Census of Oman*. Muscat: Sultanate of Oman. On WWW at www.omancensus.net. Accessed 18.2.10.

Oxford, R. and Ehrman, M. (1995) Adults' language learning strategies in an intensive foreign program in the United States. *System* 23, 359–386.

Politzer, R. (1983) An exploratory study of self-reported language learning behaviors and their relation to achievement. *Studies in Second Language Acquisition* 6, 54–65.

Sears, C. (1998) *Second Language Students in Mainstream Classrooms: A Handbook for Teachers in International Schools*. Clevedon: Multilingual Matters.

Stauft, N. (2007) Application and evaluation of the Oxford Strategy Inventory for Language Learning when used with ESL primary school students at an international school. *Moray House School of Education*. Edinburgh: University of Edinburgh.

About the author

Nancy Stauft began her career teaching Special Learning Needs in Canada 30 years ago. She earned an MEd TESOL from the University of Edinburgh and has since taught ESL to secondary and tertiary students in Japan, Quebec and the Sultanate of Oman. She was director of the Sultan Qaboos University Day Care Centre in Muscat, Oman, prior to taking up her present post at ABA – An IB World School – in 2004 where she teaches Elementary ESL and coordinates the Mother Language Program.

Chapter 6

An Amazing Journey: Making English Language Learners Successful

YOUNG SOO (KALEI) JANG-BRUMSICKLE

In this chapter the author recounts her experience as an ESL teacher in a school in Poland. In her words: 'Acquiring a second language … is the most amazing journey one can go through.' The author writes from her first-hand experience as both second-language learner and teacher and is happy for the opportunity to pass her acquired knowledge along to readers.

INTRODUCTION

Students with limited English may face difficulties in school due to not having access to effective English as a second language or effective English as a second language instruction. These challenges may originate from their linguistic or cultural differences and become more problematic over time if the instruction provided is not modified to address their specific needs. These students will continue to struggle and the difference between their achievement and that of their peers will be even more pronounced over time (Ortiz, 2001). Teachers often have difficulty distinguishing students with learning disabilities from students with limited English who struggle academically in school. A lack of appropriate assessment tools and a lack of personnel trained to conduct linguistically and culturally relevant educational assessments are a disadvantage to those learning English as a second language and to their success in school (Valdes & Figueroa, 1996, as cited in Ortiz, 2001). In addition if English language learners are identified with special needs, the shortage of trained special education teachers who will address their language and disability needs simultaneously will further hamper these students from progressing. It is important to point out that improving the academic performance of students from non-English backgrounds requires a focus on preventing failure and on early intervention for struggling learners (Ortiz, 2001).

In order to guarantee the social and academic success of English language learners (ELLs) in school, many factors are required. These include:

(1) Educators share their knowledge about effective ways to work with English language learners – educators involved should have a clear knowledge about second language acquisition, how native language proficiency is closely related to the development of English, familiarity with assessment of proficiency in the child's first langugae and English, effective instruction for first and second language, informal assessment strategies in language and literacy development to monitor student progress, and effective strategies for working with culturally and linguistically diverse families and communities.

(2) Effective teaching strategies that address student needs – all learners have the right to have access to high-quality instruction in order to help them meet high expectations in academically enriched environments. Through effective strategies designed to help English language learners, students can connect their prior knowledge to the concepts taught, which they can connect to other areas with teacher guidance and support. This will help them to narrow gaps in their background knowledge they once had.

(3) Administrative support.

(4) Authentic and meaningful assessment tools.

(5) Collaborative relationships between the school and community – parents of students learning English are as capable advocates for their children and as valuable resources in school improvement efforts (Cummins, 1994, as cited in Ortiz, 2001). Educators learn to respect different cultures and their backgrounds, and soundly understand social, linguistic and cultural contexts of their students by being involved with families and communities of English language learners.

(6) Training, support and cooperation of both mainstream teachers and parents in maintaining the balance between the child's mother tongue and the school's language of instruction. With the support of school administration, teachers, parents, and the community, language development becomes a shared responsibility between classroom teachers, other staff members including special education teachers and ELL teachers. School staff and teachers should understand that native language instruction (and maintaining) provides the foundation for achieving high levels of English proficiency (Cummins, 1994, as cited in Ortiz, 2001; Krashen, 1991, as cited in Ortiz, 2001; Thomas & Collier, 1997, as cited in Ortiz, 2001). Some of the training tips for parents of English language learners are highlighted later in this chapter.

THE ESL PROGRAM AT THE SCHOOL IN WARSAW

The goal for all

Ideally, young ELLs in my school in Warsaw would have an adult in the classroom who speaks their native language, but with many schools having anything up to 70 languages represented, it is an impossible standard for most schools to measure up to however much they want to. There are, fortunately, other ways to provide an improved level of comfort as well as a condusive learning environment for these children and raise their academic achievement. Preventing school failure begins with the creation of school climates that foster academic success and empower students (Cummins, 1989, as cited in Ortiz, 2001). This statement aligns with the assumption that all students can learn and that teachers are ultimately responsible for helping them learn. There are several critical factors that characterize positive school environments; strong administrative leadership; high expectations for student achievement; challenging, appropriate curriculum and instruction; a safe and orderly environment; ongoing, systematic evaluation of student progress; and shared decision-making among ELL teachers, classroom teachers, administrators and parents.

Most learning problems can be prevented if students are in positive school and classroom contexts that accommodate individual differences (Ortiz, 2001). Unfortunately, some students still experience challenges despite being in a supportive environment. Implementing early intervention strategies for those who struggle is necessary if problems are persistent and are detected repeatedly. Early intervention means that 'supplementary instructional services are provided early in students' schooling, and that they are intense enough to bring at-risk students quickly to a level at which they can profit from high-quality classroom instruction' (Madden *et al.*, 1991: 594, as cited in Ortiz, 2001). The purpose of early intervention is to provide regular education support to help improve academic performance for those who struggle academically in school, and to help reduce unnecessary special education referrals. Some of the early intervention strategies used include teaching for understanding, peer coaching/teacher collaboration, and collaborative team teachers.

Teaching for understanding

First teachers teach students skills, concepts, or content of subjects. Then they reteach them using different strategies or methods for those who struggle to meet the expectations of the initial instruction. This differentiated instruction helps meet specific needs of students that are concerned. After the teaching is done, informal assessment is followed which is curriculum based to identify the areas of improvement, to monitor progress and to plan and modify instruction (Ortiz, 1997, as cited in Ortiz, 2001; Ortiz & Wilkinson, 1991, as cited in Ortiz, 2001).

Peer coaching/teacher collaboration

Teachers can share instructional resources and strategies, observe each other's classrooms, and offer feedback to each other to improve their teaching practice, student learning and student behaviours. ELL teachers can share effective instructional strategies with classroom teachers so that they can use them to integrate English language learners in mainstream classrooms. Several ELL strategies are highlighted later in this chapter. It is natural to say that in positive and supportive school environments, teachers work as a team of community and share their common goals of supporting students with their learning and teachers themselves as learners no matter in what programs students and teachers are involved.

COLLABORATIVE TEAM TEACHERS

Peers and experts work collaboratively with classroom teachers to address students' learning problems, and to implement recommendations for intervention (Fuchs *et al.*, 1990, as cited in Ortiz, 2001). A group of 4–6 general teachers including the one who asks for help can form a team to design intervention strategies for students who struggle in school. The group members can decide what the nature of the issue that the student presents, help prioritise intervention, help the teacher select intervention strategies appropriate for the student in need, make recommendations for the teacher to carry them out, monitor student progress. It is the teacher's responsibility to then implement the whole plan and subsequent meetings are held to discuss student progress.

If all suggested prevention and early intervention strategies don't work to solve the student's learning difficulties, a referral to special education is recommended. In our school, special education referral committee is called Student Support Team and they meet once a week. The SST (Student Support Team) is made up of a variety of specialists including the Principal, special education teachers, ELL teachers, school counsellor, and the teacher who refers the student. The team members bring their own expertise such as assessment, diagnosis, background knowledge on especially cultural and linguistic areas, and specialized instruction and strategies to solve the problem. The data gathered through prevention and early intervention processes is used as a basis of SST's making decisions on the student whether the student needs special education services or not. The data includes whether the child is provided a positive and supportive school environment, if the teacher used effective instructional strategies for English language learners, both teaching for understanding and intervention recommended by the collaborative team teachers didn't resolve the student problem. If students continue to struggle in spite of various efforts provided to individualize instruction and to accommodate their learning characteristics, they most likely have a learning disability (Ortiz, 1997, as cited in Ortiz, 2001).

First I would like to put forward an explanation of the kinds of models used for organizing young children for ESL instruction, not usually required in a formal sense until first grade. What follows is a description of the program carried on at my present school which I hope will be of use to new teachers in a similar situation.

For pre-Kindergarten and Kindergarten

At this school, there is no specific ESL program for Pre-K (age 4) and Kindergarten (age 5). Classroom teachers and ESL teachers are in agreement that these young children learn and acquire language naturally through social interaction as well as through communicative and hands-on activities provided in the classroom. Mainstream teachers also feel that much of the curriculum they use is the same as the one that first-language learners would experience. Therefore, children can learn and acquire language more spontaneously without the studied intervention of an ESL teacher.

The program for Grades 1–3

The best way to include second-language children in the mainstream classroom, to make them feel welcome and to foster a sense of belonging, is to show an interest in their language, their country and their culture. This can be done initially by inviting their parents to bring into the classroom some cultural artefacts from home. This helps them to soften the difference in their surroundings, allowing some contact with their own cultural milieu. It helps to make a smoother introduction to their new environment.

My colleagues and I began by implementing a push-in model for every ESL student in Grades 1–3. As an advocate of the use of their first language by all children in the classroom, I developed some strategies outlined below:

ELLs should be allowed from the start to use their own language in the classroom where possible. If there are others who speak it, one child, for example, could help to clarify the meaning of something the teacher has said that another might not have understood. Occasional forays into their own language not only help them maintain their cultural and linguistic identity, but also help their English-speaking classmates to complete the picture they have of them as human beings.

During reading or other activities, ELLs find it helpful to be paired with others who speak the same language. I suggest that both ESL and mainstream teachers bear this in mind as it will help if one who understands is able to clarify the meaning of the language for those in the group who do not.

I also urge ELLs to use their first language in writing, especially when they are only just beginning to learn English. Parents or older siblings in the same school can be asked to help in monitoring this. Young beginners are intimidated and overwhelmed by the newness of the language, and for them to write in English when they don't even know 'A' from 'B' is clearly asking too much. And if they cannot yet write in their first language, they can draw whatever they feel is appropriate; this enables them to participate in some way, avoiding the feeling of being so different from others.

Bringing first languages into the classroom is considerably facilitated by having a small classroom library of books in all the first languages represented in the classroom. I always ask children to bring books in their first language so they can have something to read during Silent Reading period in the classroom.

Starting out

Starting in this school in Warsaw as an ESL teacher, I was assigned to a second-grade class where 90% of the students learned English as a second language. The class consisted of 18 students: three identified as non-English speakers, five as very limited in English, eight at an advanced level of English and two native speakers. From the very beginning of the year, I started to teach ELLs within the classroom (the push-in model) only to find there was a limitation on what I could do because the children were on so many different levels. Out of necessity, I formed a small group within the class of those with the greatest need. I soon came to the conclusion, however, that this strategy was not the best way either. Non-English speakers would not open up to say a single word. Lots of tears were shed and they expressed repeatedly their unhappiness in coming to school.

After several meetings with classroom teachers, I finally decided to pull these beginning ESL children out of their classroom every morning during their literacy block for about one to one-and-a-half hours. Within a week, these children started laughing, talking, writing and reading – which was progress, although in a limited way. They started to open up and share their similarities amongst themselves to find their common ground. These children felt they had a voice and a place they could go to express themselves. Some found friends among those who spoke the same language. Their comfort level increased and their progress was remarkable as far as I could tell. They had so much more to show and share in their classroom than they did before. Teachers should understand that beginning English speakers understand much more than they can express. They open up within the environment they feel most comfortable in. Receptive English grows at a much faster rate than expressive English, which, in this case came about when they were in the ESL class where they felt safe enough to risk displaying their burgeoning English. Now in November they are back in their mainstream classroom with more confidence and a sense of comfort, ready to continue.

During the pull-out time, I used activities that were communicative, that is, where students could form words and sentences to express themselves, and to encourage their verbal interaction. This prevented students from remaining silent for an extended period of time. I also might recite a short poem as part of a reading activity, write sentences in connection with their reading and use listening activities with visual cues to build on their vocabulary.

As a passing time activity, I always made some journal papers available so that they could draw and write about small moments in their lives at their own pace. I usually gave them a choice of writing in English or in their mother tongue. But, interestingly, when they came to the ESL class, as opposed to when they were in the mainstream classroom, they did not want to write in their mother tongue. Instead they all tried to write in English and they all steadily became better, although at different paces.

As their English develops, ESL students can produce reading responses by drawing pictures and labelling them with words or phrases. They can participate in puppet shows, choral readings, reader's theatre (similar to choral reading but with sound effects and actions that go with reading), can mime to a story read aloud and organize a simple play with guided-writing scripts.

The value of performance

What I have done in the past is to have children present their work to lower grades as well as to their own classes. These kinds of activities involve reading and listening for a purpose, vocabulary building, writing and speaking to an audience, which boosts their confidence. Choral reading involves negotiation and discussion amongst students (who will read what and how?), as well as the collaboration and cooperation involved in group and individual work, and finally a presentation to other classes and to their parents. Miming to a story read out loud is also an interesting way to involve students at a beginning level. The teacher reads a story aloud while students choose the part of a character to act out. ESL students at a beginning level develop more receptive than expressive language. This activity allows students to be active listeners and have a sense of purpose in presenting to an audience. When team-taught with classroom teachers using these strategies and group techniques, opportunities exist for effective involvement of the ESL students with native speakers in a whole class effort. As a consequence, it helps to reduce the anxiety of the ELLs, providing them with an opportunity to be themselves and also to be part of the wider group, to raise their confidence and to help them acquire the language at an optimal level.

Teacher-training workshop

It is also important to have a teacher-training workshop of sheltered instructional strategies for the whole faculty, stressing the importance of the mother tongue in the process of acquiring a second-language. During the teacher workshop we emphasize the importance of teachers' understanding the feelings of second-language learners by putting themselves in their situation. Different instructional strategies should be used by teachers (see below) to enable them to teach their ESL students language and content at the same time in a more inclusive setting – not language first, and content later in an isolated setting. This training also helps teachers in the process of language acquisition, emphasizing the benefits of being patient in dealing with ESL students, and encouraging them to use all the expertise the school has access to, before considering the possible presence of a learning disability.

Some strategies for teaching ESL students in mainstream classes

Fish Bowl is an activity for ESL students in mainstream classes. A small group participates in this lesson with the teacher who teaches a concept using manipulatives and other visual cues and aids. The rest of the class observes. After the concept is taught to a small group, and the large group has finished watching, the children talk about the activity. If an ESL student is involved in the activity, he/she learns about the concept through language, body gestures, as well as manipulatives or other visual cues. If the ESL student watches the activity, she/he listens to the language spoken both by the teacher and the participants, and observes the manipulatives or other visual aids to help understand the concept being taught. Both the inclusive setting and the strategy help the ESL students not only to understand the concept and acquire language in an authentic and meaningful way, but also helps them feel a part of the larger group.

Wait time is a strategy that the teacher uses simply to allow enough time for students to formulate their responses to questions.

Think-pair-share is a strategy which the teacher uses after having presented a lesson to students designed to have them think about the lesson presented. The teacher has students pair up with another person to share their thoughts. They would then practice the lesson using the same or different scenarios, depending on the situation. This strategy will help students to listen and process information provided by the teacher and will give them a chance to organize their thoughts which they will then share with others, providing a way to make sure they can apply the concepts taught appropriately. In this approach, ESL students are again forced to use the language and learn the content at the same time. They definitely feel included and important by being actively engaged in the activity.

Greetings: is a good example. Have at least two pairs of volunteers participate in a lesson while the rest of the class watches. After the lesson the students will think about it, focusing on what has happened and would then be paired up to share what they have learned about the lesson, finally practicing the 'greeting's with their partner. After this, the teacher might call a volunteer to share with the whole group.

Training parents of ESL students

Educating parents of ESL students is as important as educating teachers in this area. We bring their attention to some general misconceptions and misunderstandings that parents frequently have, such as trying to speak to their children in English, whether they have mastered that language or not. By providing them with a general overview of successful L2 acquisition they will see that they can help their children at home, not by involving themselves in the teaching of English, but by concentrating on speaking their own language and encouraging their children to continue growing in it. Having a meeting with parents was the first thing the other two ESL teachers and I did in school this year. This was an eye opener for many of them.

A sample:

- How can parents help their children?
- By continuing home language lessons, if available.
- By reading to their child in the home language and discussing it afterwards.
- By inviting classmates home who speak your language as well as English.
- By watching quality films in the home language as well as in English.
- By finding books in the home language that explain what their child is learning at school in English.

In general by seeing that the home language continues to be developed.

Assessment

Assessment is another important component of the work with ESL learners to ensure their success in school. I do a formal assessment twice a year using IPT (Idea Proficiency Test), one in the autumn and the other in spring. In addition, informal anecdotal notes and observations, ongoing communication with the classroom teacher, Bonnie Campbell-Hill's oral language continuum, and a student portfolio for pull-out classes were also used. We are in the process of modifying Bonnie Campbell Hill's reading and writing continuum to meet ESL student needs.

CONCLUSION

Early intervention and problem prevention strategies for struggling English learners in school are the foremost important responsibilities for classroom teachers in an inclusive classroom in international schools. If these students are not adequately provided with supportive school environments and instruction that is not tailored to meet the needs of culturally and linguistically diverse students, their success in school is not guaranteed. If the intervention focuses mainly on remediation of student learning and their behaviour problems, it would be difficult to expect successful student outcomes.

By implementing early intervention and problem prevention strategies, classroom teachers' ability to accommodate student needs will increase. Also teachers' increased ability and competence to deal with culturally and linguistically diverse group of students will reduce the perception and the number of students considered to be at risk. This will result in decreasing the number of inappropriately referring these children to special education programs and inaccurately identifying them as having a disability. As a result, students' academic and social achievement will increase.

REFERENCES

Ortiz, A. (2001) English language learners with special needs: Effective instructional strategies. Retrieved from http://www.idonline.org/article/56223theme=print

About the author

Young Soo (Kalei) Jang-Brumsickle was born in Seoul, South Korea where she received a BA in French. She also has an MA in Education from Washington State University and an ESL certification from UCLA. She is a certified international school counsellor currently working on an International Counselling master's degree through Lehigh University in Pennsylvania. This is her ninth year teaching ESL, before which she taught French, Language Arts, Social Studies and Grades 3 and 4 at international schools in various locations. Her three lovely children go to The American School of Warsaw, where both she and her husband work.

Chapter 7

The Importance of Maintaining Mother Tongue and Culture in the Classroom

ANITA HAYIM-BAMBERGER

In this chapter the multilingual author looks back at the way she learned languages as a young child. She discusses basic theories of second-language acquisition and how they underpin the work of teachers in international school classrooms. The importance of mother-tongue maintenance is stressed and ways of incorporating their first language and culture in the work of the classroom are suggested.

INTRODUCTION

How my daughters and I learned two languages

I was brought up as a passive bilingual listening to my parents speaking Arabic to one another when they did not want me to understand what they were saying. What better motivation could there be to want to understand everything they said! Looking back, however, I still wonder how I did it. As a young child we went on holidays to Israel and France on alternate years to visit the family, and once again I wondered how I knew what people were saying when nobody taught me their languages. I knew I had to try to speak French and Hebrew so that I could communicate with the people around me. My forays into communication were fearless: I did not care whether what I said was correct or not, as long as I was understood, and in the end I was successful. At secondary school I studied French and it was the first time I came across French grammar. I found it somewhat irrelevant as I had managed perfectly well up to that point without it. It was not until after I had completed my A levels and a degree in French and was living in France that I started to recognize grammatical structures in songs and in conversations, and it all finally clicked.

My eldest daughter Jenny was born in France and we lived there until she was six years old. I was the main source of her English so she had a perfect English accent and was able to translate from the age of two for visitors if they spoke the 'other' language. She is today a French/English bilingual and it was interesting to watch her languages develop and change as we moved from France to England. On the other hand, my youngest daughter, Stephanie was only two months old when we moved from France to England and is a passive bilingual: she responds in English when her father speaks to her in French. The most interesting observation I made from this experience is that a bilingual usually favours the use of one of the two languages for specific topics. Perhaps it is because a child is rarely exposed to the same vocabulary in each language.

Valuing our linguistic heritage

One of the main challenges facing international schools is the provision of an appropriate education in English for culturally and linguistically diverse children. While living in France I met a Portuguese mother who said, 'I might as well not have any children if I can't talk to them in my language.' Although we want the children to learn English it is important that they maintain their mother tongue to remain connected to their family and to avoid a sense of alienation that is detrimental to a child's sense of well-being. The visibility of linguistic and cultural diversity at inter-national schools sends a strong message to the families about the value of languages and cultures. This starts from school policies and classroom practices.

Language learning is a means of promoting intercultural understanding, and children are quick to sense, even at an early age, if their language is not valued in society or that certain languages and cultures are more valued than others. Often as a result children might decide not to speak their native language outside the home. This was true in my case: my parents feeling their language was of low status and thus being embarrassed by it, denied their origin. I feel saddened that no value was attached to different languages and cultures when I was growing up, possibly because Manchester, where I was living, was not as cosmopolitan as London, but this caused an alienation from my parents' culture as a teenager. It is therefore doubly important that, at school, languages should be given equal value. Andersson and Bayer (1970) points out that the sense of pride that children have in their second language is dependant on 'whether the minority language and its speakers have high or low prestige among other children' (pp. 81–95). Our identity is conveyed in our language, and in our expressions and engagements, distinctiveness and alle-giances. As Shaules (2007) points out 'Learning a language is not only indicative of possessing a code in order to communicate but it implies having gone through adaptive changes in one's own communication' (p. 101). It is a symbolic system representing a social reality. A positive and encouraging attitude to a child's home language is motivating and can only have favourable repercussions.

Norton (2000) found that a learner's motivation to speak a language is tied up with the 'learner's identities and their desires for the future'. Alladina (1995) wrote that children who grow up using more than one language are able to understand that there are different ways of talking about things we experience. As Masahiko Minami (2002) points out: how children tell their narratives is a reflection not only of their age but also their culture. In her book on this subject, Gallagher (2009) emphasizes the importance of additive bilingualism and biculturalism.

THE ADVANTAGES OF BILINGUALISM

Colin Baker (2007) tells us that bilinguals are able to understand the symbolic representation of words earlier than monolinguals as they see words printed in two different ways. That in turn may facilitate earlier acquisition of reading. Galambos and Hakuta (1988) also found that when a child's proficiency in more than one language is developed their metalinguistic ability to note and correct errors is enhanced. Furthermore, a child's difficulties in his home language can be indicative of an underlying problem. In the case of an ESL learner, this can often be overlooked in the initial stages, as a child's difficulty is often attributed to struggling with the new language. As to the length of time it takes to learn a new language, Cummins identifies two levels of language proficiency: BICS (basic interpersonal communication skills) taking up to two years and CALP (cognitive academic language proficiency) taking up to seven years.

Linguistic and cultural diversity in schools

Globalization increases the number of people crossing national and cultural boundaries and changes how people interact with those from other communities. A consequence of population mobility is the linguistic and cultural diversity now found in schools. Although most children adapt, moving can create internal tensions. Cummins points out that the negotiation of identity in the interactions between educators and students who speak little or no English is central to their academic success. Culture is a way of making sense of the world. Language is a social system that represents our social reality; it is also a manifestation and product of a culture. A harmonious community is achieved by celebrating the language and culture of all the children in a school.

Edward Sapir and Benjamin Lee argue that language shapes our view of the world to such an extent that speaking a different language constitutes a different perceptual world. Shaules (2007) confirms that 'language is a symbolic system that represents the conceptualisation of the values and worldview of some of its speakers, and speaking a language implies membership of a community of speakers of that language' (p. 101). Cummins concluded that the development of competence in one's native language serves as a foundation for proficiency that can be transferred to the second language. Children learn concepts and intellectual skills in their minority language that are equally relevant in the majority language. For example, in order to tell the time in the second language they do not need to relearn the concept of telling the time they simply need to acquire new labels or 'surface structures' for an intellectual skill they have already learned. Similarly, at more advanced stages there is a transfer across languages in academic and literacy skills (e.g. sequencing events). Language acquisition is personal as children learn by hypothesizing about rules and structures. Cummins also emphasizes the fragility of children's mother tongues which are 'easily lost in the early years of school' (2000). As Goethe (1749–1852), the German writer and philosopher, said, 'A person who knows only one language does not truly know that language.' It is through comparing the syntax of a child's mother tongue to the new language that a real comprehension of the grammar is understood. The children in upper primary could compare the syntax of the same sentence in English and their mother tongue to help them understand the pitfalls.

The role of the international school teacher

Teachers need to build on a child's cultural and linguistic experience in the home as it is the foundation of future learning. By having more than one language a child has a greater understanding of how language works. Minami (2002) observed American and Japanese children in the classroom and found that cross-cultural differences in socialization are discernable with children of different cultures along with syntax, vocabulary and grammar. Culture, history and literature are all part of their heritage. It is important to practise 'additive bilingualism', that is when the second language is learned without neglecting the maintenance and development of the first. Menken and Barron (2002) found testing in New York schools to be inappropriate for second-language learners as it was done in English. She recommended that a language policy be implemented in schools and that testing be done in a student's home language. This would enable the school to document the potential of an emerging bilingual as well as to obtain a more accurate reflection of a student's ability. This would go a long way to ensuring that no learners are left behind.

All teachers are language teachers, whether they realize it or not. It is therefore essential that the ESL (English as a second language) teacher and mainstream classroom teacher work collaboratively. The urgency of a child asking a question is natural; the frustration of children who cannot find the words to ask a question is tremendous. The ESL classroom, like any other, is a community where students work collaboratively and in which students of the same language background can help one another. The essential differences are class size and language levels. ESL classes ideally have no more than six children with everyone at roughly the same level in their acquisition of English. With all the children in a similar position linguistically, they tend to have great empathy for one another.

Language is most effectively learned in natural contexts. In international schools such as mine, where the International Baccalaureate (IB) programme is followed, language is learned in context. This supports the functional and interactional theories of Halliday (1993) and other linguists who hold the view that children have to learn to use language for a range of purposes and in a range of cultural and situational contexts. Therefore, rather than viewing language as a finite set of rules which must be 'acquired', it is viewed as a set of choices from which speakers select according to the particular context they are in – in other words, making a particular choice from a range of possible options; hence, the notion of language as a system – a set of resources rather than a set of rules. This makes it possible to consider the appropriateness or inappropriateness of language choices in a given context.

There is a relationship between meaning and context, and context and language. Halliday claims that all meaning, hence all learning, is at once both action and reflection. As Eggins (1994) points out, 'spoken language typically involves turn-taking, is context dependant and dynamic in structure'. It is characterized by 'spontaneity such as false starts, incomplete clauses and hesitations; uses every day lexis and non-standard grammar and is grammatically intricate and lexically sparse'. Written language on the other hand is more formal, independent and synoptic in structure, 'polished rather than spontaneous, uses prestige lexis and standard grammar and is grammatically simple and lexically dense'. It also requires greater reflection. Furthermore, having the opportunity to write in one's mother tongue not only builds confidence but also demonstrates true proficiency in writing. The teacher might suggest that children write on a topic or subject in their own language and then translate it into English. Krashen (1982) claims that input alone is enough and that grammar teaching would not improve language acquisition. This is confirmed by my personal experience of language learning. Having children compare the similarities and differences of the structure of their mother tongue with the structure of English is an effective way of helping them to understand how the English language works in the classroom.

The ESL lessons in an IB school often, though not exclusively, support the Units of Inquiry where asking questions, problem solving and exchanging information are intrinsic to the programme. Research has shown that children learn best by 'doing'. Teaching and learning are about situated meaning whereby children learn in context. Scaffolding learning makes it tangible, and visual aids can be a tremendous asset to ESL teachers, as they can make information more comprehensible.

Many of the Units of Inquiry can be developed in ESL lessons to include research on the child's home country. For example, by 'Mapping the Earth', children could look at maps of their home countries and compare them with one another. They can also compare schools and celebrations from their home country's newspapers and magazines and those around the world. They might also look at Japanese cartoons, and prepare dual-language identity texts about themselves and their families.

As a library activity, children might read stories from their home countries (both in English and their home language). Looking at food around the world, or even asking children to bring in their favourite home food is always popular – at least with the teachers! *The Guinness Book of Records* is useful when looking at health as it covers the healthiest diets around the world (this usually makes Japanese children very proud!)

In fact most Units of Inquiry lend themselves to the incorporation of the children's home cultures while developing their vocabulary. They can look at explorers, constructions, beliefs, inventions, their currency (exchange bureaus can be set up), types of energy, artefacts, sculptures from their home countries – the possibilities are endless. Even the weather can be a source. When there was a snow day last winter the Russian and Canadian children were keen to explain how much more efficient they are in Russia and Canada in dealing with snow as there is so much more of it there. This triggered a discussion about weather around the world. It is important that there be flexibility in an ESL classroom as it should be a secure place where children feel confident enough to express themselves spontaneously and at length. Some children are keen to share songs in their mother tongue and this should be encouraged as it helps develop their confidence and can impress the rest of the class too!

There are countless opportunities to incorporate a child's culture into the lessons – from losing a tooth (discussing tooth fairies or their equivalent), to sneezing (what do you say/do), singing happy birthday (what it sounds like in other languages) and tongue twisters. All are excellent vocabulary developing exercises while at the same time giving importance to their home culture. Flags from around the world and a world map on the walls, international food evenings for all the family, multicultural book fairs, celebrating Mother Tongue day, children sharing their favourite books in their mother tongue or having their parents read them to their class, signs around the classroom in their different languages as well as bilingual dictionaries and library books all contribute to a culture-friendly environment, a crucial element in an international school.

It is important to remember that simply supporting second-language learners temporarily is not enough. As Carder (2007) suggests, 'there must be a well devised, theoretically and practically based programme to educate second language learners'. At my school we have recently set up language-enrichment classes to support the students who have developed a level of oral fluency – BICS – but need support with their more formal academic fluency – CALP.

SUMMING UP THE ADVANTAGES

Bilingualism is a rich resource as there is so much to be learned from other cultures. Furthermore, research has shown that well-balanced bilinguals may have advantages over monolinguals in thinking and in academic achievement. By learning another language a child has more than one way of naming objects and thinking about them. It is important to give nonnative speakers the opportunity of reaching their full academic potential in English without sacrificing their mother tongue. At the Vienna International School it was found that students who received good instruction in the ESL programme became top achievers in the higher grades. It is also important that parents are aware of the advantages of having their children maintain their mother tongue at home; they may feel pressure to expose their children as much as possible to the school language to learn it more quickly.

Pavlenko (2005) found that bilingualism can provide varied and alternative conceptualizations which enable flexible and critical thinking. Language is very emotive and is central to one's identity: using and developing a child's home language makes his personality blossom and more complete. Respect is a key to a child's confidence; thus, respecting a child's culture is of great importance. There is a wealth of languages to be discovered. There is a complex relationship between language, culture and identity. Language is not simply a tool; it is part of the social experience of a culture, a way of thinking and feeling. 'What a child can say, has learned or experienced cannot be completely transferred to another culture or language.' To quote the headmistress of a bilingual nursery school in Paris, 'Language has more meaning because of culture; culture gives importance to a language.'

Multicultural schools in an increasingly mobile world encourage tolerance, open-mindedness and understanding. Breaking the link that connects children to their language may affect them deeply. It is important for children, indeed it is their right, to use in school the language with which they identify alongside the second language so that they can reach their potential in the academic world and in later life. In Cummins' words, 'to reject a child's language is to reject a child', and to respect a child's culture and language is to 'respect who they are and where they come from'. Valuing each child's language and culture is an ideal way to begin the task of promoting intercultural understanding and in the end a more peaceful world.

REFERENCES

Alladina, S. (1995) Being bilingual. In M. Carder (ed.) *Bilingualism in International Schools.* Clevedon: Multilingual Matters.

Andersson, T. and Bayer, M. (1970) *Bilingual Schooling in the United States.* Austin, TX: Southwest Educational Laboratory.

Baker, C. (2007) *Foundations of Bilingual Education and Bilingualism.* Clevedon: Multilingual Matters.

Carder, M. (2007) *Bilingualism in International Schools.* Clevedon: Multilingual Matters.

Cummins, J. (2000) This place nurtures my spirit. In *Creating Contexts of Empowerment in Linguistically Diverse Schools.* University of Toronto.

Eggins, S. (1994) *The Study of Second Language Acquisition.* Oxford: Oxford University Press.

Gallagher, E. (2009) *Equal Rights to The Curriculum: Many Languages: One Message.* Multilingual Matters.

Goethe, J.W.V. (1749–1852) On WWW at Google language quotes.

Galambos, S. and Hakuta, K. (1988) Subject-specific and task-specific characteristics of metalinguistics awareness in bilingual children. *Applied Psycholinguistics* 9.

Halliday, M. (1993) Towards a language based theory of learning. *Linguistics and Education* 5.

Krashen, S. (1982) *Principles and Practice in Second Language Acquisition.* New York: Pergamon Press.

Menken, K. and Barron, V. (2002) What are the characteristics of the bilingual education and ESL shortage? *Ask NCELA* 14.

Minami, M. (2002) *Culture-Specific Language Styles.* Clevedon: Multilingual Matters.

National Clearing House for English language Acquisition and Language Instruction: Educational Programs. Washington.

Norton, B. (2000) *Identity and Language Learning: Gender, Ethnicity and Educational Change*. Essex: Pearson Education.

Pavlenko, A. (2005) *Bilingualism and Thought*. Oxford: Oxford University Press.

Sapir, E. and Lee B. (1958) The status of linguistics as a science. In D.G. Mandlelbaum (ed.) *Culture, Language and Personality*. Berkeley, CA: University of California Press.

Shaules, J. (2007) *Deep Culture, the Hidden Challenges of Global Living*. Clevedon: Multilingual Matters.

About the author

Anita Hayim-Bamberger was born in Manchester and was brought up as a passive bilingual in Arabic. She is fluent in French and able to communicate in Spanish and Hebrew. She lived in Paris for seven years where she completed an MA in linguistics. Anita is currently training to be an English–French interpreter. She has been a language teacher for more than 20 years and is currently an ESL teacher at the Southbank International School in London.

Section 2

Chapter 8

Young Mathematicians: Global Learners

MAULFRY WORTHINGTON

This instructive chapter describes a classroom of young learners who are encouraged to use their own graphical marks and symbols to support their mathematical thinking, thereby helping them subsequently to make sense of the abstract symbolic written language of mathematics. Furthermore, as the author explains, '... any lack of fluent English need not be a barrier to children's understanding ... provided they can build on their early understandings of graphical marks and symbols'.

INTRODUCTION

Concerns about standards of children's mathematics have increased in our global society and with this, increased concerns about curricula and pedagogical approaches: these concerns appear to be universal. One aspect of mathematics that has received far less attention is the beginning and development of children's 'written' mathematics and how it impacts on their understanding.

This chapter explores young children's mathematical thinking through their own graphical representations. This emphasis differs from the approaches teachers commonly use and is termed *children's mathematical graphics* (Carruthers & Worthington, 2005, 2006). Children use their *mathematical graphics* to support and communicate their mathematical thinking as they come to understand the abstract written symbolic language of mathematics as a deep level.

The chapter explores a number of new examples from multilingual children aged four and five years as they reflect on their personal and family experiences, play games and solve problems. They may challenge current practice and should encourage teachers to reflect on children's experiences. The chapter also charts children's trajectory of learning in this area, providing guidance on ways in which teachers can 'tune into' children's mathematical thinking and offering an effective means by which to assess children's graphicacy in mathematics.

Introducing children's mathematical graphics

Each weekend Giorgio travels from his school in Zurich to his home in Rome, a long journey for a four-year-old. Giorgio's teacher explained that he was obsessed by trains and loves the metro. One day after reading a book about trains with his teacher, he spontaneously drew a train (Figure 8.1). He explained that the zigzag squiggles were 'peoples'.

Giorgio was exploring his feeling about returning home combined with his passion for trains. At the same time he was expressing his thoughts about 'lots of people': his personal use of zigzag symbols was sufficient for him to communicate his large number of ideas.

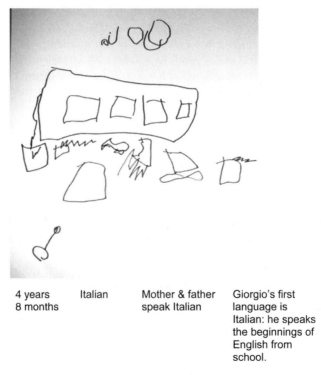

| Giorgio | 4 years 8 months | Italian | Mother & father speak Italian | Giorgio's first language is Italian: he speaks the beginnings of English from school. |

Figure 8.1 Giorgio's train

Whereas in their drawings and writing children freely explore emotions and feelings of attachment, there are far fewer opportunities for such explorations in mathematics, particularly in adult-led written mathematics (Worthington, 2009). Early 'written' mathematics is also often divorced from real experiences and without personal meaning for young children unless (as here) they can make such connections themselves. For the youngest children such feelings about home are natural and their representations may often include aspects of mathematics. In another example from the same school, Gaya was thinking about her Grandad's forthcoming birthday.

Gaya drew a 'Hello Kitty' cake (Figure 8.2) around a small cutting board to achieve the shape that she wanted for 'Kitty's' face. She explained 'Grandpa's really old; he's 30'. The pink squiggles represent candles and when her teacher asked how many he would need, she replied 'Thirty, of course.' Gaya is Israeli and, like her parents, her first language is Hebrew; like Giorgio, she is learning English from school.

For most young children birthdays are highly significant events to anticipate and savour and Gaya was drawing on her personal experiences. She knew that the quantity of candles for a birthday cake should match the age of the person whose birthday was celebrated and this knowledge helped her determine the number needed for her Grandad's cake.

Gaya's thoughts about her Grandad's birthday are coupled with her interest in popular culture: she likes 'Hello Kitty' (a character that originates in Japan) so it seems logical to her that this is the very best cake for her Grandad. We can see that not only do languages cross cultures but that global cultures are rapidly shared though modern

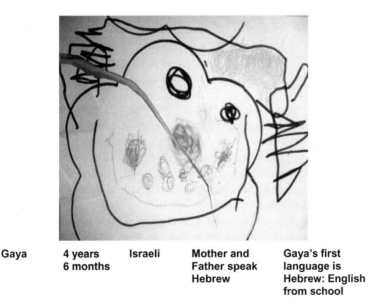

| Gaya | 4 years 6 months | Israeli | Mother and Father speak Hebrew | Gaya's first language is Hebrew: English from school |

Figure 8.2 Gaya: A birthday cake for Grandad

media (Marsh, 2006; Worthington, 2010a). Giorgio's and Gaya's representations are examples of *children's mathematical graphics* in which children represent their internal, mental representations through external graphical representations. Each chose *how* they would represent their thinking, that is, drawings and invented or personal symbols such as Giorgio's zigzag sign for 'peoples' and Gaya's use of circles to mean 'candles'. Other children might have drawn, or written words or numerals to represent people or candles. Children benefit from choosing how they will represent their mathematical thinking that best fits their purpose, the particular mathematical context or idea they are exploring in play or the calculation or the problem they wish to solve.

Multiple languages

The examples featured in this chapter are from children who are bilingual or multilingual and attend an international school in Europe and, as the examples show, using their own graphical representations is no barrier to children's ability to explore and communicate their mathematical ideas. *Children's mathematical graphics* are inclusive, supporting young learners everywhere and helping children of all abilities including the most gifted, and those who are second-language learners.

The symbolic language of mathematics (spoken and written) has itself been described as a 'foreign language' (Hughes, 1986; Pimm, 1981) and like learning an additional language, children learn mathematical notation best in meaningful contexts, building on what they already know.

Early Childhood mathematics

In our global society concerns about standards of mathematics in schools have increased. These concerns appear to be universal and increased international, national, local and school pressures are no doubt experienced by most teachers in curricula changes, testing and data comparison (e.g. *The Trends in International Mathematics and Science Study*, TIMSS, 2007).

Young children's understanding and development of 'written' mathematics has received far less interest when compared with the extensive research and publications on early writing, and is seldom acknowledged in early childhood curricula. However, due to the nature of its abstract written language, mathematical notation has been found to cause children the greatest difficulties (Ginsburg, 1977; Hughes, 1986) and becomes increasingly important as they move through school. Consideration should be given to the significant gap that exists between young children's early understanding of 'written' mathematics and the standard, written symbolic language of maths. Showing children what to write (or draw) and how to do it; asking them to trace over, copy or colour in or providing published worksheets or teacher-given written mathematics actually *obstructs* deep understanding (Carruthers & Worthington, 2006). This bridging function is highly important in early written mathematics and was identified by Hughes (1986) as the gap between the children's informal understanding and formal 'school' written mathematics.

TEACHING MATHEMATICS: DIFFERENT BUT THE SAME?

In 2000, Robin Alexander published his comprehensive study of Primary education in France, Russia, India and the United States. The examples of mathematics lessons in the four countries make interesting reading and include several mathematics lessons with children of six years of age (though unfortunately none from younger children). One of Alexander's conclusions was that mathematics teaching worldwide is heavily influenced by textbooks and worksheets: this was also the case in England. Of course there are local and national considerations that influence teachers in different countries. In England the dominance of worksheets in the past has been corroborated by Brooker (2002) in her research on young children starting school. And research we conducted with almost 300 teachers into how they taught early written mathematics in England revealed similar findings for mathematics teaching with children of three to eight years (see Carruthers & Worthington, 2006). Low-level 'colouring-in' items children have counted, or copying written numerals may result partly from a misunderstanding that mathematics is a 'hard' subject and that since these are young children, things need to be made 'easy' if they are to understand. Yet, our evidence is that from three years of age many children explore quite complex mathematical ideas and problems provided they are set within meaningful contexts and they can choose whether to use their own graphics to support their thinking.

Another feature that impacts on teaching and mathematics curricula is the age at which children begin school, since this is likely to influence the curriculum content. For example, in England four-year-olds are commonly in reception classes (the first year of school) and recently school entry was fixed at the September following a child's fourth birthday (DCSF, 2009a). The Netherlands is the only other European country where children can start school at such a young age; in Europe and the rest of the world six years is more common, with some countries setting school entry at age seven.

It is difficult to find a country where mathematics teaching genuinely supports young children's developing understanding of early written maths in ways that make personal sense, although the *Realistic Mathematics Education* (REM) in the Netherlands invests in this through a structured approach for children from six years of age. On the other side of the world in Queensland, Australia, Zevenbergen argued that 'whilst there are tokenistic references made to children's informal understandings, these are not central to curriculum design' (Zevenbergen, 2000: 4).

Mathematics in England (birth–5 years)

When the 'Foundation Stage' was first launched in 2000 it was hoped that this would result in more appropriate experiences for children throughout this phase. Yet, due to continuing concerns about the levels of children's achievement, the mathematics curriculum appears often to be interpreted in ways that limit the four- and five-year-olds' experiences. One study of teaching and learning (Inside the Foundation Stage: Recreating the Reception Year) for this age group found that whereas teachers 'emphasized the need for spontaneity and independence in children's learning' they 'also worried about whether children would achieve the specified targets, especially in literacy and numeracy, and planned tightly structured tasks to ensure that they did so'. This resulted in an 'emphasis on the smallest and most basic mechanical units of literacy and numeracy' (Adams *et al.*, 2004: 21/27) and there is evidence that the primary school curriculum, Ofsted inspections and SATS tests continue to exert considerable downward pressure.

Since 2007 children from birth to five years of age in England have experienced a 'play-based' curriculum: However, although the section on *Problem Solving, Reasoning and Numeracy* asserts that practitioners should value young children's 'graphic explorations' in mathematics (DfES, 2007: 61), it unfortunately fails to include any guidance on this. Yet, in England since 2002 the inspection system has repeatedly raised concerns about young children's mathematical achievement: these include the need to establish links between children's mental and written mathematics; children's over-reliance on formal written methods and their reluctance to use informal written mathematics; and concerns about calculations and problem solving and their limited 'use and application' of mathematics.

In 2008, a two-year government-funded review was begun of mathematics teaching in Early Years settings and primary schools. It was known as the 'Williams Review'. The final report highlighted the significance of children's mathematical graphics for 'children's cognitive development', citing our taxonomy (DCSF, 2008a: 34/35) and raised concerns about the very limited extent that children 'use developing mathematical ideas to solve practical problems' (DCSF, 2008a: 41). This report was followed by a general guide for Early Years teachers and practitioners titled *Mark Making Matters* (DCSF, 2008b), as well as a booklet for teachers and practitoners titled *Children Thinking Mathematically* that we were commissioned to write (DCSF, 2009b).

The Netherlands

Whilst children in the Netherlands usually start school at four years of age, formal introduction to reading, writing and arithmetic is delayed until they are seven. Although there is no official requirement to use a specific mathematics curriculum, many schools introduce the REM curriculum developed by Freudenthal, who, rather than seeing mathematics 'as a subject matter that has to be transmitted', stressed 'the idea of mathematics as a human activity' in which students are given 'guided opportunities' to 're-invent mathematics by doing it' (Van den Heuvel-Panhuizen, 2001: 3). However, the youngest that children are taught this curriculum is age six to seven, and their 'guided opportunities to re-invent' mathematics is closely related to sections in the REM textbooks (e.g. working out candles on a birthday cake or people getting on and off a bus), then guided to specific ways of representing calculations. Although the approaches used in the REM curriculum are said to 'bridge the gap' between informal and formal written mathematics it does not appear to acknowledge children's spontaneous representations that originate either in their play or in other contexts outside mathematics lessons and the REM curriculum.

A smaller percentage of Dutch Primary schools use the 'Developmental Education' curriculum based on Vygotsky's work, and some introduce 'schematizing', a way of representing ideas visually which has been shown to support understanding of written calculations (Poland & Van Oers, 2007).

CHILDREN'S MATHEMATICAL GRAPHICS: THE SYMBOLIC WRITTEN LANGUAGE OF MATHEMATICS

Our research began in 1991 in the nurseries and schools in which we taught as we searched for a more effective means of supporting children's understanding of mathematical notation. We began from an 'emergent writing' perspective, encouraging children to use their own marks, symbols and representations to support their mathematical thinking. We found that they do this spontaneously in their play and in adult-led groups, provided the culture of the setting or class supports this 'meaning-making' or semiotic approach. Since children's own representations build on what they *already* know and understand about representing meanings with marks, *mathematical* understanding is supported at a deep level (Carruthers & Worthington, 2005, 2006). *Children's mathematical graphics* encompass all aspects of mathematics for children from three to eight years (e.g. written number and quantities; calculations and data handling), and are also relevant for the mathematics of shape, space and measures. They are part of a continuum that begins in the nursery.

Beginnings

Children's meaning-making with marks, symbols and visual representations (graphicacy) begins with gestures, actions, sounds and language and in their imaginative symbolic play (see the taxonomy on page 91).

In their play children come to understand that, just as artefacts and materials can be used to 'mean' or symbolize something else, so can graphical marks and symbols. These various ways of representing meanings are known as 'symbolic tools': they help us to solve and communicate 'mental' problems just as tools such as hammers, spades and scissors help us to solve physical problems. Vygotsky (1978) recognized the importance of symbolic tools for children's cognitive development. This ability to use one thing to signify something else is at the base of the symbolic languages of writing and has now been shown to underpin the symbolic written mathematical language (Worthington, 2009, 2010b).

This perspective is important since it helps us to understand the significance of imaginative, symbolic play. Children explore and communicate their meanings in a variety of ways with a range of materials and media as *multimodal* (Kress, 1997). For example, noticing the zigzag edges of the paper she cut with pinking shears, Jemima referred to it as a 'crocodile'. On another occasion Hamzah was drawing and made lots of tiny circles explaining his drawing as 'cars': it seemed that for him it was the wheels of cars that were their most significant feature. Children also make junk models to explore their meanings: for example, Nathan made what he explained was 'an astronaut flying to the moon': its meaning became clear when he used actions and added sounds and the words 'blast off!' (Worthington, 2010b).

In their role play, cut-outs, models and drawings, children focus on particular features (or 'affordances') to signify something else (e.g. a crocodile, wheels or an astronaut 'flying to the moon'). What may sometimes appear to adults as 'just play' is of considerable importance for young children. Part of its potential value is cognitive, helping them understand how marks, symbols and other visual representations made with a pen or other drawing tool on a surface can also carry meaning. Both Vygotsky and Kress have focused on the relationship between young children's meaning-making in play and how it underpins their writing. Recent research has extended this to chart the relationship between imaginative play and *children's mathematical graphics* (Worthington, 2010b, c). Van Oers (2005) proposes that, through play children develop more abstract forms of activities, arguing that the 'potentials of imagination' are the emergence of abstract and divergent thinking. An additional category of imaginative play that relates to calculations has recently been added to those developed by Van Oers (Worthington, 2010b, c).

Understanding and assessing children's mathematical graphics

In the course of our research we gathered together hundreds of examples of *children's mathematical graphics*. Analysis of over 700 examples enabled us to chart children's mathematical thinking through their representations: we identified 10 distinctive aspects covering written number and quantities and the development of calculations. Children's early explorations with written number and quantities are represented in the first part of our taxonomy (Figure 8.3).

The five dimensions shown in the taxonomy above are explained more fully below.

Early explorations with marks – attaching mathematical meanings
Young children's early marks – sometimes referred to as 'scribbles' – have significance for the child. Over time children's graphics develop, allowing them to explore and express ideas and meanings through drawings and early writing and begin to attach mathematical meanings to some of their early marks and representations.

Early written numerals
Children refer to their symbols as numbers and some of their personal symbols relate to standard written numerals.

Numerals as labels
This is when children use numbers they see in their environment as symbols or labels. Knowing and talking about numbers is not the same as writing them. When children choose to write numbers in context, they have converted what they have read and understood into symbols of the standard symbolic language of mathematics.

Representing quantities that are not counted
Children either attend to the link between their early marks and meaning as a quantity in a general sense, or use the paper to arrange items and numerals in a general sense.

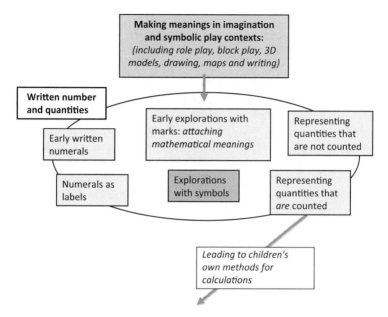

Figure 8.3 Taxonomy: Children's mathematical graphics: Beginning in play. © Carruthers & Worthington, 2011.

Representing quantities that are counted
During the same period that children represent un-counted quantities, they may also begin to count the marks or items that they have represented, and represent items they have counted. This is the first half of the taxonomy showing how children's thinking begins in play: this development leads to early calculations and all other aspects of written mathematics. The taxonomy charts a trajectory of children's mathematical thinking through their representations but it is not hierarchical and should not be directly taught. Many teachers find that the taxonomy helps support their understanding and is valuable for assessment. The various ways children represent their mathematical thinking are dependent upon the mathematical ideas they want to explore and communicate: for example, through their drawings of people and candles, Giorgio and Gaya showed that they were *representing quantities that are not counted* (pages 85 and 86).

Bi-literacy

Research has shown how some children combine aspects of their first and second *written* languages, for example, 'code-switching' (a feature common in second-language learning) to combine letters or characters from their two different languages or writing systems, or the directionality of writing or grammar (see e.g. Drury, 2007; Kenner, 2004). However, whereas writing requires children to use one written 'code' (i.e. the letters and words of their culture's alphabet or other writing system), *children's mathematical graphics* allows them to choose how they will represent their mathematical thinking. This can be particularly valuable for young bilingual children. As the examples in the remaining pages of this chapter show, children speaking several languages will confidently use their own *mathematical graphics* when the classroom culture supports a more open way of thinking. In a sense all young children code-switch as they move between their informal understandings of graphics for mathematics and the more formal abstract written language of mathematics: in our research we found many examples of children code-switching within their *mathematical graphics,* particularly in their calculations (Carruthers & Worthington, 2006, 2008).

The following examples are from children who speak a range of languages and all include details of the mathematics the children were exploring at the time (see Figure 8.3). Figures 8.4 and 8.5 were triggered by the arrival in the classroom of some new sand timers that were causing great excitement! Nicholas's teacher wanted to help the children understand how they might use the timers and suggested they invent a game, to 'race' the timer.

Nicholas decided to see how many blue items he could collect whilst the timer ran through, and several other children decided to join in. Nicholas took all of the items he had collected, lined them all up in one long line and sorted them into things he determined belonged together. He added the lines, stating it 'looked better like that'. Nicholas had drawn dinosaurs and other toy animals (the figures left and right), buttons and highlighter pens, and as he drew each, he counted the current total to see how many he had.

Nicholas was *representing quantities he counted.*

Blank paper is of the greatest value to *children's mathematical graphics* and rather than teachers drawing lines or grids on a page it is helpful if children can also make decisions about layout (as Nicholas did by adding lines). Later this skill will be valuable as children make decisions about layout with written calculations and data handling.

Paulina joined in with Nicholas's game, representing the details of each item including a ruler and a 'gel' pen.

The circular shape with lines radiating from it is a table. It is interesting to note that whereas Paulina represented the items she had counted, when drawing the table she indicated 'many' legs rather than a specific quantity. Whilst she could easily have counted the number of legs on the table, she appeared to be representing her idea of several chairs tucked into the table – which together would have accounted for lots of legs! When faced with a large quantity of something, children often represent their personal sense of a large (uncounted) quantity.

The heart shape at the foot of the page was a gel hand-warmer to keep in her pocket and that Paulina had brought from home.

Paulina was also *representing quantities she counted and representing quantities that she did not count.*

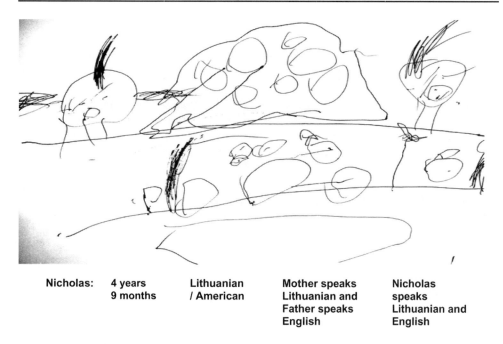

| Nicholas: | 4 years 9 months | Lithuanian / American | Mother speaks Lithuanian and Father speaks English | Nicholas speaks Lithuanian and English |

Figure 8.4 Nicholas's sand-timer game

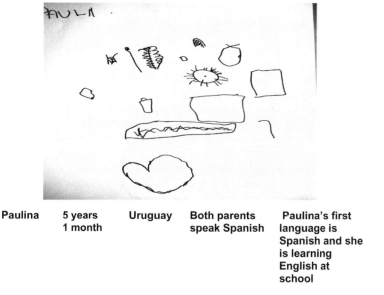

| Paulina | 5 years 1 month | Uruguay | Both parents speak Spanish | Paulina's first language is Spanish and she is learning English at school |

Figure 8.5 Paulina plays the sand timer game

Like zigzags and crosses, hearts have strong visual impact and also often appear in such popular cultural contexts as comics, jewellery and clothes. Whereas Paulina's heart shape was a specific item, girls often include heart shapes in their drawings, writing and mathematical graphics. Matthews (1999) shows how infants and very young children use a range of marks such as dots, lines, arcs and zigzags that form the basis of the symbols they will later use in drawings, writing and mathematics, arguing that from what appear to be 'chaotic actions' and random 'scribbling' these marks are significant in young children's development. Just as they make choices about the materials and the means they use to represent an animal, a car or an astronaut flying, children in nursery and school make choices and decisions about the graphical marks they use.

Children 3–5-years old have been found to use specific signs in various contexts, for example, using crosses not only as kisses on a birthday card, but in drawings (e.g. as an aeroplane or as hands); as a symbol to represent written speech; as a symbol to designate scores in a ball game; as part of a sign for 'shop closed'; in mathematics to signify 'add' or as a form of tally when gathering data. This flexibility of thinking and sign-use underpins children's understanding of the symbolic written language of maths at a deep level (Worthington, 2009).

David was the 'snack helper' one day and decided that he wanted to make his own list. In these two examples David used crosses to show the quantity of each snack item the children could have. In Figure 8.6(a), the four crosses at the top meant that children could have 4 pieces of apple each. The zigzags (another graphical symbol that children often use to mean different things) are David's labels that refer to the names of the food items for snack time (e.g. 'apples').

a. In this example David was *representing quantities he counted*.
After he had made his first list David turned his small whiteboard over and this time explained that the letter/number-like symbols (like an 's' or '5') showed how many items of snack each child could have.
b. In this example David was *representing quantities he counted and using his own early written numerals*

Gabrielle enjoyed playing with the teddy bears in her classroom. Noticing that there were three different types of bears she grouped them together and decided to see how many there were in all. She drew one bear to represent each type, finally writing the total amount of each type above (or on) each bear. This was Gabrielle's own idea and was quite a sophisticated way of representing 37 bears (i.e. the combined total of 12, 15 and 10).

Gabrielle was *representing quantities she counted* and using *numbers as labels*.

(a)

(b)

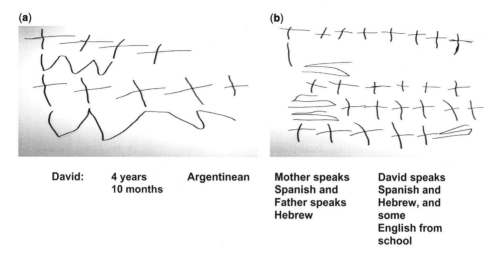

| David: | 4 years 10 months | Argentinean | Mother speaks Spanish and Father speaks Hebrew | David speaks Spanish and Hebrew, and some English from school |

Figure 8.6 (a) David's snack list (b) David's snack list (reverse side)

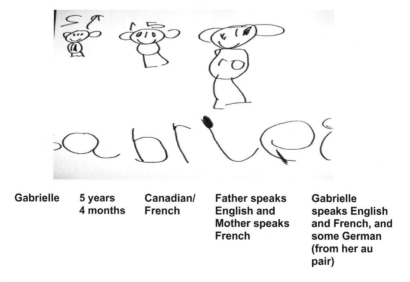

| Gabrielle | 5 years 4 months | Canadian/ French | Father speaks English and Mother speaks French | Gabrielle speaks English and French, and some German (from her au pair) |

Figure 8.7 Gabrielle – counting bears

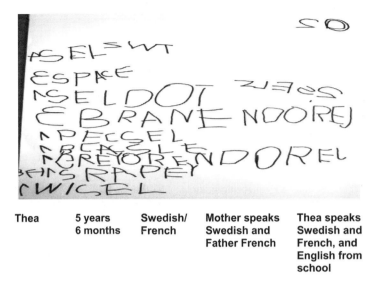

Thea	5 years 6 months	Swedish/ French	Mother speaks Swedish and Father French	Thea speaks Swedish and French, and English from school

Figure 8.8 Thea – playing the 'counting game'

Noticing what Gabrielle was playing, Thea decided to collect toys herself. Unlike the other children, Thea decided she would use words, spelling words phonetically. She has focused largely on capital letters (very evident in advertising and in the media) and also included some personal signs that suggest either the numeral '1' or a '7', and a '3'.

Although she spoke Swedish, French and English, Thea only *wrote* in English at the time and used her own writing. For example, the second item in her list is 'spike' – the term she decided to use to describe a pyramid-shaped block and the fourth item is 'brown and orange', which she wrote to describe some coloured glass pebbles she'd found.

Thea was also *representing quantities that she counted.*

Anoushka was playing with some toy vehicles, arranging and rearranging them in various patterns on the floor. She wanted to take a photo of what she was doing but the camera's battery had run out, so she decided to use a paper and pen. The shapes represent vehicles though she only added wheels to the tiny ones in the centre. Anoushka added dots as a strategy to help her check how many she had (finding it somewhat difficult to keep track of where she was). During the course of her play she counted 36 items in total and then added her own number symbols (top right) to signify this.

Anoushka was *representing quantities she counted* (and also counting quantities she'd represented), and using her own *early written numbers.*

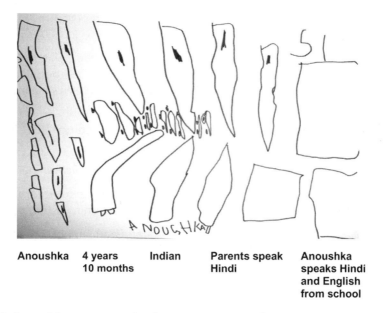

| Anoushka | 4 years 10 months | Indian | Parents speak Hindi | Anoushka speaks Hindi and English from school |

Figure 8.9 Anoushka – representing her arrangements of toy cars

When young *children's mathematical graphics* are supported, they enable a trajectory of learning that develops to include their own informal written methods for calculations. We charted this developing understanding in the second part of our taxonomy (see Carruthers & Worthington, 2006, 2008).

RESEARCH INFORMING PRACTICE

Children's mathematical graphics emphasize the *processes* of mathematical thinking, focusing on children's own thinking, meanings and understanding about mathematical notation. In contrast, *recording* what they do following a practical activity places the emphasis on marks and drawings as a *product* and is a lower level of cognitive demand (thinking) in mathematics. Children do not need to record mathematics if they can do it mentally; neither do they need to be asked to record something they have already worked out in a practical context. The difference between *representing mathematical thinking* and *recording* is one of quality and depth of thinking.

Recent research into children's meaning-making in play has highlighted a number of key points that can make a difference to children's understanding of 'written' mathematics (Worthington, 2010b). It showed that whilst teachers and practitioners may use the same play-based curriculum, they often interpret play and their roles differently. This research suggests that the most notable difference is the extent to which teachers and practitioners take an interest in children's *meanings*. The pedagogical implications from this research highlight the importance of imaginative, symbolic play; specifically:

> Adults who focus on young children's own *meanings* in their play; Learning environments that provide open-ended resources and extended periods of time for children's symbolic play; Adults who focus on young children's meaning-making as they use marks, symbols and drawings.

Symbolic play underpins *children's mathematical graphics*, in turn highlighting the importance of:

> Adults who value and take an interest in children's *mathematical* meanings;

> Collaborative dialogue to scaffold children's thinking about their *mathematical graphics*, enabling them to negotiate and co-construct understanding;

> Reflective adults who work together to understand and support children's thinking, involving parents in sharing and celebrating young children as powerful meaning-makers and competent young mathematicians.

The children's examples explored in this chapter show that any lack of fluent English in an English-medium school need not be a barrier to children's understanding of the abstract written language of mathematics, provided they can build on their early understandings about graphical marks and symbols. Learning a second language, children subconsciously build on what they know from their first language of how languages 'work'. In similar ways children's knowledge of how graphical marks and symbols can carry mathematical meanings enables them to build understanding of standard mathematical notation, effectively bridging the gulf that would otherwise exist. But none of this is possible unless teachers create learning cultures in which children feel empowered to explore their own mathematical meanings, thereby providing strong foundations for understanding mathematical notation – wherever they live in the world.

With special thanks to Emma Hookey and the children at Zurich International School, Switzerland.

REFERENCES

Adams, S., Alexander, E., Drummond, M.J. and Moyles, J. (2004) *Inside the Foundation Stage: Recreating the Reception Year.* London: Association of Teachers and Lecturers (ATL).

Alexander, R. (2000) *Culture and Pedagogy: International Comparisons in Primary Education.* Oxford: Blackwell Publishers.

Brooker, L. (2002) *Starting School: Young Children Learning Cultures.* Buckingham: Open University Press.

Carruthers, E. and Worthington, M. (2005) Making sense of mathematical graphics: The development of understanding abstract symbolism. *European Early Childhood Education Research Association Journal* (EECERA) 13, 57–79.

Carruthers, E. and Worthington, M. (2006) *Children's Mathematics: Making Marks, Making Meaning* (2nd edn). London: Sage Publications.

Carruthers, E. and Worthington, M. (2008) Children's mathematical graphics: Young children calculating for meaning. In I. Thompson (ed.) *Teaching and Learning Early Number* (2nd edn). Maidenhead: Open University Press.

Carruthers, E. and Worthington, M. (2011) *Understanding Children's Mathematical Graphics: Beginnings in Play.* Maidenhead: Open University Press.

DCSF (2008a) *Independent Review of Mathematics Teaching in Early Years Settings and Primary Schools.* London: DCSF.

DCSF (2008b) *Mark Making Matters.* London: DCSF.

DCSF (2009a) *Independent Review of the Primary Curriculum: Final Report.* London: DCSF.

DCSF (2009b) *Children Thinking Mathematically: PSRN Essential Knowledge for Early Years Practitioners.* London: DCSF. On WWW at http://nationalstrategies.standards.dcsf.gov.uk/node/257449?uc=force_uj. Accessed 17.1.09.

DfES (2007) *Practice Guidance for the Early Years Foundation Stage.* London: DfES.

Drury, R. (2007) *Young Bilingual Learners at Home and at School.* Stoke-on-Trent: Trentham Books.

Ginsburg, H. (1977) *Children's Arithmetic.* New York: Van Nostrand.

Hughes, M. (1986) *Children and Number: Difficulties in Learning Mathematics.* Oxford: Blackwell.

Kenner, C. (2004) *Becoming Biliterate: Young Children Learning Different Writing Systems.* Stoke-on-Trent: Trentham Books.

Kress, G. (1997) *Before Writing: Rethinking the Paths to Literacy.* London: Routledge.

Marsh, J. (ed.) (2006) Popular culture, new media and digital literacy. In *Early Childhood.* London: Routledge Falmer.

Matthews, J. (1999) *The Art of Childhood and Adolescence.* London: Falmer Press.

Pimm, D. (1981) Mathematics? I speak it fluently. In A. Floyd (ed.) *Developing Mathematical Thinking.* Wokingham: Addison-Wesley.

Poland, M. and Van Oers, B. (2007) Effects of schematising on mathematical development. In *European Early Childhood Education Research Journal* 15, 269–293.

TIMSS (2007) *The Trends in International Mathematics and Science Study.* Washington: Institute of Education Sciences. On WWW at http://nces.ed.gov/timss/. Accessed 2.7.09.

Van den Heuvel-Panhuizen, M. (2001) Realistic mathematics education in the Netherlands. In J. Anghileri (ed.) *Principles and Practice in Arithmetic Teaching.* Buckingham: Open University Press.

Van Oers, B. (2005) *The Potentials of Imagination. Inquiry: Critical Thinking Across the Disciplines* 24, 5–17.

Vygotsky, L.S. (1978) *Mind in Society: The Development of Higher Psychological Processes.* Cambridge, MA: Harvard University Press.

Worthington, M. (2009) Fish in the water of culture: Signs and symbols in young children's drawing. *Psychology of Education Review* 33, 37–46.

Worthington, M. (2010a) This is a *different* calculator – with computer games on: Reflecting on children's symbolic play in the digital age. In J. Moyles (ed.) *Thinking about Play – Developing a Reflective Approach.* Maidenhead: Open University Press/McGraw-Hill.

Worthington, M. (2010b) Play is a complex landscape: Imagination and symbolic meanings. In P. Broadhead, L. Wood and J. Howard (eds) *Play and Learning in Educational Settings.* London: Sage Publications.

Worthington, M. (2010c) Symbolic play and the emergence of graphicacy in early childhood mathematics: A semiotic perspective. Paper presented at the British Congress in Mathematics Education (BCME-7), Manchester, April 2010.

Zevenbergen, R. (2000) Using mental computations for developing number sense. *Teaching Mathematics* 25, 29–33.

About the author

Maulfry Worthington has conducted extensive research in children's mathematical graphics and young children's play and is currently engaged in doctoral research (Free University, Amsterdam). She has taught young children for over 26 years and has had several other roles including Early Years consultant; National Numeracy Consultant and university lecturer. Maulfry has many publications including *Children's Mathematics: Making Marks, Making Meaning* (Sage Publications, 2006), co-authored with Elizabeth Carruthers. They are winners of several national awards and their work on children's mathematical graphics is featured in a number of government documents in England, including the *Williams Maths Review* (DCSF, 2008a) and *Children Thinking Mathematically* (DCSF, 2009b). They are founders of the international 'Children's Mathematics Network'.

Chapter 9

Meeting the Needs of Young Second-Language Learners who Struggle

FRANCES BEKHECHI

A seasoned teacher in a large international school describes the difficulties of trying to assess and deal with the problems some young non-English speakers have in learning a second language. She relates some of the challenges she encountered in this area and describes in detail the way she learned to manage them.

INTRODUCTION

The problem

According to the results of the longitudinal studies done by Collier and Thomas in the United States and Jim Cummins in Canada, acquiring a second or additional language is a lengthy process and reaching an appropriate level of academic language proficiency can take on average five to seven years, or possibly even longer if the student is not yet literate in his primary language. As teachers, however, we have all come across students whose learning curve, within these parameters, was worryingly out of sync with the norm. If the students concerned are of an age when literacy skills should be well in place in their first language we perhaps have a better chance of determining whether the difficulties they are experiencing can be attributed to second-language issues or an underlying learning disability. If they are aged between two-and-a-half and six or seven, the author maintains, trying to establish the cause can be considerably more problematic.

Takashi's story

Some years ago, Takashi arrived in our kindergarten as a complete beginner in English. He presented as a bright and alert little boy, who, despite his lack of English, seemed totally unfazed by his new surroundings. He immediately gravitated towards all the colourful hands-on materials available in the class, and right from the start displayed a natural aptitude for spatial problem-solving and an ability to produce extremely complex structures using blocks or Lego. Circle time, however, proved much more of a challenge for him, and he was far more likely to be found rolling on the floor than sitting crossed legged attending to the discussion or to the shared reading of a Big Book. Consequently, his oral language was slow to develop and by the end of the year he was still communicating in single words or short phrases, the pronunciation of which often made it difficult to understand – at least for the teacher.

For some reason, the children in the class had much less difficulty understanding what Takashi was trying to say. They had become adept at deciphering his telegraphic speech and would often act as interpreters between him and the teachers, 'translating' what he said and filling in the gaps as necessary. Takashi was, in fact, very popular with his peers. He was full of energy and mischief, and was already exhibiting all the attributes of a future athlete. As the star goal-scorer in any playground soccer match, he was in high demand and the boys were constantly vying with each other to have him on their team.

In 1st grade, Takashi's artistic ability really came to the fore. He showed a fascination for different forms of transportation, in particular aircraft, sports cars and fast trains, which he could draw from memory in the minutest detail, with a use of perspective that would have been impressive even in a 6th grader. His progress in language remained slow and this was not helped by the fact that he had a ready-made group of interpreters, always willing to step in and translate his message into correct English, thus removing one of the basic motivators for improvement: the need to make oneself understood. In many ways, Takashi was the antithesis of the stereotypical Japanese student, and his mother, before the teacher could even get a word in, always began any parent–teacher conference by apologizing for her son. He had an older sister who was a model student, quiet and studious, incredibly motivated and clearly destined to achieve great things. It already seemed apparent that the baby of the family, despite his obvious talents, was not going to follow the traditional route.

By 2nd grade, Takashi's teachers were beginning to express real concern. He had made progress in the early stages of reading and it was hoped that working with simple repetitive texts would help him develop a more correct use of grammatical structure in his speech, as he was clearly a visual rather than an auditory learner. Midway through the year, however, there was still no evidence of this happening, and his writing also continued to display the same basic structural errors, which seemed to resist all efforts to correct them. What was very clear was the enormous disparity between his extremely high ability in anything math related and his considerable struggle with all aspects of language. In every other area, he was obviously a very intelligent little boy.

As with most of our Japanese students, Takashi was attending Japanese school on Saturday and, according to his mother, was making good progress with literacy. This was encouraging. Perhaps he was just taking a little longer than usual to acquire English and more time was needed. We all knew from the long-term studies the time it can take for second-language students to reach grade-level proficiency, and this was after all only his third year in English. By the end of the year, however, there was still little sign of improvement, and so Takashi remained in an intermediate ESL class in 3rd grade. This corresponded to his level of functioning as regards both his oral and literacy skills, although a number of students in the class were considerably more advanced than he was, despite having started as complete beginners only the year before.

At this point, the need for formal testing was suggested as a way of getting to the bottom of Takashi's difficulties. The presence of a specific learning disability is generally determined by means of standardized intelligence tests, where the scores indicate a significant gap between 'potential ability' and current levels of achievement. However, it was felt that Takashi would still be disadvantaged by the level of language used in the test, and that any results would therefore be invalid. This, of course, raises one of the major problems with using the discrepancy model to identify disabilities in second-language learners through the medium of an English-language test, as it would be perfectly normal for several years for them to score lower on verbal than on nonverbal tasks, whether or not a learning disability was present. Catch 22.

And there were others: Takashi sticks out in my mind as being exceptional, but over the years I have of course come across other students whose learning caused me concern. Like the Norwegian girl who arrived in 4th grade, bright in so many ways and already orally fluent from her previous schooling in English, but exhibiting real difficulties with print. Was she dyslexic or had she just not had the right kind of ESL support in the early years? Then there was the little Greek boy who, at the start of 1st grade, was already reading end-of-second-grade texts with fluency and expression. No apparent cause for concern there, except that he was totally incapable of answering the most basic questions about what he had read. It seemed even more surprising when we discovered that he was able to retell word by word from memory the entire text of a fairytale he had at home on CD-ROM, complete with sound effects ('click on the wand to see what happens – whoosh!') and still could not say anything at all about the contents of the story. As time went on, his other behaviours began to suggest a possible disorder on the autism spectrum, but his parents refused to recognize there might be a problem that needed investigation – and then he moved.

The mobility factor

This highlights one of the aspects that define most international schools and set them apart from those in national systems: the whole question of mobility. The majority of our students come from families where the father, or in some cases the mother, works for a multinational company or an embassy. They are generally here on a three- or four-year contract before either moving back home or going on to another international posting.

The life of a global nomad can be challenging for children, and there can be any number of reasons why they might have adjustment issues when they first arrive: disrupted schooling; differences in teaching methodology and expectations between their previous school experience and this one; sadness at the loss of best friends; loss of contact with extended family; having to leave a much loved pet behind; being thrown into a situation where they do not understand the language and where the culture is totally foreign to them; picking up on the culture shock experienced by a parent who may not even want to be here in the first place.

In a way, the amazing thing is how so many of them seem to thrive! But of course there will always be those who struggle, and trying to determine the cause of the problem is perhaps one of our biggest challenges, particularly in the case of very young children who are in the early stages of acquiring English, while still laying the foundations of their primary language. Given the great number of possible causes which could explain their difficulty, there is always the temptation to 'give them time', to make allowances. The risk is that, in doing so, precious time may be lost. Before we manage to work out exactly what is going on and initiate a program of remediation, the child may already be on her way to another school in another country, where there, too, they decide to give her time to adjust.

ASSESSING THE DIFFICULTIES OF STRUGGLING SECOND-LANGUAGE LEARNERS

Over the 20 years that I have been teaching ESL in our school, we have seen a significant demographic shift in our population. In the 1980s, 70% of our students came from North America, with the other 30% being made up of 40 or so different nationalities. Now, less than 30% of our students are American, we have more than 70 different nationalities represented on campus, and well in excess of 50% of our students do not have English as their mother tongue.

A recent study in the States indicated that approximately 14% of the total school-age population has some sort of learning disability (U.S. Department of Education, 2005). The actual proportion of second-language students in the equation was unclear. Professional literature is, in fact, replete with references to the considerable challenge of distinguishing between the normal difficulties experienced in the process of acquiring a second language and the presence of a language-based learning disability. On the surface, the behaviours can often appear very similar. The underlying causes, however, may not be the same, nor in most cases would they be the type of remediation required.

In the absence of reliable data, one must assume that the percentage of students with learning disabilities among native and nonnative speakers of English should be fairly similar, and that this same percentage, give or take, will be reflected in international school populations.

One might, of course, hypothesize that the figure could actually be higher in the case of international schools. For students struggling in a local system that perhaps lacks our facilities, parents may feel that our smaller classes, differentiated instruction and system of learning support will be a better option, even if, in some cases, it means starting afresh in another language.

Seeking appropriate assessment tools

In any case, given our overall increase in numbers of second-language students, we can certainly expect to see a corresponding increase in the number of ESL students whose learning curve, for whatever reason, appears to fall outside of the expected parameters of normal language acquisition. The question is, when this happens, what do we do about it?

In an open-admissions school such as ours that has as its mission statement: 'Everyone included, everyone challenged, everyone successful', it is particularly important to start off with a very clear definition of what success looks like. In order to hit a target, you first have to be able to see it! Over the last few years, major curriculum revisions have provided us with a set of standards and benchmarks which define expectations in all subjects at all levels, Nursery through Grade 13. In conjunction with the grade-level literacy benchmarks, we have devised a set of ESL stages inspired by the Ontario English as a Second Language Curriculum and the New Zealand English Language Learning Progressions, which link specific literacy scores with our levels of ESL instruction (see the Appendix). All of this is underpinned by a Language and Literacy document that clearly articulates our beliefs, principles and practices, and makes specific reference to the importance of the home language and culture as a base on which to build and extend children's understanding.

In our Early Childhood Center (ECC), all new students in Pre-Kindergarten – 2nd grade, with the exception of ESL beginners, are screened on entry. Appropriate sections of the Brigance are used, along with the draw-a-person test, letter recognition and letter sound knowledge, mathematical knowledge and depending on the age of the child, an oral reading and comprehension test, and a writing sample. This guides initial placement in our language program (English or French as a Foreign Language) for students in K-2, and already alerts us to those who may need careful monitoring.

Assessment

Literacy instruction in the ECC is delivered through a balanced program of shared, guided and independent reading and writing in a variety of genres, differentiated to meet individual needs, including those of second-language learners. Children's progress in reading is assessed using benchmark books and we have created our own continuum for recording progress in writing. Clear grade-level expectations have been established for different times of the year, and these determine when a student is deemed to be working on grade level, our major criterion for allowing second-language students to exit the ESL program. Literacy data are officially recorded on a database in September, February and May in order to chart and evaluate progress. For the last three years, we have also isolated the scores of our ESL population to allow us to compare individual student performances with those of the peer group. This has helped us create our own set of norms against which to measure student achievement over time.

The English Language Development program in our Early Childhood Center is provided by a joint team of ESL teachers and Learning Support or Literacy specialists. From Kindergarten through 2nd grade, students receive a half-hour of instruction daily in either English or French, during which we call our Language Block. In 1st and 2nd grade, ESL beginners receive an additional 50 minutes a day in a withdrawal class during the regular homeroom literacy hour, and in-class support is also provided by the ESL teacher assigned to the grade level.

Ongoing assessments identify where a student stands in relation to expectations and determine movement between levels and ultimately exit from the programme. While we do not believe that the introduction of another language at this stage will necessarily impede progress in English, we recognize the importance of establishing solid literacy skills in the language of instruction, while supporting in every way possible the continued development of the child's primary language (see other chapters that deal specifically with this important issue) and choose, in the early years, to make this our priority. Research validates our belief that literacy skills, once in place, generally transfer very successfully across languages, in which case time spent building solid foundations in English and in the primary language should in theory serve only to make the acquisition of subsequent languages more successful when the time comes.

We in fact apply this same principle to native and nonnative speakers of English alike and, at each grade level, we have native English speakers who receive additional literacy support during the Language Block rather than taking French. Some groups actually include orally proficient second-language students who exhibit similar literacy needs. In all cases, the grade-level literacy benchmarks determine exit from the programme.

Anticipating some students' difficulties

At any point during the year, but particularly at the designated times when literacy data are officially recorded, any student whose performance appears to fall outside of the norm is red flagged. This also applies to ESL beginners by mid-year if, for example, they seem to be having significant difficulties with phonemic awareness. The procedure is then as follows: concerns are raised with the grade-level team and the Learning Support specialist attached to the team; the ESL specialist is included in the discussion and observations noted. The counsellor may be asked to observe informally, both in class and on the playground, and record behaviours, the idea being to have as complete a picture as possible of how the child functions in a variety of contexts. The ESL specialist is able to provide insights into matters relating to language and culture, and if the counsellor suspects the presence of emotional problems, she may suggest therapy sessions in the home language.

At this early stage, the first step is generally for the learning support specialist to include the child in a small literacy group that meets for 20 minutes in the morning. This is a pre-referral strategy which can sometimes be sufficient to get some students on track. It also allows additional data to be collected for a future referral if this is deemed necessary. How the student responds to intervention will be carefully monitored and will inform subsequent decisions on how to proceed.

If after a period of time it is felt that ongoing support will be needed, parents are contacted and an official referral is made to the head of Learning Support. Information regarding the child's past history, including medical records if available, is gathered from the file, along with any relevant comments from previous report cards. Baseline and current literacy data are assembled, and information regarding the level of development of the primary language is sought. All teachers who work with the child are asked to fill in a referral form, which includes an evaluation of the child's learning with reference to motivation, an ability to stay on task, an ability to follow spoken instructions and to verbally express ideas, wants and needs, as well as an indication of general behaviour, organization of self and materials and relationships with others. The opportunity is provided to elaborate on any aspects that would help to better understand the child's learning profile, as regards particular strengths, weaknesses, challenges or interests. There is also a section that deals with differentiated strategies/modifications already tried, and how successful or otherwise they were.

The next step is to schedule a Child Study meeting, which is attended by the head of Learning Support, the child's homeroom and ESL teachers, the Learning Support specialist for the grade level, the Speech and Language therapist and the school psychologist. Together they consider all the information available and draw up a combined plan of action to target the student's areas of difficulty. This may include additional small group work with the Literacy specialist, one-on-one sessions with the Speech and Language therapist, occupational therapy and perhaps working with the school psychologist, in addition to regular differentiated ESL and classroom instruction. The team reconvenes at regular intervals to evaluate progress and to readjust the learning objectives as necessary. Depending on the outcome, a full battery of psycho-educational testing may be recommended, in English and in the home language. In Brussels we have access to an organization that is able to provide this service in an ever-increasing number of languages. When testing in a particular language is unavailable, this has to be done in the home country, usually during a school vacation. Once this stage is reached, a case manager is assigned and an Individualized Learning Plan (ILP) is drawn up and shared with all the teachers who work with the child. If this is not deemed necessary, the small group literacy support will continue for as long as required. Had Takashi been in our ECC now, this is the procedure we would have followed.

The LD/L2 of Else Hamayan

Although our support programme is not officially referred to as an RTI (Response to Intervention) model, it closely mirrors the approach advocated by Else Hamayan in both her professional presentations and her writing. I first heard Else speak at an ECIS conference, where her session was called 'Distinguishing between Learning Disabilities and Language Learning Difficulties in ESL Students'. Coincidentally, Veronica, a Learning Support colleague, and I were presenting a session at the same conference, sharing our own personal journey, still in its early stages, towards trying to support these children who seem to fall between two stools. We had chosen to call our session 'ESL or Special Needs?' As we were scheduled at the same time as one of the invited speakers, we expected to have a handful of participants at best. In fact, the room ended up full to capacity and we had to bring in extra chairs. It was clearly already a hot topic.

Compared to our fairly anecdotal account, Else's session outlined a very systematic approach to gathering and assessing of information. She considered various descriptors of student performance in light of possible LD explanations, while at the same time making the point that they could easily be simply indicators of a struggle with second-language acquisition. She discussed the impact of culture and of previous educational experiences on a child's ability to adjust to the demands of a new learning environment, and she provided a flow chart of precise steps to follow and questions to ask before coming to a determination as to whether or not to refer an ESL student to special education.

Since then, I have never missed an opportunity to hear Else speak. She has a wealth of knowledge and experience to share, and everything she says is grounded in sound common sense and coloured by an obvious commitment to meeting the needs of second-language students at all stages of their development.

I saw her again at a recent conference where she referred to what had come to be known 10 years ago as her 'LD/L2 Workshop', and in which she had attempted to disentangle long-term disabilities from normal second-language difficulties. She explained how, over the years, there had been a shift in her thinking, and how she had come to realize that asking if it was L2 or LD was really a 'futile question', certainly in the initial stages. She now looks on a struggling L2 child as 'ESL+/–LD', to be determined at a later date. While still emphasizing the necessity of extensive information gathering, she now focuses on the importance of establishing a strong collaborative model for supporting students whose learning is cause for concern. She sees a team approach as essential, as the problems in the case of bilingual children are multifaceted and no single professional can have all the answers. She calls these collaborative groups ECOS teams (for Ensuring a Continuum of Services). It is they who are responsible for assembling all the necessary information about the student, for considering possible interpretations of the observed difficulties, for suggesting interventions and finally for monitoring progress. The importance of not waiting until a specific label can be attached to the cause of the problem before providing support is emphasized. The interventions suggested are all underpinned by the provision of a solid ESL programme, and by a culturally inclusive curriculum that recognizes the primary language as a valuable resource to be developed concurrently with English. As the Collier/Thomas research highlights, the role of the mother tongue in all of this cannot be overestimated. Schools need to ensure that parents are well informed of this from the outset and conscious efforts to support the mother-tongue should be seen as a requirement by the school.

Takashi revisited

With appropriate interventions in the early stages, many of the students will turn out to be ESL-LD. Others, of course, will actually have a specific learning disability. Takashi, our little Japanese student, was finally tested in 5th grade, after six years of English-medium instruction, using the WISC-III (Wechsler Intelligence Scale for Children). By that time, it was deemed that he had had sufficient exposure to English to make the test results valid. What we discovered reflected our early observations. Here was a child who was scoring at the 98th percentile in nonverbal intelligence and at the 16th percentile in verbal IQ. It was noted that he demonstrated excellent nonverbal reasoning skills, an ability to synthesize complex patterns and to understand how parts relate to a larger image. His results on the Visual Auditory Digit Span Test highlighted his difficulties with auditory processing and verbal and written recall. The diagnosis was a language-processing disorder which, it was thought, might be evident in his primary language. Speech and language therapy in English was recommended, as well as testing in Japanese. To our knowledge, the latter was never done. Takashi was exceptional in more than one respect, not least because of the extremes indicated by his test scores. He was also exceptional in that he remained with us from Kindergarten till the end of 9th grade. Very few of our students stay that long. As I was aware of his past history, his middle-school English teacher asked for suggestions as to what he might include in a reference for Takashi's new school. (He was returning to Japan, but planning to attend an English-medium high school there.) Here is part of what I wrote: 'Takashi is a very special case. The testing that was done when he was in 5th grade showed him to be highly gifted in certain areas (spatial problem solving, mathematical reasoning, etc.) but with serious learning difficulties in anything language-related ... In order for Takashi to get the kind of support he needs, the school must be made aware of both his considerable talents and his areas of difficulty. My hope is that he can somehow "get through the system" and then go on to a Japanese university where he can perhaps focus on architecture, engineering, art or technology. If such an exceptionally talented young man isn't given the opportunity to be successful, it will be a crying shame'.

Problem solved?

Whenever I come across an ESL student in a similar situation, I often wonder if they would have fared better had they focused on just one language, but it seems there is no definitive answer to that question. Studies that have considered the issue appear contradictory. Some would claim that, in the case of severely dyslexic students at least, the challenges of functioning successfully in more than one language are just too great. Others that compared learning disabled students in immersion programs have found that they ended up functioning as well in their second language as their monolingual learning disabled counterparts in regular English-medium instruction.

What seems clear is that international schools often have considerable resources at their disposal for providing the best kind of support available. We are also much better informed now than we were some years ago as regards the need to provide a culturally inclusive curriculum that recognizes the development of the students' mother tongue as being of fundamental importance in their acquisition of other languages. In addition, we are in the privileged position of being able, when a student does struggle, to cut through much of the red tape that can tie national systems up in knots and make the referral process interminable. In fact, the only red tape we really have to deal with is of our own creation, and we can choose to make the system as easy or as complicated as we wish.

As Else says, when a second-language student is struggling, to spend time trying to ascertain whether we are dealing with an ESL or an LD problem is futile. What counts is providing as much support from all angles as our resources allow, and this as soon as the problem is first observed. Her book *Special Education Considerations for English Language Learners: Delivering A Continuum of Services* co-authored with Barbara Marler, Cristina Sanchez-Lopez and Jack Damico, is, in my opinion, the definitive guide on the subject. What it proposes is an alternative to a system where ESL students have to 'wait to fail' before their difficulties are considered serious enough to warrant additional support. The sooner interventions are provided, and response monitored, the more chance there is of closing the gap. What better place to start than in Early Childhood!

APPENDIX

Excerpts from the Language and Literacy Document for Grades K-2[1]

Beliefs

- Developing literacy for every child is a shared responsibility of families, communities and early childhood educators.

- Children develop literacy in ways related to the language and cultural practices of their home and cultural context.

Policy Principles

- Be aware that support for first language is fundamental to literacy development.
- Be aware that the ISB community consists of people from vastly diverse linguistic and cultural backgrounds and with an equally diverse range of personal experiences.

- Recognize that children enter the Early Childhood Centre having begun to learn to communicate and make sense of their experiences at home and in their communities.
- Identify and meet the needs of all children, including those from non-English-speaking backgrounds and those with diverse learning styles.
- Respect the child's home language and culture and use that as a base on which to build and extend children's understanding of language and literacy.
- Recognize that an ongoing assessment of children's progress in language and literacy is essential to planning appropriate educational experiences.

Note

1. *Courtesy of the International School of Brussels Early Childhood Center.* For Resources for ESL Stages see: *The Ontario Curriculum, Grades 1–8: English as a Second Language and English Literacy Development – A Resource Guide* (2001). On WWW at http://www.edu.gov.on.ca/eng/document/curricul/esl18.pdf (pp. 28–31).

About the author

Frances Bekhechi began her career in the United Kingdom as a teacher of French and German before moving into the world of ESL. For the last 20 years, she has been teaching English to second-language learners in grades K-6 at the International School of Brussels. In 2000, she took a sabbatical to obtain certification for working with dyslexic students. She is currently Head of the English Language Development department in the Early Childhood Center of ISB, and is a member of the ECIS ESL/MT Committee. She is a tutor trainer for ESL in the Mainstream and Language and Literacy-classroom applications of functional grammar.

Chapter 10

The Benefits of Sign Language in the International Preschool Curriculum

DYLAN YAMADA-RICE

This well-documented chapter considers a relatively new and very stimulating idea: the use of signing as a simple means of communication in a multilingual classroom. The author maintains that this language is easily learned by young children as well as teachers, and its use in the multilingual classroom allows communication from the first week of school. This would surely improve things for the teacher who cannot understand the languages of many of her pupils, and for those of her pupils who cannot understand anyone at all.

INTRODUCTION

This paper is based on work carried out during a period of time in which I was the Assistant Director of a private international preschool. The school is set in a rich and affluent part of inner-city Tokyo and serves primarily American and European expatriate children and some Japanese. This mix provides the school with a combination of monolingual native English, multi/bilingual and speakers of English as a second or additional language. It is a multilingual environment facing inclusion difficulties like other schools with diverse student backgrounds. The school uses an internally produced curriculum, for which I was in part responsible. The private nature of the school means the curriculum is unmonitored by outside authorities, allowing freedom to make adaptations and changes as needed. Such freedom provided the opportunity for signing to be incorporated in the curriculum for all ages from 15 months to five years in 2005. Although these changes were relatively recent at the time I wrote this paper, they had already begun to create a very different school environment.

Part 1 of this paper focuses on the belief that language and inclusion are closely connected in international schools. It considers the language backgrounds of children who attend such schools in Japan, the adverse effect – that instruction in English only can have, leading inevitably as it does to exclusion.

Part 2 is an evaluation of how recent research on American Sign Language (ASL) in hearing children's classrooms by Daniels (1996, 1997, 2001a, 2001b, 2003) could be used to address language exclusion issues in international preschools.

PART 1: INTERNATIONAL SCHOOLS: A MULTILINGUAL LEARNING ENVIRONMENT

The makeup of international schools varies the same as any other type of school. However, where English is the language of instruction students can be characterized mainly as children whose languages fall loosely into the following categories: monolingual native English speakers, multi/bilingual and those who are in various stages of learning English. I am aware that, as verbal languages are an extensive and far-reaching area of study for which I have limited space for discussion, an overview is needed to understand the unique forms of exclusion in multilingual classrooms and why an inclusive environment is so important. After this the argument for the use of signing as a tool to counterbalance language differences will be better understood.

Monolingual native English learners

On the whole, monolingual native English speakers have grown up in an environment that considers the use of English to be paramount. Both parents are usually, although not always, native English speakers and the children come from backgrounds where there is a 'lack of status afforded to literacies other than English in the educational system' (Kenner, 2000: 13). However, when these children move to another country they are thrown into an environment where they will be exposed to at least one new language in their out-of-school lives. This might open up for the first time an awareness of languages other than their own, which could have either positive or negative outcomes depending on how students are supported. Before the introduction of signing at the school where I worked, native English-speaking children often seemed to have little tolerance for those who could not understand instructions or class materials as well as they did.

Bi/multilingual learners

Kenner (2004), like many other writers on bilingualism, stresses on the flexibility of children who can speak more than one language. 'In situations where everyone is bilingual or multilingual, people switch between their different languages within conversations to maximize communication' (Kenner, 2004: 108). This is known as code-switching, where children look through their repertoire of languages for vocabulary to suit their needs regardless of whether they are mixing languages or not. Code-switching clearly shows how bi/multilingual children are used to having flexibility with language use. This is often naively interpreted by monolingual native English speakers as meaning children are unable to differentiate between different languages. This is not the case. On the contrary, bilingual children at my school often use their language abilities to translate material for ESL learners; a good example that 'difference is not necessarily a source of difficulty [but] also a stimulus for new ideas' (Kenner, 2004: 124). Baker (1988) suggests other advantages to being bilingual: speakers have superior divergent thinking ability, which leads to 'creative, imaginative, open-ended and free-thinking skills', increased language fluency, flexibility, originality, elaboration of thought, an increased richness of meaning and cultural connotations (Baker, 1988: 23). Both Kenner (2004) and Baker's (1988) words illustrate the necessity of promoting bilingualism in international schools, where flexibility of thought and language are an essential part of living in a diverse multicultural language environment. Above all, supporting children to understand language differences should be considered an essential aspect of preschool curricula. Preschool provides a good opportunity for children to be taught about other cultures as a means of lessening prejudices and stereotypes at a later age.

Learners of English as a second language

In international school settings in Japan, ESL students are by and large native Japanese speakers whose parents wish to provide them with a head start in the learning of English which will allow them greater access to future work and educational opportunities. The recognized advantages are that bilingualism has cognitive benefits that are very valuable to ESL pupils (Roberts, 2005). However, caution should be aired as children can be negatively impacted when required to perform in a second language they are not proficient in. In particular, ESL learners can have difficulty accessing and performing well within the confines of an English-based curriculum (Baker, 1988). Such problems grow in light of the fact that ESL students are often put into environments where their language requirements are left unsupported. At preschool level especially it is often assumed that children are at the age of optimum language retention and will catch up in time. This is true for some but I would suggest not all, and possibly not even the majority. From my observations the resulting factor is that children form groups based on their strongest language, which they use regardless of the fact that the instructional language is English. In doing so, the process of developing an inclusive learning environment is undermined. Lastly, it is worth mentioning that while ESL learners only make up a third of my previous school's student intake, a number controlled by school admissions policy, in many other comparable international preschools in Tokyo the number is unregulated. In such circumstances the problems mentioned previously may be well intensified.

The previous three categories demonstrate how English as the only instructional language in multilingual classrooms is not inclusive for all learners. ESL students clearly have the hardest time, as they are unable to reach their potential in a language that they cannot fully understand. From my professional observations I would suggest that this has knock-on effects of lowered self-esteem and frustration. In contrast, while at first glance it might seem that the system is most favourable to native English speakers learning in their first language, there is a danger that 'when standard English is accorded ... power, there is a consequent lack of value attached to other languages and literacies' (Kenner, 2000: 25). I believe this causes an erosion of tolerance and understanding towards other language speakers, which goes against the creation of an inclusive educational environment. This is as harmful to native English speakers as it is to other members of the class. Thus, it appears to me that the most advantaged students are the bilingual children who are not only able to access the learning environment but also have flexibility and cognitive benefits that come with being able to communicate in more than one language. Overall, these imbalances in the classroom mean that the best learning environment is not being achieved for any of its students.

Inclusion and language

Research and academic writing on inclusion is a well-worn topic (see e.g. Clough & Corbett, 2000). The area spans, amongst others, special needs, race and disabilities but rarely language. The term inclusion in education remains contested. However, I find Nutbrown's (2006) definition to be all encompassing: 'learning which involves and belongs to all members of that community' (Nutbrown, 2006: 64). Using the term community to refer to the international school classroom, and considering inclusion as it relates specifically to language, this definition provides an appropriate starting point for issues specific to this paper. While most educators would agree that young children have the right to access a curriculum that supports and affirms all, there are specific needs in international schools. Siraj-Blatchford states that:

> From an early age, young children are beginning to construct their identity and self-concept and this early development is influenced by the way others view them and respond to them and their family. (Siraj-Blatchford, 2001: 105)

The topic of identity is also central to Souza's (2006) research, which found children to describe their own and others identities in terms of language and birth place. This strong connection between identity and language was also replicated in my previous work place. Teachers often commented that children can quickly distinguish which languages new classmates speak and make initial attempts to communicate based on their appearance and ethnic background; regardless of the fact that the instructional language is English. Similarly, Sneddon (2003) observed children to have a strong awareness of languages and their uses. Such examples illustrate that children themselves understand that identity and language are closely connected. Thus, each child's language should be at the roots of their education. By denying a child usage of a language we are confining and distorting their identity. Such connection between language and identity ties issues of inclusion in international schools strongly to language. The need to raise awareness of cultural and language differences is intensified in international schools, like other schools with diverse student backgrounds. As Hessari and Hill (1989) rightly point out, in a multicultural classroom, all cultures and languages should have equal importance. However, such considerations can also be problematic where curricula are required to be taught solely in English, as was the case at my school. In such circumstances it likely remains that the outward tranquility projected from most early childhood settings is masking underlying inequality (Siraj-Blatchford, 2001). Such inequality is disadvantaging children who are already experiencing the diversity of an international environment. Instead the multicultural, multilingual learning environment should celebrate differences and use them to develop and grow (Fish, 2002).

Achieving language inclusion

The Department of Education and Science (DfES) Report (2002) provides guidelines on the inclusion of ESL learners. However it is extendable to all schools aiming to create an inclusive teaching environment with diverse language backgrounds. Module two of the report provides an operational model for achieving inclusion. The model is based on a belief that three areas: (1) Setting suitable learning challenges, (2) Responding to pupils diverse needs and (3) Overcoming potential barriers to learning are an essential key to inclusion attainment. Within this framework the report considers the needs of ESL pupils to feel safe, settled, valued and having a sense of belonging to the class, as fundamental factors. Very similar findings are presented by Hessari and Hill (1989) who considered that in order to achieve inclusion in multicultural classrooms five aspects of personal and social development are fundamental.

These are:

- Self-esteem, a sense of self-worth and feeling valued for contributing to the class.
- Self-awareness, the fundamental understanding of sameness.
- Awareness of others, the ability to empathize with others.
- Relationships.
- Thinking and questioning.

It might seem that I am stating the obvious but such factors as presented by DfES (2002) and Hessari and Hill (1989) are unachievable without teacher intervention. We must think what we can do as educators to include all children. Smith's (2003) findings from the 'Dealing with Differences' programme which looked at creating an inclusive environment in a multicultural high school in the United States, illustrates that such actions also need to be fitted into school structure and policy, and further that such policy must be a collaborative effort by students and staff alike. Hessari and

Hill (1989) agree. It would be hard to disagree that the message of inclusion will be much stronger if it is included into the whole-school structure.

One way of achieving this aim is to include other languages into the school's curriculum. Such methods build on language diversity awareness and 'illustrate the universality of language' to create a less insular environment (Hessari & Hill, 1989: 139). Many agree with the importance of the idea of allowing children the chance to express themselves in languages other than the main instructional language (Blair *et al.*, 1998; Dryden & Hyder, 2003; Hessari & Hill, 1989; Souza, 2006). Not only are international schools in Japan, such as the one in which I am employed, working against this, they are actually encouraged to do so by parents.

It is my opinion that there is little desire by parents for any language other than English to be brought into the classroom, making these schools in Japan stand apart from multilingual schools in the United Kingdom. My understanding is that in the United Kingdom, there is a concern that children will feel isolated if unable to bring their culture and language into the classroom. By and large guardians of language-minority children want home languages to be part of their children's school lives. By contrast, the transitional nature of international schools in Japan and the vast opportunities for children to interact in other environments and return to their home countries regularly means most parents are seeking something different. In general, monolingual native English speakers want their children to follow a curriculum similar to one in their home country and view the addition of other languages in the classroom as restricting their child's ability to learn in their native tongue. Bi/multilingual parents see the necessity to keep up English in a country where it is only spoken naturally at school, and possibly believe they can provide access to other languages outside of school. Lastly, ESL learners fall into two categories, native Japanese speakers who wish their child to get a head start in English, which is seen as very prestigious and beneficial in later life, or ESL learners of other nationalities who have similar wishes to the previous bi/multilingual group. While the parents' wishes might be taken into account, I have no doubt that the nonnative English-speaking children left to face these classrooms must still meet problems similar to those of the language minority children in the United Kingdom. Thus, how can language inclusion issues be addressed in international school environments? It is my belief that the only way to maintain an English-only speaking environment while addressing the imbalances caused by teaching in a language which is not native to all is by the addition of sign language into the curriculum. I shall consider this next.

PART 2: SIGN LANGUAGE

I shall now discuss how sign language can be used as a tool to address the language-related inclusion issues raised in Part 1. I have chosen to focus on American sign language (ASL) as this is the form of signing included in my school's policy to support an American curriculum. It is also the language studied by Daniels whose research will form the backbone of this second part.

An introduction to American Sign Language (ASL)

'Sign language is a term that refers to many languages that have evolved through-out the world in situations in which spoken language was not possible' (Daniels, 2001a: 7). Contrary to common misconceptions of inferiority, signing contains language elements such as, social, regional and personal variations, differences between female and male usage, slang and formal structures – the same as you would expect to find in any verbal language (Daniels, 2001a; Stokoe, 2001). The visual nature of Signing makes it especially useful to children who 'garner significant benefit from a greater involvement with visual learning' (Daniels, 2001a: 124). In addition, the nature of ASL which uses the hands to form shapes as opposed to the mouth to form words might make it an especially useful tool for children who 'effortlessly use their hands for comfort, communication, and acquisition of information from the time of their birth' (Daniels, 2001a: 129), meaning that children are already naturally adapted to the acquisition of such a language. More importantly, in relation to the international school environment, the visual quality of signing makes it the only language that can be combined simultaneously with another (Stokoe, 2001). This unique feature is especially important to schools that only have one instructional language.

A review of Daniel's research on including signing in the curriculum of hearing children

Much talk has taken place on the benefits of baby signing in early language acquisition but what about its use in the curriculum of older children? I believe baby signing is only the tip of the iceberg and that sign language can have much deeper benefits, including creating inclusive multilingual learning environments. I will discuss this in more detail later, but first I wish to consider the writing of Daniels, a major researcher on the inclusion of signing in the curriculum of hearing children. Due to space limitations I have decided to concentrate on the work of one researcher. However, it should be noted that Daniel's findings have been supported by other researchers such as Heller *et al.* (1998) and Good *et al.* (1993).

Daniels (2001a) reviews her individual research projects to date. The findings are widely advantageous for children learning English. Specifically, they include advancement in English acquisition; improvement in vocabulary, reading ability and spelling proficiency above those found in children who have learned without signing. Obviously, the accelerated attainment of English vocabulary is particularly useful to ESL learners in an all-English environment, where any new vocabulary will be useful immediately, but it is also beneficial for native English speakers. Daniels (2001a) further suggests that it is advantageous to teach ASL in the preschool years where it is possible to 'take advantage of the small window of optimal opportunity ... for young children to acquire language readily' (Daniels, 2001a: 34). Other benefits found by Daniels' research include better self-esteem and comfort in expressing emotions on the part of the English language learners, and for the teacher, it helps in classroom management, and creates a comfortable and positive learning environment. Additionally, Daniels (1996) found that signing benefits did not lessen over time even when the children began kindergarten to find that ASL was no longer in the curriculum. The reasons Daniels offers for what she describes as this 'Magic' (signing) is that 'presenting words visually, kinesthetically, and orally offers an advantage to young learners' (Daniels, 2001a: 42).

During her research projects, Daniels wondered if a teacher's ability to sign fluently affected the results that could be achieved in the classroom and undertook the project 'Teacher enrichment of the pre-kindergarten curriculum with sign language'. The outcome indicated that the fluency with which signing is introduced into the curriculum seems unimportant if consistently added. She suggests instead that teachers only need to stay one lesson ahead of students. And even if this is not possible, as in the case of a teacher forgetting signs more rapidly than her students, to learn together does no harm to the outcome. While Daniels believes this is especially great because little training is required, I would argue that when teachers are untrained many lack the confidence necessary to use signing in the classroom. This is an area unmentioned by Daniels but one I have noticed in my work. My belief is also reiterated in a separate work by Heller *et al.* (1998), who found teachers to grow in appreciation and understanding for the language with training. Indeed Daniels herself found that when signing was implemented by 'a native signer who used ASL in a voice-off mode to transmit normal kindergarten curriculum content . . . most children attained age-appropriate bilingual ability in English and ASL' (Daniels, 2003: 53). Although this is different from her earlier research that showed little training to be needed for some large rewards; clearly even larger gains can be made when teachers have training. I suspect the aid of a fluent sign teacher boosted both child and teacher interest and confidence.

Nevertheless, this seems to suggest that ASL could, if implemented fully by trained teachers, bring all the flexibility and cognitive benefits of bilingual learners to all children (mentioned in the earlier 'bi/multilingual learners' section). Signing advantages stretch to all members of the classroom but provide the biggest benefits to disadvantaged students. In the case of Daniels' (2001a) research this refers to African-American students of lower socio-economic status. However in the case of students in international schools, I suspect signing could provide the biggest advantage to nonnative English speakers who are also disadvantaged learning in a language which is not their first. Although Daniels makes no reference to this effect, many of the areas listed are particularly relevant to classrooms with wide language diversities.

How do the benefits of Daniels' findings relate to the promotion of inclusion in multicultural classrooms?

To date I have looked at the needs of different language groups and the importance of addressing inclusion in order for all students to be able to access the curriculum equally. The National Curriculum defines inclusion as: 'providing learning opportunities for all pupils' (DfES, 2002). At present, this is not being achieved in many international schools in Japan. In Part 1, I considered the ways in which inclusion could be achieved. To summarize, studies suggest that all children need to feel safe, settled and valued at school, and that this can only be achieved when all are provided with suitable learning opportunities and barriers preventing access to the class material are removed. In order to achieve this, inclusion policies must be written into the school's mission and curriculum. If implemented successfully the school will increase self-esteem in its pupils and promote a greater awareness of others. The achievement of these aims would surely provide a more positive schooling environment for all concerned – pupils, teachers and staff.

How does the use of signing address these findings? I believe that signing provides suitable learning opportunities for all. Children are naturally drawn to sign language because it is a real language and very visual, which also seems to add to the ease with which children pick it up. Indeed in my work many teachers commented how children seem able to pick up new signing vocabulary more quickly than the teachers themselves. Whatever the reasons, signing provides a very real way of removing barriers, allowing children not only to access class material but also to communicate with one another. All members of the class, while being instructed in English, are simultaneously learning together in a language (ASL) that is secondary to all. When barriers are removed and suitable learning opportunities are presented, all children will feel safe, settled and valued, resulting in increased self-esteem; especially, as Daniels research shows, among the least privileged students, in this case ESL learners. In addition, language also promotes understanding of others especially for monolingual-native English speakers who may previously have had no understanding of how it feels to learn in another language.

This was illustrated by research in the United Kingdom (Daniels, 2001b) which successfully included two deaf students in a hearing class using BSL (British Sign Language) and English, as opposed to English-only which is the norm. In doing so, one of the noted benefits was the hearing children's new understanding of the deaf and BSL as a language. As in this study one of the main reasons I believe signing could be so successful in multicultural classrooms is because it actively devalues the priority of English above other languages. This devaluation of English allows all children to feel a sense of belonging in terms of language, and brings an understanding that other ways of communicating are also valued in the classroom, even though the main language for instruction may not be their native tongue. Without a common unbiased language the sheer number of different languages alone causes exclusion. 'Inclusive education is as much about helping children to behave inclusively as it is about including particularly marginalised groups of society' (Nutbrown, 2006: 68). Sign language removes the priority of English above other languages, providing children with a tool with which they can behave inclusively. Without doing so, children may be restricted from acting inclusively even when it is not their intention to do so. As a result signing will decrease cliques caused by languages in classes and promote a healthier acceptance of other languages. 'Primary schools [or preschools] do not have to be places where children are encouraged to think in one-dimensional ways' (Cole, 1997: 49).

Signing offers children the chance to interpret the world in a different way, in a setting where differences are very apparent to them. I believe this supports and adds to the student's international education as language provides one of the biggest barriers in understanding another culture. Thus, I fully support the inclusion of sign language into international school curricula as a means of providing multicultural inclusion. Indeed, having witnessed the increased interactions of children with different native languages since the implementation of signing at my school, I would even go as far as to question whether a curriculum *without* signing can expect to be inclusive where students come from varied language backgrounds and English is the only language used in the classroom.

How can signing be included in the curriculum?

According to Daniels' (2001a) research, there is no set way to incorporate signing into the curriculum; a teacher needs no prior knowledge of signing for the benefits to be effective. Signing can be implemented in either ASL or English word order. The only thing she warns against is making up signs. Like all aspects of teaching, the results are best where teachers have high expectations for the outcomes and also involve parents. These findings have definitely been reflected in my work place. Signing was included in the curriculum at the beginning of the academic year with teachers receiving very limited training and access to materials. At first the introduction of signing caused concern among many parents, especially those with monolingual English backgrounds, who were worried that the new language might affect their child's speech. To support parents, the school provided a question and answer open night, and ongoing communication kept them informed on new signs and signing songs and so on being taught at school. The inclusion of parents helped our program flourish as they regularly provided the teachers with positive feedback. Furthermore, full inclusion requires the involvement of *all* members of the school and thus extends to parents as well.

Since the introduction of sign language until my departure a couple of years later teachers noticed the benefits it had on the school in terms of providing a more inclusive learning environment for children with diverse language backgrounds. Teachers remarked that friendship patterns changed and that there were more crossovers between different language groups. Lastly, like Daniels, teachers at my place of work remarked on the huge benefits signing brought to classroom management. Although this could be viewed as a side advantage it is especially important in multilingual classrooms where management phrases often need to be repeated many times for all to understand. Teachers were able to sign these phrases without disrupting the flow of their teaching. The observations made by teachers at my school support Daniels' findings and also could be a possible starting point for future research. The changes seemed so big in such a short time that it would be interesting to specifically research and record the differences in multicultural classrooms before and after the introduction of sign language. Indeed how best to incorporate sign language into the curriculum could be a possible area for future research as well. Finally, why start in preschool? Because these are the most important years of a child's life:

> What happens during children's earliest years shapes whether they become open to or fearful of people with different skin colours and customs. It determines whether children learn to feel proud or ashamed of their heritage. (Chang, 2006: 1)

CONCLUSION

In conclusion it can be seen that it is essential to create inclusive environments in international schools where language backgrounds are diverse and the sheer number of native languages alone appears to be causing exclusion. At the most basic level inclusion benefits all by allowing every student equal access to educational opportunities and a chance to achieve their full potential. As mentioned earlier, the devaluation of English is one way to achieve inclusion in international schools like the one I worked in where it was impossible to add other verbal languages to the curriculum. Further, this devaluation of English is also beneficial for all children. Simultaneously ASL can act as a second language, developing bilingual advantages in all children, while English remains unaltered as the only spoken classroom language. Thus, ASL and English combined can maintain the native level of English speakers, while improving the vocabulary attainment of all. These benefits, as Daniels (2001a) illustrates, can be achieved with very little teacher training or effort on the part of the students. This makes sign language not only an inclusive tool but also one that's easy to implement. Lastly, I believe: 'Inclusion is a process, not a fixed state' and should be addressed through 'imaginative approaches to the curriculum' (DfEE, 1998: 23/27). Thus, if it can be found that signing helps to provide a more inclusive environment in international schools, we must be imaginative in our approach and move forward to make the use of signing school policy.

On a final note, I have noticed, in the course of my reading, that signing in hearing children's curricula is an area that appears to be gaining interest with researchers. However, most of my reading also suggests that the results of research to date are inconclusive or unfinished, with many researchers calling for further studies in the area. As I was unable to find any writing on the idea of signing as a means of inclusion in multilingual classes, let alone in international schools I would suggest that this is a starting point for future research in this area. More research needs to be undertaken to discover the actual benefits rather than mere speculation about its place in international schools. It might help signing to become more common in international schools and multilingual settings in general, providing better access to the curriculum for every student and a happier school environment for all. An idyllic image and one that I believe is not impossible to achieve.

REFERENCES

Baker, C. (1988) *Key Issues in Bilingualism and Bilingual Education*. Clevedon: Multilingual Matters.

Blair, M., Bourne, J., Coffin, C., Creese, A. and Kenner, C. (1998) *Making the Difference: Teaching and Learning Strategies in Successful Multiethnic Schools*. Department for Education and Employment, Research Brief No. 59. On WWW at http://www.naldic.org.uk/docs/resources/documents/RB59.pdf. Accessed December 2010.

Chang, H. (2006) *Many Languages, Many Cultures: Ideas and Inspirations for Helping Young Children Thrive in a Diverse Society*, Scholastic Early Childhood Today. On WWW at http://www2.scholastic.com/browse/article.jsp?id=4278. Accessed December 2010.

Clough, P. and Corbett, J. (2000) *Theories of Inclusive Education: A Students' Guide*. London: Paul Chapman Publishing Ltd.

Cole, M. (1997) Equality and primary education. What are the conceptual issues? In M. Cole, D. Hill and S. Shan (eds) *Promoting Equality in Primary Schools* (pp. 48–75). London: Cassell.

Daniels, M. (1996) Seeing language: The effect over time of the use of sign language on vocabulary development in Early Childhood education. *Child Study Journal* 26, 193–209.

Daniels, M. (1997) Teacher enrichment of pre-kindergarten curriculum with sign language. *Journal of Research in Childhood Education* 12, 27–33.

Daniels, M. (2001a) *Dancing with Words: Signing for Hearing Children's Literacy*. Westport, CT: Bergin & Garvey.

Daniels, M. (2001b) Sign language advantage. *Sign Language Studies* 2, 5–19.

Daniels, M. (2003) Using a signed language as a second language for Kindergarten students. *Child Study Journal* 33, 53–70.

DfEE (1998) Developing a more inclusive education system. In *Meeting Special Educational Needs: A Programme for Action* (pp. 22–27).

DfES (2002) *Supporting Pupils Learning English as an Additional Language*. On WWW at http://www.standards.dfes.gov.uk/primary/publications/literacy/63381. Accessed February 2006.

Dryden, L. and Hyder, T. (2003) All about supporting children new to English. *Nursery World* 1st May, 15–22.

Fish, L. (2002) *Building Blocks: The First Steps of Creating a Multicultural Classroom*. On WWW at http://www.edchange.org/multicultural/papers/buildingblocks.html. Accessed December 2010.

Good, L., Feekes, J. and Shawd, B. (1993) Let your fingers do the talking: Hands on learning through signing. *Childhood Education* 70, 81–83.

Heller, I., Manning, D., Pauvur, D. and Wagner, K. (1998) Let's all sign!: Enhancing language development in an inclusive preschool. *Teaching Exceptional Children* 30, 50–53.

Hessari, R. and Hill, D. (1989) *Practical Ideas for Multicultural Learning and Teaching in the Primary Classroom*. London: Routledge.

Kenner, C. (2004) *Becoming Biliterate: Young Children Learning Different Writing Systems*. Stoke on Trent: Trentham Books.

Kenner, C. (2000) Biliteracy in a monolingual school system? English and Gujarati in South London. *Language, Culture and Curriculum* 1, 13–30.

Nutbrown, C. (2006) *Key Concepts in Early Childhood Education and Care*. London: Sage Publications Ltd.

Roberts, C. (2005) English as an additional language. *Times Educational Supplement* 30th September.

Siraj-Blatchford, I. (2001) Diversity and learning in the early years. In G. Pugh (ed.) *Contemporary Issues in the Early Years: Working Collaboratively for Children*. London: Paul Chapman Publishing.

Smith, R.S. (2003) Coping constructively with interethnic conflict: A pilot study of the "Dealing with Differences" program. *Current Issues in Education* 6. On WWW at http://cie.asu.edu/volume6/number13/index.html. Accessed December 2010.

Sneddon, R. (2003) *Tri-lingual 11-Year-Olds in Hackney Outperform Monolinguals in Reading Tests and Tell More Elaborate Stories.* On WWW at http://www.naldic.org/docs/BRB3.doc. Accessed February 2006.

Souza, A. (2006) *Children See Language as a Feature of their Identity.* On WWW at http://www.naldic.org.uk/docs/BRB5.doc. Accessed December 2010.

Stokoe, W. (2001) The study and use of sign language. *Sign Language Studies* 1, 369–406.

About the author

Dylan Yamada-Rice was born and grew up in the south of England. She has lived and worked in Japan in the field of education for more than a decade, most recently as the Assistant Director of an international preschool in Tokyo. She is presently a full-time PhD student at The School of Education, University of Sheffield.

Chapter 11

Addressing Transition and Mobility Issues with English Language Learners in the Early Childhood Years

DEBRA RADER

In this chapter the author describes important ways in which international school educators can help young children deal with the challenges brought about by entering a new school or transferring from it to another, or simply staying behind when a friend leaves. These changes are magnified when the child has not yet learned the language of instruction. It is suggested that schools that wish to help their students in transition should go one step further and include such activity in the written curriculum.

INTRODUCTION

Transition issues affect children who move, particularly from one country to another where they are faced with a new culture and language in addition to a new home, school and neighbourhood, and the loss of much that is familiar. This chapter explores the transition and mobility issues facing young English language learners who attend international schools in the early childhood years; pre-school through Grade 2. It provides educators with an understanding of the issues, and ways to support these children during the transition process, celebrating the benefits and addressing the challenges to maximize their international school experience. In addition it discusses the need for culturally relevant and responsive classrooms to not only support young children in transition, but to contribute to the development of children's cultural identity, and to develop an appreciation of and respect for cultural diversity beginning at an early age. Suggested children's literature resources, ideas and activities are included as well.

EARLY CHILDHOOD EDUCATION AND THE INTERNATIONAL SCHOOL SETTING

The early years are the most important years in a child's life; years when they are shaped in significant and fundamental ways by their family. This is equally true for children entering nursery or pre-school, because it is where they first begin their interaction with the world outside the family. It is a significant responsibility for teachers of these young children as they begin to build on the foundation established by parents. Educators must be well informed and responsive to the young child's social, emotional, physical, intellectual as well as cultural, language and learning needs, all of which will have an impact on the child's personal and academic success, and will contribute to building a strong foundation for subsequent learning and the development of self-esteem. Young children who attend international schools have a distinct school experience. International schools have many defining characteristics. However, they are particularly unique in that most of them serve highly mobile populations and children from a wide range of cultures.

Moving to another country and culture brings both benefits and challenges for both children and adults that need to be addressed. Children and their families continually arrive and depart throughout the school year and this affects not only those who move, but also those friends, classmates and teachers who are left behind. The multicultural nature of most international schools is a tremendous resource. Children learn, work and play with children from cultures different from their own; sometimes hearing, learning and speaking languages different from their mother tongue. However, for English Language Learners, learning another language compounds their experience of transition.

Most international schools recognize that they have a role to play and a responsibility to support their students and families through the transition process, and have implemented programs and strategies to do so.

Educators can best serve the internationally mobile students in their schools by becoming informed about the experience and process of transition, and the issues facing the children and parents in their school community. This includes acquiring knowledge about and an understanding of transition issues and the transition process, cultures and second-language acquisition.

It is helpful for educators to reflect on and be aware of their own experiences with transition, their own cultural identity and their own beliefs and biases about different cultures.

Understanding the transition and mobility issues facing young children

Our world is a highly mobile place with families continuing to move around the world for a variety of personal and professional reasons. We know from our personal experience and the experiences of our family, friends, colleagues as well as the students and families we work with that moving internationally has tremendous benefits and also presents significant challenges. While it is a rich and exciting experience to live in another country and to learn a new language, both children and adults face many issues as they make the transition from one country to another, and adjust to a new home, new neighbourhood, new school, new culture and often a new language all at once! While these issues affect the entire family, I focus on addressing them with young children for the purpose of this chapter, although educators will find themselves both educating and supporting the parents about transition as well.

There are many factors that affect internationally mobile children as they adjust to living and going to school in a new country. Not only are they adjusting to a new language and culture but to new sights, smells, sounds, tastes, climates and ways of doing things. Children also miss people, places, pets, activities or sports and certain belongings that could not come with them, and often feel a sense of loss on leaving them behind. Children of five or older worry about what their new school will be like, if they will fit in, leaving family, leaving old friends and making new ones; and may experience some degree of culture shock in the new location. Moving is particularly stressful for young children as they lose their sense of security and often feel disoriented when their routine is disrupted and all that is familiar is taken away. Children aged three to six are quite literal in their thinking and along with their relatively short life experience are unable to imagine the new place and understand that their special belongings will come with them. Parents who are normally attentive to their young children may be less focused on their young child's needs and are understandably distracted by the logistics of the move and their own transition issues. Children take their cues from their parents and young children often pick up on their parents' stress. It is important for teachers of young children to be aware of the signs of stress as they may be in the best position to be caregivers and to inform parents. This may include regressive behaviours, expressing increased fears and anxiety, temper tantrums or withdrawal, clinging to parents and difficulty with separations, concentration and sustaining play activities.

Children and their families also go through marked stages in the process of transition. While many models have been developed Pollock and Van Reken (1999) developed a model describing the process of transition individuals move through which is based on their work with internationally mobile families. It includes the following five transition stages:

Involvement: In this stage we have a sense of belonging to the community we live in, and we feel settled, comfortable and 'at home'.

Leaving: Once we learn we are moving we enter the leaving stage. This stage brings many mixed emotions as we say goodbye to people and places that are important to us, and begin to focus on the future.

Transition: This stage begins once we actually leave the place we are living and ends once we arrive at the new destination and begin to engage in life there. Some people never fully engage in the new location and remain in the transition stage during the entire time they live in another country. Life is quite unpredictable during this stage, often characterized by chaos and anxiety!

Entering: During this stage we may feel particularly vulnerable as we begin to learn about the new country and culture in which we are now living. Culture shock and cultural adaptation usually occur during this stage. Emotions may fluctuate as we begin to adjust to our new lifestyle, and feel the loss of people, places and pets we have left behind and miss.

Re-involvement: In this stage we finally have a sense of belonging in the new community.

At any given time children and their families in international schools may be going through some stage of the process of transition described above. This means that there are always those who are newly arriving, those who are beginning to settle in, those who feel a sense of belonging and those who are preparing to leave for their next destination. Transition affects everyone including those who stay behind. As we all learn more about the experience of transition we can better support our school community and one another.

Many teachers include transition activities to facilitate the arrival and departure of their mobile students. Assigning a buddy for new students or creating a memory book for those moving on, are examples. Some international school educators are now integrating transition education into their existing curriculum as well. There is an important distinction between transition activities and transition education. Transition education goes beyond transition activities and helps children develop the knowledge, understanding and skills needed to successfully manage the transitions involved in moving to a new location. This also includes cross-cultural skills, and essential life skills such as problem-solving, communication and decision-making. Transition education can be easily integrated into the existing curriculum and should be ongoing throughout the school year.

Teachers are in an ideal position to address children's concerns, to provide a sense of security and to support them through the transition process. They recognize the importance of establishing a balance between affirming and celebrating their students' unique experiences and backgrounds and focusing on helping them adjust to the new place.

Educators can learn more about the concept of transition education which has been comprehensively developed in the publication, *New Kid in School: Using Literature to Help Children in Transition* (Rader & Sittig, 2003).

Consideration of a child's culture is essential in addressing the transition issues faced and supporting the children in our care. While children usually respond to a warm, caring and supportive school environment, their sense of self and safety is enhanced when their cultural and language backgrounds are recognized, evident and celebrated in the classroom and in the wider school environment. Culturally relevant and responsive classrooms reflect the cultures represented in the classroom and school community. Not only do such classrooms provide a sense of security, as needed during the transition process, but they also help children to develop at an early age both their personal and cultural identity as well as a respect for diversity, both important educational goals.

Ways educators can support young English language learners in transition in international schools

Below you will find ideas for addressing the transition and cultural needs of young English language learners in international schools. The international school classroom and environment presents authentic contexts that lend themselves to facilitating positive transition adjustment and valuable cultural learning. Educators in international schools have an excellent opportunity to teach children explicitly about culture and to move beyond the cursory and superficial. As you read below about some of them here I hope you are inspired to supplement them with ideas of your own.

Build a strong sense of community in your classroom where all cultures and languages are welcomed, valued and celebrated.

Ensure that your displays and materials reflect the cultures and languages of your students in authentic ways. Include items such as books, dolls, games, photographs, art and musical instruments. This not only facilitates cultural learning, seeing familiar objects displayed in the classroom or school reassures children who have recently arrived that they are welcome.

Establish familiar routines, and create and maintain classroom rituals such as Circle Time activities as these provide a sense of security during times of change.

Consider inviting young children to bring a special toy or photograph that brings them comfort during the early days of school.

Use Circle Time to engage children in discussions about changes and new experiences, sharing your own experiences as well. Young children are often very interested in hearing about their teachers' experiences and this can lead to effective conversations about moving and transition.

Learn key words and phrases in the children's languages and learn to pronounce your students' names correctly. Teach the other children in the class to pronounce their classmates' names correctly as well.

Assign an English-speaking buddy to your new student. It is helpful to have a buddy in the class who also speaks the same mother tongue and can help ease initial anxiety about understanding what is said. You can include all members in your school community who speak the child's language – parents, faculty, students across all ages – to be available to reassure and guide new children, and to answer their questions, speaking to them in their mother tongue.

Look for ways to include your students' languages through learning poems or songs, colour words, days of the week or counting in the children's home languages. The importance of developing a child's mother tongue has been well established, both as part of strong cognitive development and cultural identity. Some schools have established mother-tongue lunch days, story times with parents reading to children in their mother tongue and after school activities led in the children's mother tongue.

Learn and incorporate strategies for second-language acquisition into your instructional practice. This might include the use of real-life objects and materials that are familiar, which can help English language learners make connections between the knowledge they have in their own language and the new material being presented. Use short, clear consistent phrases to facilitate the learning of English, and explicitly teach and use the academic language of the classroom, rephrasing ideas when necessary.

Integrate transition education into your curriculum. Help your students to learn about and understand the experience and process of transition by reading and discussing children's literature that addresses this. (See suggested literature list.)

Enlist the help of your students' parents to learn more of the cultures represented in your classroom and apply it to your instructional practice. Demonstrate the value of and build on the knowledge and skills students bring from their home cultures. Consider ways to bridge children's home and school experiences through using examples and materials from your students' lives. Young children may experience confusion when there is a mismatch between the home and school culture. Consider appropriate ways these differences can be addressed with children and parents.

Model a respect for difference, and a curiosity and interest in other cultures. Look for and provide learning opportunities that recognize and honour the cultural traditions of the children in your class, school community and the wider world. Incorporate meaningful themes that lend themselves to culture learning such as *Families, Celebrations, Cultures Around the World, Homes, Transportation* and more. These are often part of Early Childhood education and are reflected in international programs such as the International Baccalaureate Primary Years Program and International Primary Curriculum.

Develop strong and positive relationships with the parents of the children in your class. While this is important with all parents it is particularly important with the parents of Pre-school and Kindergarten children, who may, along with their children, be quite anxious. Pre-school teachers often invite the parents to an orientation before school begins, where they may be asked to complete a questionnaire about their child and their home culture. Many international school educators also provide the opportunity for parents to tell each other about their children, their likes and dislikes, their developing personalities, and their cultural backgrounds and home culture including the languages spoken at home and with other family members.

Provide a *Moving Plan* for your mobile students appropriate to the children's ages. As Junior School Principal at an international school in Italy, I addressed transition issues with new families as part of the admissions process. It was explained that while moving can be exciting it also presents challenges. However, moving can be made easier if we plan for it and know what to expect. We discussed the importance of having positive closure in the old place to facilitate a positive start in the new one. In addition, I met with parents preceding a move and met with the children who were leaving to explain and provide the children with a *Moving Plan*. Parents often reported that this had a very positive effect on their children's adjustment. *(For more information on the Moving Plan, see Appendix 1.)*

Explore the many ways you can use photographs to create displays that contribute to a sense of belonging and help children settle in to the new place. You might display and label photographs of teachers and other school staff at work in their classrooms or offices. Some teachers have enlisted parents' help in creating displays of children's personal timelines and/or photographs of the children and their families in their home country, previous homes and their new home in the host country.

Some schools have created Transition Teams to co-ordinate the transition programming and resources throughout the school, and support families and children of all ages.

Provide your students with a Trip Journal to record trips home or to other countries they visit that will later be shared with the class. Children write and draw about their experiences and include mementoes, brochures, ticket stubs and so forth that they have collected, as well as evidence of something new they learned in their travels. This provides an excellent way for children to share their cultures and/or rich cultural learning gained from their travel experiences. *(For more information on the Trip Journal, see Appendix 2.)*

Acknowledging children's feelings and experiences can be an intervention in itself. Invite children to share their special memories, experiences and feelings about moving through poetry or narratives written in Writer's Workshop. Consider publishing bilingual texts with your students as well. This is highly beneficial as students can then share them with members of their families who do not speak English, and is a way to stay connected with family members living far away. Younger children can dictate their 'moving stories' which they can then illustrate and share as a class book.

Invite the parents of children from different cultures to share their national holidays, celebrations and traditions. Many educators include international parents in cooking with the children and some have explored the ways bread, rice and other foods are prepared and eaten in different cultures. Include the different ways birthdays and other rites of passage are celebrated as well as dance, art, music, games and storytelling traditions.

Dramatic play provides ample opportunity to explore the experience of transition and develop a greater awareness of cultural differences. Pre-school and Kindergarten teachers might consider creating a Moving House corner as a theme for dramatic play including space allocated for both packing up and unpacking belongings. Based on the children's own experiences of moving and the books you have read about moving you could decide what you would need and create a list together. This might include boxes, labels which the children could make with pictures and/or words, toys, books, clothes, treasured objects such as a favourite stuffed animal and more.

Consider ways the classroom Home Corner could reflect different cultures including those present in the classroom. Include clothing such as kimonos, saris or kente cloth and develop a collection of hats and shoes from different cultures. You could also include international food containers that give the children the opportunity to learn more about foods from different cultures, and see different languages in print and how foods are packaged in other countries. You could also include cooking and eating utensils from different cultures such as a wok, waffle iron or chopsticks. This provides an authentic opportunity to discuss similarities and differences between cultural objects and practices.

The host country offers rich opportunities for learning about culture in addition to national holidays and traditions. Look for ways to help children learn about and engage with the host culture through activities and field trips.

Suggested literature and resources

Literature can be used by both parents and educators as a springboard for discussion about transition issues and to explore different cultures. Below is a sample list of titles recommended for use with young children.

Asch, Frank (1986) *Goodbye House*, New York: Aladdin Paperbacks (PS-Grade 2)

In this story Baby Bear and his parents say goodbye to each room in their house before moving on. Parents can use this book to say goodbye to their home with their children before a move. This book can be used by teachers to tour the school with their students who are moving and give children the opportunity to say goodbye to the playground, art room, music room, library and various classrooms, and share their special memories as part of forming closure before a move.

Baer, Edith (1990) *This is the Way We Go to School: A Book About Children Around the World*, New York: Scholastic, Inc. (PS-Grade 2)

This book explores the way children in different countries travel to school, and can be used to learn about transportation in the different countries your students have lived in or are from.

Brandenberg, Aliki (1998) *Painted Words and Spoken Memories,* **New York: Greenwillow Books (K-Grade 2)**

This story is told in two parts, describing the experiences of a young Greek girl who moves to the United States. She tells her story first through her paintings and then through her words. It can be used to explore the experiences of moving to a new country and being faced with a new school, new customs and a new language.

Civardi, Ann (1992) *Moving House,* **London: Usborne Publishing Ltd (PS-K)**

This book can be used to talk about and learn about the experience of moving with very young children. Invite the children to talk about the ways their families' moves were the same or different.

Dooley, Norah (1996) *Everybody Bakes Bread,* **Minneapolis, MN: Carolrhoda Books (K-Grade 2)**

This book explores the way bread is made, eaten and used in different cultures, and can be used as a springboard to explore culture through bread making with your class.

Fox, Mem (1997) *Whoever You Are,* **New York: Harcourt Books (PS-Grade 2)**

The message in this beautifully illustrated book is that even though we look different, live in different homes and countries, go to different schools and speak different languages, we children around the world have many similarities as human beings.

Morris, Ann Around the World Series (PS-Grade 2)

Consider the following titles to support cultural learning with young children as each topic is presented in various countries around the world.

Bread, Bread, Bread
Shoes, Shoes, Shoes
Hats, Hats, Hats
Houses and Homes
On the Go

Penn, Audrey (2007) *A Kiss Goodbye,* **Terre Haute: Tanglewood Press (PS-Grade 2)**

Chester raccoon and his family are moving and this sequel to *The Kissing Hand* provides an opportunity to discuss the concept of 'home', fears associated with moving and special memories.

Penn, Audrey (2007) *The Kissing Hand,* **Terre Haute: Tanglewood Press (PS-Grade 2)**

This is a charming story of the way Chester raccoon and his mother eased his anxiety when beginning school. It can be used to ease the separation from parents for young children when beginning school and having moved to a new place. Colleagues and I have used it successfully with children from Pre-school-Grade 2 and parents have found it reassuring to read to their young children at home. Several parents translated it into their mother tongue to share with their children with positive results.

Rader, Debra and Sittig, Linda (2003) *New Kid in School; Using Literature to Help Children in Transition,* **New York: Teachers College Press**

This comprehensive resource presents a model for transition education which has affirming and celebrating students' unique experiences and backgrounds at its heart, and includes the following components; The Common Experience of Mobility, the Process of Transition, Friendships and Relationships, Cultural and Personal Identity, Problem-solving and Moving Back. Using quality children's literature as a springboard, it provides educators with ideas and strategies to teach children about transitions and help them develop the understanding and skills to manage them effectively. Appendices include Tips for Teachers, Tips for Parents, Suggested Transition Activities and Approaches to Transition.

Stimson, Joan (1996) *A New Home for Tiger,* **London: Scholastic Children's Books (PS-Grade 2)**

In this story a young tiger discovers the meaning of 'home' after moving to a new place. It is an excellent vehicle to explore the concept of home with children, and provides an opportunity for children to share their special memories of their past home/s.

REFERENCES

Pollock, D.C. and Van Reken, R.E. (1999) *The Third Culture Kid Experience; Growing Up Among Worlds.* Yarmouth: ME Intercultural Press.

Rader, D. and Sittig, L. (2003) *New Kid in School; Using Literature to Help Children in Transition.* New York: Teachers College Press.

APPENDIX 1

Create a moving plan and include the following headings on separate pages. Adapt the text for different age groups. (Teachers' words are in *italics*)

My moving plan

Moving can be both exciting and sad. You can make it a bit easier if you take time to think about your move and make a plan for leaving. This project is meant to help you do exactly that! And more!

Think about the time you have lived in_____. You are bound to have many memories! There will be things you will miss and probably things you will be glad to leave behind.

My thoughts about moving

When I leave (city) or (school) I will miss: _____
I will be glad to leave behind: _____
I look forward to (for example) making new friends
I am concerned about (for example) my new school, and saying goodbye (One of the most important things to remember when you are moving is to take time to say goodbye to the special people and places in the area where you have lived) : I want to say goodbye to these people (including how I would do it) : Mr Cary – I plan to stop by the Music Room and have a chat.

Before I leave (city) or (school):

I want to go to_____one more time.
I want to say 'thank you' to_____.
I want to take pictures of_____.
I want to exchange addresses with _____.
I want to _____.
Think about the thoughts or feelings you might want to share.
Example: I want to tell Sam that I'm sorry I lost his T-shirt.
I want to tell _____ that _____

You have learned many new things while you have been in (city) and at (school). Think about the skills you've gained and how you might use them in the future.

Skill   Using the skill in the future
How to make new friends   Make friends in my new school

APPENDIX 2

Create a Trip Journal and include the following headings on separate pages. Adapt the text for different age groups.

My Trip Journal

Name_____

Date_____

Destination_____

I went to _____

It is located in _____

Draw a simple map to show where you went. Label your starting point and your destination. In what direction did you travel?

Who went with you on your trip? Put a photograph or draw their pictures below. Label their names.

How did you travel on your trip? Write and draw about the type of transportation you used.

Did you collect any souvenirs like brochures, pictures, maps, postcards or ticket stubs? Draw or put some of them here.

Who did you meet when you got to your destination? Draw some of the special people here. Tell them about your journal. Have them put their names by your drawings of them.

Did you go anywhere special? Write and draw a picture about it.

Did you have any special meals or celebrations? Write and draw a picture about it.

How did you use maths on this trip? Write and draw a picture about it below.

Write and draw a picture about your favourite part of the trip.

What is something new you learned on your trip? What were you curious about? Write and draw a picture about it below.

About the author

Debra Rader has worked in international schools for 25 years. She taught at Hampstead International School (IS) and Southbank IS, London; was Primary and Middle School Principal at Southbank IS (Kensington); and Junior School Principal at the IS of Florence. She holds a BS in Elementary Education from Keene State College in NH; Certification and Post Baccalaureate Studies in Special Education from Kentucky University in Lexington, KY; an MS Ed in Instructional Leadership: Curriculum and Instruction from Illinois University at Chicago (partly undertaken at Bath University, UK); a Cambridge ESOL CELTA from International House, London; and an IS Leadership Certificate from the Principal's Training Centre. Having developed a model for Transition Education, she has become a specialist in this area, presenting numerous workshops on this subject at international school conferences. She is co-author of *New Kid in School: Using Literature to Help Children in Transition* (see above).

Chapter 12
Music: The Universal Language

STEPHEN LUSCOMB

A seasoned music teacher identifies ways in which both the English language learners and the native speakers can benefit from the lessons in his music room. And while his ideas can be used on their own, taken from these pages and transplanted to the classroom, they are really intended to spark the imagination of any teacher, who will then modify and adapt them to the needs and abilities of his or her own music class.

INTRODUCTION

The music classroom is a most welcoming place for the English- and non-English-speaker alike. While serving well the native English speaker, it also offers English language learners a place to feel quickly and easily at home, to participate and to understand. I follow the Orff–Schulwerk method, which is music and movement education, using movement to prepare and reinforce musical concepts and skills. It emphasizes improvisation from a very early age, offering children an opportunity to own their own creations. It uses traditional media such as the spoken word, dramatic play and a wide range of classroom instruments, from xylophones, metallophones and glockenspiels (the pitched or barred instruments) to cymbals, wood blocks, gongs, shakers and all varieties of drum.

The school offers an Orff–Schulwerk music experience to first through fourth grades. More than 50% of the students are learning English as a second language. The first and second grades prepare a major concert event each spring, in which all the children participate. Although this changes over time, the most common languages at school today, aside from English, are French, Italian, Hebrew, Japanese, Korean, Dutch and Spanish.

The instruments are used to support poems with the creation of 'sound carpets', to accompany songs and for the performance of instrumental pieces. Children are brought to improvise on all these instruments and with their voices. The recorder is also used in the Orff–Schulwerk classroom. One might refer to the Orff approach, but not to an 'Orff method', as there is no prescribed sequence of activities and skills to be followed in a correct order. Orff spoke of the creation of 'elemental' music, a simple, child-oriented sound, which can at the same time be musically complex. The Schulwerk approach makes use of the children's natural sense of curiosity and wonder, expanding these as they grow more confident and familiar with what they can do.

Children are encouraged to contribute their own ideas for creating sounds and soundscapes. They are exposed to the ideas of movement, and allowed to combine their own ideas with those of others. Such an environment for music-making and dance provides fertile ground for children of any language background, and places few barriers before those students who do not yet speak much English, the language of instruction in our school.

Group participation: Learning to learn in a group

The beginning of each school year is a moment for learning to learn in a group, or 'group participation', as Jane Frazee[1] has called it. I try to start the first few lessons without words, gesturing to show the children where to sit and what to do. The first order of business in the group participation category is an activity in which the children copy the actions of the teacher. After they are seated I put my hands on my knees and begin moving my hands slowly up. The children seem instinctively to know that they should copy this. To keep things interesting and rivet the attention of the children, I throw in 'tricks', suddenly dropping my hands back to my knees, for example, then starting over. The ESL children, who often enter the room with a very serious expression, perhaps worried about being faced with yet another teacher who does not speak their language, are quickly in smiles.

A next step for group participation is simultaneous imitation: I sing a song and add a beat-related movement. The children join the movement without yet knowing the song. The native English speakers are soon singing with me, and the others often follow quickly. Ideally, the song would suggest beat-related movements.

A group participation activity for older groups of children might be a drumming activity. I start the year with a poem about drums. The poem includes a few catchy rhythms, and the children are asked to play the rhythm of the words on hand drums. When this is secure, we say the poem aloud, and then in canon. Then we play the poem in canon, and add a simple conga drum accompaniment. Next comes movement, also performed in canon. This leads us into territory appropriate for any fourth grader: drumming technique, movement with a poem, the performance of rhythmic canons, the addition of an accompaniment and form, probably letting the class decide the final form of our piece, making selections from the series of steps we went through together. Non-English speakers will be challenged to keep up with the pace of this activity, but will not need the linguistic ability to participate in the final performance.

None of these activities is aimed particularly at the non-English-speaker (being intended instead to deal with the way in which one learns in a music classroom – as a group, not as individuals), but both work well with a student population of second-language students.

Listening: The development of auditory memory

Students are frequently asked to echo rhythms clapped for the class. The music specialist would know these as body percussion rhythms. The teacher stamps, pats, claps or snaps short rhythmic motives, for children in grades two and lower, probably of four-beat durations, for children in second-grade and above, in eight-beat/one-phrase durations. The class echoes the rhythm of the teacher. This has purely musical goals – mental/rhythmic/musical warm-ups, preparation for a particular song that will be taught later in the same lesson – as well as addressing the goal of exercising auditory memory, an important skill for all children. Body percussion rhythms are also an attention-getting means for the classroom teacher to support the music teacher's work, as well as being a friendly way to give the signal for classroom work to begin, or to call the class to order.

ESL children can do all this comfortably because no words are used. This practice can then be extended into a vocal warm-up using vocables (la, la, la or mi, may, ma, mo, mu, etc.), speaking these 'non-sense syllables' in rhythm, or sliding up and down with the voice, but without using any real words. While these activities are helpful to the English language learner, they are important for all music students: all of them need to have a good auditory memory.

During the latter part of the school year, when listening has become listening to a piece of music, classical or otherwise, the children will often be asked to 'move like a ...' during a certain section of a piece. The children might be asked to move like most anything: an animal, a baby, a robot – so long as the chosen thing might move to the sort of music being played. One would not ask the children to move like turtles while playing fast music. Both the creativity involved in doing this, and the awareness of form, for example, are spot on the music curriculum for all students, both native and beginning English speakers. Form would be just one example of something on which one might focus a listening activity.

PHONICS: REINFORCEMENT IN THE MUSIC CLASSROOM

Many of the songs and poems used in the music classroom support the work of the mainstream teachers. When poems or songs are displayed on visuals, the teacher can point to the words as they are sung or spoken. Children can be asked to find the rhymes, and with little sacrifice of valuable contact time the music teacher can examine with students the differences in spelling that still yield up rhymes (e.g. train and plane, true and shoe, raid and made, etc.). Alliterations are also common in poems and songs, and are easily pointed out to the children not only as phonics-support tools but to assist the entire class in memorizing the texts of songs and poems. Numerous songs and poems play with the rhymes in captivating ways and are great fun. Examples include 'Down by the Bay' and 'Apples and Bananas', well-known standards available in many published collections of children's songs. When it is possible to have children work in small groups to create new verses for songs, or just a new final line to a song or poem, the ESL children have an opportunity to be part of the group and also learn from their more proficient English-speaking classmates at work with this 'language play'.

When visuals are used to introduce the words of a song or poem, another common Orff–Schulwerk activity is touched upon – the performance of instruments when designated 'special words' are spoken. The visual showing the poem might then have particular words circled to show, for example, that a drum should be played when the child says a given word. Accuracy of performance demands that the children say the poem, aloud or in their heads.

These specially marked words will often end up being the rhyming words that come typically at the ends of the lines or phrases.

For all the children, these productions of poems with instruments on special words provide a demonstration of the sorts of sounds and the ways of using instruments that they will later be called upon to do on their own.

'Sound carpets': Participating without speaking

One much loved activity among the first graders is the preparation of 'sound carpets', instrumental accompaniments for poems that support the text itself. For example, using a poem about rain, the children would choose classroom instruments that produce 'rain sounds' (some shakers, hand drums played very softly with finger tips, etc.). The final product is owned by the students (and I try to stay out of the choices, even when I do not agree with them, or find that other instruments would be more appropriate), and they are delighted to perform their creations for the homeroom teacher when he or she returns to pick up the children after music class.

Sound carpets are popular with all grade levels. With first graders the poems chosen tend to have a concrete topic, but as the children grow older the poems can move to the more abstract level, calling on the children to use vocal or instrumental sounds as symbols for something else. One might, for example, chose for older children poems on topics such as sadness or loneliness, calling forth an entirely different musical soundscape than that used for a first-grade poem about elephants, and drawing upon a more mature intellect.

Another project being tried at our school for the first time involves the art teacher: she is asking fifth graders to choose a song and then to create a nonrepresentative art work based upon their chosen song. As far as the fifth graders know, this is the end of the activity. She will choose some of their works, and I will be asking my fourth graders to produce short (two-minute) pieces of music from them. As far as my fourth graders are going to know, this is the end of the activity. But they will be recorded and returned to the art teacher, who is then going to ask her fifth graders to once again produce a nonrepresentative art work based upon the music created by the fourth graders. When the whole project is complete, we will lead the fourth and fifth graders through the succession of artistic works – song become visual art become musical piece become visual art again. Whole realms of philosophical discussion of the possibility of accurate translation of thought and language are open to us, and none of it leaving out the students with weaker abilities in English.

Rhythm syllables: Reading rhythms

Rhythm syllables are another painless way for ESL children to participate and feel included. Different music teachers use different systems of rhythmsyllables to teach classes to read rhythms, but all of those systems allow beginning English speakers to join quickly in the group's work. (A commonly used system is: ta's and ti-ti's, etc.) The rhythms can be spoken in preparation for something the children might later be asked to play, or simply read from the board. Children unfamiliar with them quickly learn to decipher this new sort of reading, and at that point the veteran ESL children and new-to-the-school English speakers are in the same boat.

In my classroom, rhythm activities are a frequent moment for small-group work. Some non-English speakers have their moments in the sun with this sort of thing, feeling often enough inhibited in English but able to hear rhythms and manipulate rhythm-cards, for example. They provide all students with an opportunity for small-group social interaction, but allow those with limited English to work on something that is 'not English'.

Classroom instruments

All varieties of classroom instruments can be used competently by children, irrespective of their ability to speak English. The Orff–Schulwerk music classroom usually includes a host of child-friendly instruments, ones that produce a good sound on the first or second try. They are able to see what to do, then begin to play. The students might be asked to remove bars from xylophones before playing, and again, are able to simply copy the work of their classmates. If the teacher demonstrates a rhythmic pattern to be performed, the ESL student is just as capable of playing it as any of the other children. At the same time, they are learning the vocabulary of playing – mallets, bars and so on and the vocabulary of musical concepts – quiet, slowly, and so on, as well as the entire range of verbs that are used in music and everywhere else at school: watch, wait, listen and so on. The excitement of using instruments competently makes all the children feel good about their work, but even more so the English language learner, for whom no linguistic barrier exists to inhibit accurate performance.

Once again, all students are well served by this work, being given an opportunity to learn to accurately manipulate the instruments and mallets, preparing them for further musical growth at a later age.

Improvisation: Supporting rhyme and phrase structures

From second-grade (more or less) the Orff–Schulwerk teacher will be making an approach to the important musical skill of improvisation. (Improvisation has been described as 'playing it your own way'. Books have been written on this topic, but for now let us describe it as 'making it up on your own', but within certain structures determined by the music teacher.) This will take place in several ways. Children, having already had experience with the echoing of four-beat rhythms, are usually able to create their own four-beat rhythms. Given a drum, they will soon be creating their own beat-aware rhythms, and obviously a knowledge of English is not a prerequisite for doing it well or quickly.

Improvisation on the basis of the text of a poem or song is another step along the road to free improvisation. Children are first taught a poem, perhaps going through a series of steps towards internalizing the rhythm of the poem (saying the poem aloud, saying the poem aloud while patting knees to the words of the poem, whispering the poem while patting, saying the poem with 'magic [silent] lips' while patting the words on knees). When the rhythm of a poem or song has been internalized, the teacher can follow the words by watching the silent lips move together with the hands patting the knees. This also allows the music teacher to assess performance and understanding of many children at one time.

Finally, the children transfer this internalized rhythm to barred, classroom instruments (xylophones, metallophones or glockenspiels). The music teacher will be primarily concerned with accuracy of rhythm, but the children have also learned the text through numerous repetitions. The music teacher will then move on to musical fine-tuning such as adding appropriate endings to the improvised phrases and so on and all these activities remain perfectly open to every child.

When the children move on to the free creation of rhythms of full phrase length, the ESL child will see and hear this happening and will once again join in as a matter of course, uninhibited by not yet speaking much English.

Even before second-grade, activities will be offered giving children a chance to move freely to music in various meters, to create dances to go with, simple songs or instrumental pieces. They might be given a chance to 'read' from paper: changing drawn lines and curves into instrumental or vocal pieces.

Movement activities to help develop musical concepts

English language learners need little to bring them into the mainstream of classroom activities when movement work is involved. They see the others move, and join in immediately. These activities can begin with movement to music in various meters. Whether played on the piano, a guitar or on a drum, the teacher can provide music for free movement, and this nonlinguistic activity will quickly have everyone moving and participating fully. Children may be asked to move 'with style', and the English speakers will soon be leading the others into self-expressive activities that clearly require no further communication. Movement activities can be designed to support such music concepts as phrase length or awareness of note durations, longer than the single beat, and all of it remains open to the whole class. All students need to feel comfortable with their own bodies and the way they move, and this provides a moment in which the nonnative speaker will often do a nicer job than those who 'understood the instructions', just taking off on their own in a way that seems to fit with the sounds they hear.

Another activity for the early years – but also enjoyed by older students – involves the slide whistle. I ask the classes to put their hands on their knees and follow the sound of the slide whistle. Everyone quickly understands what to do, but the students usually use their eyes rather than their ears to follow the instruments. So I will hold the instrument up in the air, bring my hand down while the sound goes up, or maybe raise the entire instrument without moving the slide, forcing the children to use only their ears to 'move with the sounds'. The activity works for all the children, focusing on their ability to hear up-and-down movement, and doing it without words.

With older students, usually fourth graders, I use an activity which involves the use of hand drums, the addition of movement to rhythms, and small-group work. Groups of four to six students (divided so that I always have four groups in total) are asked to create 16-beat rhythms they can remember and perform together on hand drums. By the fourth-grade, the students have a reasonably large passive, rhythmic vocabulary (by which I mean that they can use a rhythm when playing but cannot yet write it down or read it). I notate their rhythms, and then ask them to add movement to their rhythms. We spend a lot of time on watching each other's creations, making (positive only) comments on the work of the other groups, then refining and adjusting their work. When each group is ready to perform their final product we have a 64-beat piece, performed by one group immediately after the other. Then two groups who have more or less complimentary rhythms are asked to combine their separate movements in one space, while keeping their two distinct rhythms. This is a serious challenge to the students' ability to work together and cooperate, leaving children with limited English free to make both rhythm and movement suggestions without having to delve too deeply into wordy explanations. All of the students benefit from the group work and the creative exercise.

As a sort of follow-up on this activity, I print the rhythms they have created and put them on the overhead, going over the familiar and, as appropriate, the unfamiliar rhythms with the class, serving also a music literacy end.

Dramatic activities

All first graders love animals. They do a unit of study on animals and their habitats, which includes a visit to the zoo. In both French and ESL classes, children learn the names of animals, often testing the linguistic abilities of parents whose English or French may be good but not in the area of zoology. This game reinforces the names of the animals, and also serves musical ends appropriate for all the children.

A beat-related song/activity in my classroom is the use of the song 'Who's That Knocking at the Window?' Children stand and sing the song with the teacher while also patting the beat; they then drop to the floor and turn into something else as the teacher sings the song again but now with the verse changed to 'Butterflies are knocking at the window', and so on. The names of the animals are reinforced while also working on beat awareness. The names of the animals in combination with the sounds and faces of their classmates lead to an easy understanding of this activity by ESL learners.

Scarves or other simple and inexpensive bits of equipment can also straddle the line between drama and movement activities when added to slow-moving music, or ethereal contemporary music. With older children one might act out the stories of short books. We recently spent one 45-minute session adding sound and movement to Uri Schulevitz's book, *Snow*; when we finished for the day, all the children asked to continue the next day (despite my feeling that we had more or less exhausted what we could do with the book). Working a bit more formally, we have added songs and dramatic sound effects to various folk stories (a second-grade unit of study at our school). Very successful among these were *The Stone Cutter*, a Japanese folk Tale, and *Who's That In Rabbit's House?*, an African folk tale.

Not only are non-English speakers happy to be dealing with something familiar, but the rest of the class is treated to a heightened realization that the child who does not speak English so well is thoroughly versed in his or her own cultural world and happy to see it as part of the music class.

Inter-cultural activities

Exposure to other cultures is even more important in an international school than in many national systems of education. It provides all our students with an opportunity to learn not just about 'other cultures', but about the cultures of others in the same class.

Some examples: Near the start of each school year I do a rock-passing game with the students of the second-grade. The game takes place while singing a song, but the song is repetitive and has simple words, allowing all the students to participate, even those new to the English language. All of the children are challenged, while singing, to pick up the rock, to change hands and pass it on to the next person – all the while doing these things on the beat, as necessary in the game.

With third-grade I sometimes do a simple but beautiful Japanese song, with a complicated ostinati accompaniment on metallophones, glockenspiels and a series of those metal instruments all the children love to play. When they are able to perform this, we add a sound carpet for a poem that again suggests the use of yet more of those ever-popular metals. And still the nature of the song and poem call for, and usually receive, a gentle treatment with the metals. We would perform this in ABA form – song, poem with sound carpet, song.

Another third-grade activity: a native-American poem set to music for xylophones and drums. I let the children read the rhythms to be played on the drums, while asking them to memorize what is played on xylophones. They then break up into small groups or three to five students to prepare sound carpets with movement for a series of short native-American poems chosen randomly from a selection I have found in various library books. The results of the small group work are then performed between repetitions of the song, creating a rondo form. Work in small groups, music reading, performance of instrumental ostinati, movement creativity and dramatic reading of the poems are among the areas of focus for this activity, relevant and easily accessible to all students.

Dancing

In addition to being exciting, fun and healthy, dances support rhythmic sensitivity and awareness of musical phrases. They also offer an opportunity to introduce music and dances from other cultures, including the native cultures of the children in the class. Few things can make a student feel as much a part of the group as participating in a robust, energetic folk dance, the learning of which can be accomplished by demonstration and/or watching what the others in the classroom are doing. We recently took a simple Mozart composition for piano, featuring sections each containing six phrases, and created a six-phrase dance. Mozart might have been surprised to see the movements these first graders chose for his music, but it underlined for them the construction of the music in phrases. For older children, dances serve the purpose of reinforcing beat awareness and a feel for phrases, but they also have a social role to play, making a number of individuals into a single group.

CONCLUSIONS

Opportunities abound for the easy inclusion of the English language learner in the music classroom. Indeed music, along with art and physical education, represents a great relief from the foreign language and culture that surround these children in most of the other areas. None of the activities mentioned above need be introduced with only ESL children in mind, but all of these activities will assist them in learning both music and English. At the same time, with the opportunity to contribute to classroom work unhindered by a lack of English proficiency, they see themselves as part of the group. Furthermore, when contributing samples from their own cultures, English language learners reaffirm their own identity, and at the same time make available to other children a valuable glimpse into their world.

Note

1. Jane Frazee is Orff teacher at the St Paul Academy/Summit School and director of the Center for Contemporary Music Education at Hamline University.

About the author

Stephen Luscomb is a US and Belgian national. He did his undergraduate study at Southern Illinois University at Edwardsville. After two years teaching in south-central Nebraska, he completed a License degree in Philosophy at the Catholic University of Leuven (KUL). He has two children who graduated from the International School of Brussels, where he has taught music for 17 years.

Chapter 13

Italiano Sì! Sì!: Teaching Italian through PE

ERNESTINA MELONI

Italiano Si! Si! is an award-winning Italian language program at primary level, based on language teaching through other disciplines. One of the projects developed is described in this chapter. It was the result of a successful collaboration between the author as language teacher, and Susan Ogle the PE teacher.

INTRODUCTION

Italiano Si! Si! is an innovative and creative approach to language teaching and learning, and it is the purpose of this chapter to explore the ways a foreign language might be taught alongside another lesson, in this case physical education, with very good results. But before we introduce the program we would like to present some of the research that underpinned the experiment.

Background research

There is enough research proving that children learn best when they are moving around, following a rhythm or listening to music. Music and movement are in every child and they easily fall into its rhythms.

There are studies showing that physical fitness and physical activity have an effect on cognition and academic performance (Dwyer *et al.*, 2001; Sibley & Etnier, 2003); therefore, using a language while moving or doing exercise stimulates the neurons and electrical wiring that facilitate a child's ability to take in information and learn it.

Part of this important link was established when researchers traced a pathway from the cerebellum to parts of the brain involved in memory, attention and spatial perception (Jenson, 2000). Researchers found that the part of the brain that processes movement is the same part of the brain that processes learning.

What is also important to remember is that a child's attention span does not often last longer than five minutes. We therefore need to keep instruction time to a minimum and give children the opportunity to explore, exercise and experience, instead of expecting them to sit quietly for a long time just listening. Young children are also very visual and tactile; so if we want to keep them engaged it is always advisable to allow them to touch, to move and to copy us. A movement or a gesture should always accompany instructions. Children repeat what they see and always find a rhythm to help them to memorize. We could not find a better way to learn languages, using movement and music as the focus of our lessons.

'I hear and I forget. I see and I remember. I do and I understand!': Confucius

In order to stimulate development in various ways, young children need to experience movement and music through a variety of concrete, multisensory experiences. They also need to nurture their imagination and creativity while playing in order to internalize and integrate such experiences. If we associate movement with language, allowing children to play but designing activities and games that also develop language and locomotive skills, we ought to get excellent results. For children between the ages of two and 12, we can stimulate the brain and influence and develop healthy behaviour in class, using movement as a creative tool to learn languages, or simply to enjoy them. By combining movement and language, a child is moved to explore language through music which channels energy, stimulates imagination and promotes creativity. To introduce words and sentences related to movement and physical activities is extremely powerful because children use their bodies to express things and they are not really aware that they are learning a language at the same time.

Through the use of language, while doing physical exercise, children explore words, sounds and their bodies' function; they learn about the space around them, and they learn about each other. All children should be encouraged to participate, as both boys and girls enjoy these classes, including children with communication, sensory, developmental or physical challenges. Children perceive the world through their senses, and this leads to a greater understanding of themselves and their surroundings. It strengthens the imaginative powers and increases the ability to experience life with greater meaning.

Learning a language can be facilitated when a child's entire body is involved. All senses are engaged when children explore different aspects of movement. For example, the *kinesthetic* sense, which increases as children literally feel the shapes and actions that their bodies are making. *Visually*, children respond to the images they see as well as the images they create. The *auditory* sense is stimulated as children respond to sounds and the music they make or hear. *Tactile* experiences include running with bare feet, performing specific floor movements, or swirling a scarf. These sensory experiences help children appreciate the beauty in nature, art, literature and everyday living.

Movement stimulates cognitive learning. Research shows that the right hemisphere of the brain (the sensing and feeling side) functions through activities such as music, art and creativity. The left hemisphere organizes sequential and logical skills such as language and speech. Both sides of the brain must be developed during the critical learning periods in early childhood because of the cross referencing that occurs. When children are engaged in creative movement, they are involved in activities that will increase their memory and ability to communicate. Dr Elizabeth Lloyd Mayer, a psychoanalyst at the University of California, Berkeley, eloquently said: 'Scientists are confirming what teachers have long suspected: music not only touches people's souls, it also shapes growing minds. When children sing or play music they become better readers, thinkers and learners. The more we discover about how the brain works, the more we recognize how crucial music is to children's learning'.

While children are engaged in physical exercise, they repeat automatically the sentences or words given, while remaining focussed on the exercise. Children must learn what it feels like to concentrate. Practising a language while doing exercise helps children gain more experience in concentrating, and they develop higher levels of awareness of themselves and others. Practising languages during PE also helps to build their self-esteem because nobody is listening to their pronunciation and the child is free to speak in the way he or she feels most comfortable. A child's self-esteem is also enhanced through participation in activities where their contributions are valued and where the language plays a secondary role. Repeating words or short sentences while doing physical exercises gives children the opportunity to relieve any tension and anxiety due to their performance.

Children learn best when they can make sense of their learning. Embedding language learning into school life brings benefits on many levels. It helps children to realize that there are many languages in the world (and in their school) and that speaking another language is normal, natural and valuable. Experiencing language everyday helps children to memorize new words and structures, giving children the confidence to respond to what they hear and to use the new language for real purposes. Integrating language learning into the school day makes best use of the time available and provides coherent links between different subjects of the curriculum.

An experience like this allows all children to benefit while being active in the learning process. Unfortunately we, as language teachers, are often worried about the linguistic results and we do not encourage other gifts such as creativity and musicality. Indeed, many children with these gifts are labelled 'learning disabled', 'ADD (attention deficit disorder)', or simply 'underachievers' instead of being helped to reinforce and develop their gifts.

Multiple intelligences: The many ways of learning

Howard Gardner, in his work on multiple intelligences, concludes that our schools, indeed our cultures, tend to focus most of their attention on linguistic and logical–mathematical intelligence. We tend to have respect for the highly articulate or logical people in our society and can be deeply suspicious of artists and other creative people. Dr Gardner suggests that we ought instead to recognize the other forms of intelligence, in the fields, for example, of art, architecture, music, nature, design, dance, therapy, or business and others who enrich the world in which we live. The theory of multiple intelligences suggests that teachers should be trained to present their lessons in a wide variety of ways using music, cooperative learning, art activities, role play, multimedia, field trips, inner reflection and much more (see Armstrong, 1993, 1994).

One of the most remarkable features of the theory of multiple intelligences is how it provides eight different potential pathways to learning. If a teacher is having difficulty reaching a student in the more traditional linguistic or logical ways of instruction, the theory of multiple intelligences suggests several other ways in which the material might be presented to facilitate effective learning.

They are:

- Words (linguistic intelligence).
- Numbers or logic (logical–mathematical intelligence).
- Pictures (spatial intelligence).
- Music (musical intelligence).
- Self-reflection (intrapersonal intelligence).
- A physical experience (bodily-kinesthetic intelligence).
- A social experience (interpersonal intelligence).
- An experience in the natural world (naturalist intelligence).

This does not mean that we have to teach or learn something in all eight ways, but we should see what the possibilities are and then decide which particular pathways we should pursue, or which would seem to be the most effective as teaching or learning tools. The theory of multiple intelligences is so intriguing because it expands our horizon of available teaching and learning tools beyond the conventional linguistic and logical methods used in most schools teaching PE and a foreign language at the same time.

The teaching of Italian together with PE is designed to help children develop languages while they develop motor coordination, increase spatial and rhythmic awareness and to provide a positive learning experience. The program includes rhyme, games, musical story telling, instrument playing, the use of props and the development of basic concepts like rhythm, directionality, perception and memory.

Learning a language is a continuous building process. The earlier children begin to study a second language, the greater the likelihood they will develop a high level of proficiency in it. They will also have a sense of how one lives and communicates in another language. Learning a language develops listening skills, helps in the retention of information, organizational ability, problem solving and imagination and can enhance the study of other disciplines.

When I was asked to teach Italian during a PE class, I was terrified by the idea of teaching a language while another lesson was taking place. The PE teacher did not have any linguistic background and she obviously had her own program to teach so how could I contribute to the lesson without creating confusion, friction and frustration? At the same time I was thrilled by the idea of introducing elements of Italian outside the traditional classroom. I was driven by the challenge to create and develop something completely new, and I became totally involved in the activities.

The importance of physical activity at an early age should not be underestimated. Children love running, jumping, skipping, climbing, crawling, sliding and rolling. It is a real need and helps to form them and they get enormous satisfaction from it. They enjoy exploring and experimenting, testing themselves in difficult and challenging ways and developing their coordination and skill. They watch each other, copy each other and easily follow any rhythm.

Working together

All sorts of activities are important and are designed to develop a certain awareness or to exercise a particular part of the body. There is no special formula for the introduction of the new language, but it should be done gradually. Neither teacher should be too ambitious; each lesson requires careful planning and time should be allocated for that purpose.

The way to success is based on regular meetings for planning the lessons together. Each lesson should be planned in advance and the activities designed bearing in mind that the language component need to be added. The introduction of the language to use, in this case Italian, has to be gradual and consistent. Equipment is chosen according to the activity decided upon. Usually the language has to adapt to the PE lesson, but at the same time the PE lesson can be modified or simplified in order to allow the language to be introduced during the lesson. The PE teacher does not necessarily know the language to be taught and she does not need to speak it, but she has to be prepared to allow time for the language teacher to step in and introduce some Italian words and to explain when and how to use them.

Cooperation and collaboration between teachers is the key to the success of an interdisciplinary teaching approach. Both must have a good understanding of the goals of the experience and must also share the vision, otherwise collaboration would be more difficult and, in the end, less effective.

The program and its implementation

The program is designed to help children learn Italian while they develop motor coordination and spatial and rhythmic awareness, taught through rhyme, games, musical story telling, instrument playing, props, along with the development of basic concepts such as rhythm, directionality, perception and memory. The main goal of our Italian program is not to have the children reach an immediate proficiency in the language. We do not expect children to speak fluently. What we aim for is to create a positive attitude, interest and curiosity by presenting the language in a very natural-istic way, through listening and speaking.

Teaching a language through another discipline involves total physical response (TPR) and has produced very interesting results. In a PE lesson children understand and follow instructions in Italian, and seem to retain and memorize them easily by associating chunks of language with a particular activity. They are later able to use this language with the correct pronunciation and intonation in a different context.

In the early stages of teaching a language, consideration must be given to these factors:

(1) Children may not yet have learned to read and write.
(2) Their attention spans may be short, requiring several changes during the lesson.
(3) Children need a model as they tend to imitate what they see and hear.
(4) Repetition: chanting and singing is important.
(5) The introduction of new elements must be done gradually and in a 'spiral' way, that is gradually adding more elements to a sentence to allow the child to reproduce the sentence in its entirety, fully understanding its meaning.

How the language lesson is structured and introduced

Both teachers should be present at the lesson, with the language teacher working to support and reinforce the verbal communication in general. It should not be for-gotten that the lesson is still a PE lesson, and the PE teacher must have the space and time necessary to carry out his or her lesson.

Normally, Italian and PE lessons take place only once a week in an appropriate space, either Gym or an open space like a playground. Balancing instruction time to meet the dual nature of the lesson must be a goal. The PE activities are essentially the same but are set in a variety of imaginative contexts to allow the language to slip in naturally. Sometimes a lesson might be deliberately simplified or redesigned in order to give more opportunity for the language to be used.

It is well to create a precise routine for this collaboration. For example, it could be the language teacher who greets the children and tells them where to sit using only the target language. The children would know that this is their Italian as well as their PE lesson and the mood for the lesson would be set. The language teacher would then introduce the new Italian words that they will be using during the lesson, along with a translation into English. The language teacher will next model the words and the children will repeat them, using the intonation and pronunciation they have heard. This exercise gives time for the PE teacher to set up the gymnasium and orga-nize the equipment.

Once the language teacher has introduced the vocabulary, the PE teacher gives instructions for the activities. There is usually a warming up activity, a main activity and then a closing activity. During the lesson, the language teacher takes part in the activities and supports and encourages the use of the language at the same time. The children get immediately into the PE activity and repeat aloud the foreign words while doing so; and it is all part of the game. Children do not even realize that they are learning a language. Often they create a rhythm, which helps them to memorize the words, and they use the language mechanically without thinking or making any conscious effort. The introduction of the language is progressive, and gradually a full sentence can be said and repeated during an activity. It is interesting to notice that children use the language outside the PE context and show that they recognize the meaning and value of it.

Learning a language through other activities, in this case through movement, greatly reduces the anxiety of performance and increases the motivation. Children are more focused on performing the physical exercise than on the production of a particular sentence in a foreign language. As a matter of fact the emphasis is not on the language but on the activity. Teaching languages through movement gives children a context for listening to and learning a language, providing further opportunities for reading and writing development.

> I believe in action and activity. The brain learns best and retains most when the organism is actively involved in exploring physical sites and material, asking questions that actually crave answers. Merely passive experiences tend to attenuate and have little lasting impact. (Gardner, 1999: 82)

TPR, involves listening, doing and responding to commands. This leads to the Language Experience Approach (LEA), which is a method developed by Asher (1972), who created a study based on listening to a command and responding only through movement and action. Kinesthetic activities, besides being fun, can help young learners develop decoding skills, fluency, vocabulary, syntactic knowledge, discourse knowledge and meta cognitive thinking (Sun, 2003).

Which vocabulary should be introduced?

Greeting children in the target language is the first step towards creating the right environment. Commands can be very effective, especially in enhancing listening skills in a second language. This has been confirmed by a series of experimental studies in Russian, Japanese, French, Spanish and German. The imperative drill can be traced back to 1925 when Harold E. and Dorothee Palmer (1959) observed that physically responding to verbal stimuli is one of the simplest and most primitive forms of stimulus and reaction in the whole range of speech activities. This may be the first pattern of responses by the young child to language uttered by his mother. In the past much research has been done on the learning of a second language through movements and commands and it is still very useful.

Examples of language that can be taught/used in the PE/language class:

Greetings: The language teacher welcomes children to the class in the target language and says goodbye to all of them on their way out at the end of the lesson. Children are encouraged to respond in the target language.
For example: *Buongiorno bambini! Arrivederci /Ciao Ciao bambini!*

Instructions and commands: As mentioned before, commands and instructions are very useful in the target language. Locomotor skills can be easily described in the foreign language (creeping, walking, jumping, leaping, etc.), as well as nonloco-motors (stretching, bending, twisting, shaking, etc.).
That is: *Camminare, saltellare, correre.*

Numbers: They fit perfectly in a PE lesson or a dance class. Numbers can be used to count children, keep score in team games, count items, steps, throws, and so on. Counting should always be done in the target language so that the children can get used to using numbers in Italian.
That is: *Contiamo insieme: uno, due, tre. Facciamo le squadre …*

Colours: Colours are useful for identifying children, for example, by the colour of their T-shirt or the colour they are wearing.
That is: *rosso, verde, giallo, blu, marrone, viola, arancione.*

Shapes: Spots, shapes or markers put on the floor of the play space help to develop children's spatial awareness.
That is: *Quadrato, rettangolo, cerchio, triangolo, rombo, stella, esagono, trapezio.*

Equipment: Equipment is often colourful, and has different shapes and textures. It is important to name the equipment used in the lesson in the target language: Bean bag, cone, skittle, rope, ball, racket, and so on.
That is: *fagiolino, cono, birillo, palla, racchetta, ecc.*

Directions: Left, right, under, over, inside, outside, in front of, behind.
That is: *Sinistra, destra, sotto, sopra, dentro, fuori, davanti, dientro.*

Body parts: These can be used in any activity or game to create shapes of letters, bridges, houses or animals, and so forth.
That is: *Testa, braccio, gomito, spalla, pancia, gamba, ginocchio, piede.*

Animals: Guessing the animal from its walk/move, using different actions as jumping, flying, skipping, and so on.
That is: *Farfalla, elefante, leone, formica, ippopotamo.*

Team building: Identifying months for birthdays and holidays.
That is: *gennaio, febbraio, marzo ecc.*

Examples of activities and games

The activities are introduced in a progressive order from the simplest structure through to more complex ones. Sometimes activities are chosen to allow the use of the language naturally introduced but often they are designed to engage the imagination and excite children into action while making use of the language. The program is designed to help children develop motor coordination, increase spatial and rhythmic awareness and to help provide a positive learning experience while elements of a language are introduced. The program includes songs taught through rhyme, games, musical story telling, instrument playing, props, dance and development of basic concepts like rhythm, directionality, perception and memory.

Many games and songs can be translated from English:

> *Simone dice* (Simon Says)
> *Occhi dolci* (Hokey Pokey)
> *Testa, spalle ginocchia, pie* (Head, shoulders, knees and toes)

Regina Reginella A game where children ask the Queen how many steps they have to take to reach her castle. The Queen names the number of steps.

Uno due tre … stella! A game where one child says Uno, due tre … stella! and the others have to walk fast to reach him.

Bandierina Bandierina! A team game where a child holds a handkerchief and calls a number. The children on both teams with that number must try to be the one to snatch the handkerchief and run back to his or her place.

We encourage also the introduction of traditional Italian songs and dances where activity and movement are involved:

> *La bella lavanderina*
> *Rinoceronte*
> *Il canto degli elefanti*

Stories where parts of the body and animals are involved translated into Italian, such as: *Dalla Testa ai piedi* (From head to toe) Eric Clark.

And traditional Italian dances: steps and movements are taught, using numbers and directions.

> *Tarantella* – from Naples, South of Italy
> *Tamurriata* – from Naples, South of Italy
> *Pizzica* – from Puglia, South of Italy

Post Script

In 2004 *Italiano Si! Si!* won the European language award for its innovative and creative approach to teaching a foreign language, in this case, Italian. We have continued to develop and explore different ways to teach movement, dance, music and language in the same lesson and hope our work will be useful to international school teachers in their effort to find a better way to teach a second language to their students.

REFERENCES

Armstrong, T. (1993) *Seven Kinds of Smart: Identifying and Developing Your Many Intelligences.* New York: Plume.

Armstrong, T. (1994) Multiple intelligence: Seven ways to approach curriculum. *Educational Leadership,* November.

Asher, J.J. (1972) Learning another language through actions. *The Modern Journal* 56 (3), 133–139.

Dwyer, Sallis *et al.* (2001) Relation of academic performance to physical activity and fitness in children. *Pediatric Exercise Science* 13, 225–237.

Gardner, H. (1999) *Intelligence Reframed: Multiple Intelligences for the 21st Century.* New York: Basic Books.

Jensen, E. (2000) *Learning with Body in Mind.* Thousand Oaks, CA: Carwin Press.

Palmer, H. and Palmer, D. (1959) *English Through Actions.* Reprinted eda, first printed 1925. London: Longmans, Green.

Sibley, B. and Etnier, J. (2003) The relationship between physical activity and cognition in children: A meta-analysis. *Pediagtric Exercise Science* 15, 243–256.

The training zone in the CILT website (www.cilt.org.uk) has examples of integrating languages with PE at primary level.

RECOMMENDED READING

Armstrong, T. (1987) *In Their Own Way: Discovering and Encouraging Your Child's Personal Learning Style.* New York: Tarchet/Putnam.

Armstrong, T. (1994) *Multiple Intelligences in the Classroom.* Alexandria, VA: Association for Supervision and Curriculum Development.

Armstrong, T. (1996) Utopian schools. *Mothering Winter.* (Originally published in mothering Summer, 1989.)

Biagini, A. (1993) *Gio ... cando.* Nicola Milano: Editore.

Gardner, H. (1993a) *Frames of Mind, the Theory of Multiple Intelligences.* New York: Basic Books.

Gardner, H. (1993b) *Multiple Intelligences: The Theory in Practice.* New York: Basic Books.

Landy, J.M. and Burridge, K.R. (2000) *Motor Skills and Movement Station Lesson Plans for Young Children.* West Nyack, NY: The Center for Applied Research in Education.

Paola Soccio–Francesca Bertolli (2006) *Il Tempo delle Storie.* Bolzano: Edizioni Junior.

About the author

Ernestina Meloni has a degree in Modern Foreign Languages from University of Cagliari, Italy, and an MA in Linguistics from the University of London. She is a renowned language trainer and consultant and frequently presents at conferences in the United Kingdom and abroad. She is a member of the Language Committee of ECIS and on the Board of Trustees of the Italian School in London. Among her publications are a booklet about teaching Italian through cinema (*Cinema Italia,* published by Edilingua, 2004). In the same year Ernestina was knighted by the Italian government for promoting Italian language and Culture in the United Kingdom, and received, together with Susan Ogle, the European Language Award for *Italiano Si! Si!*. In 2005 she received an Outstanding Teacher Award from Chicago University. She has been involved for the past 25 years teaching and promoting Italian language and culture in schools. Currently she is in charge of the Italian programme at the Haberdashers' Aske's School for Girls in London.

Chapter 14

The Role of the Library in Supporting Young Language Learners and their Families

JEFFREY BREWSTER

A veteran teacher-librarian describes the program he has built up at his school's library, where teachers, children and their parents find a welcome invitation to explore its rich collection of books in English or in their own language. Children learn at an early age how the library works and what it has to offer them at the various stages of their education.

INTRODUCTION

An international school library serves dual purposes: *First and foremost*, in order to meet the educational needs of all its students and teachers, the library should maintain a collection of quality print, digital and online resources in the languages of instruction in the particular school. In addition, it is essential to have a good collection of resources in the first languages of all the children in the school. This international collection will be discussed later in the chapter. It is also vital to have a trained teacher-librarian who sees his or her role as that of a co-teacher with classroom teachers and as one who has some expertise about learning and the use of carefully selected resources. An adequate support staff is also essential, so that the cataloging, processing, and many of the administrative tasks can be managed, but with the bulk of the teacher-librarians' time being allocated to teaching and collection development.

Second, international school libraries have a responsibility to function to a degree as a community library, most especially when the host country language is neither English nor one of the languages of students and their families. It is by extending our role to include community library services for families that we are able to play an even more significant role in supporting young language learners. This chapter describes the several ways that library programs and services in international schools can best meet the learning needs of their young English language learners.

What a Quality International School Library Program Should Offer

The setting

IS libraries should offer a welcoming space for children and families, with comfortable furniture of appropriate sizes, couches, natural light if possible, interesting displays reflecting the diversity of the school community and a welcoming staff that is knowledgeable and helpful.

It is essential that the visual environment communicate as much information as is possible about: what is available, how to find it, what the checkout/return procedure is, how resources are handled, and so on, as young children in general, and young English language learners (ELLs) in particular, need as much visual support as possible when navigating a new language context. Displays that students can share with parents, such as a map of the world surrounded by photocopied covers of books written in various geographic locations, with a piece of yarn connecting the two, foster library-family communication.

Book selection should be geared to the interests and the languages of the children as well as the units of study that are a part of the curriculum. As children browse through books and investigate displays librarians have an opportunity to make initial contact with them. Through discussion of a book that they have chosen for themselves as worthy of investigation, we can provide some basic vocabulary as well as sharing other resources on the same or a similar topic. This brief interaction can be the beginning of a child's understanding of what a library can offer.

If a child is literate in a language other than English, it is essential to have some resources in the child's first language related to particular topics or units of study. With these resources, children can build background knowledge in their own language while learning content in English. Sometimes parents will ask for books on particular topics so that they can discuss concepts with the children in their first language as a preparation for the time in class when they will meet that content in English. Knowing the classroom curriculum and the general interests of children of different ages empowers the teacher-librarian in an international school to support the connections that foster understanding.

For example

Currently, there are 20 different languages in the series titled *Counting your Way Through* (Haskins & Benson, 1996). The author introduces a variety of concepts from various cultures organized around the numbers from 1 to 10. Also included is a phonetic pronunciation guide for the numbers. These are wonderful resources for children who do not yet speak English and who can use the book as a means to share something about their country and language with classmates while learning the numbers in English.

In terms of collection development, international school teacher-librarians must search for bilingual books, such as:

Moon Rope by Lois Ehlert,
China's Bravest Girl by Charlie Chin,
1,2,3, Go! by Huy Voun Lee,
My Colors, My World – Mis Colores, Mi Mundo by May Christina Gonzalez,
Best-loved Children's Songs from Japan by Yoko Imoto.

Several publishers that specialize in bilingual books are included in the notes at the end of this chapter.

In addition to high-quality books in many languages, magazines, audio books and DVDs, age-appropriate online resources should be included in the collection. Some of the most valuable online resources for supporting language acquisition and concept development include:

http://www.en.childrenslibrary.org
More than 2600 books in 48 languages are available in this digital library. The site is easy to navigate and one can search in several languages. Additional books and languages are being added all the time. The ICDL is becoming a truly comprehensive library of international children's literature.

http://www.raz-kids.com
This site offers digitalized leveled texts according to the Fountas and Pinnell Guided Reading Scheme for Levels A–Z. Children are able to listen to fluent reading models while developing vocabulary and understanding. Of special interest are the sections on poetry, nursery rhymes and songs for emergent readers.

http://www.pebblego.com
This database of 240 animals has the 'read to me' option, plus video clips, sound clips, maps, fun facts and extremely well-organized basic information about each animal.

http://www.onemorestory.com
Currently, four dozen top-quality children's picture books are included in this site which is similar to a 'read aloud' program.

http://www.bookflix.com
This site provides reading support by combining a DVD of a children's literature selection (fiction) with a 'read to me' nonfiction text that is linked thematically. Over 250 'pairs' of fiction/nonfiction are divided into eight easily searchable categories.

Access to resources

Signs and labels that are easily accessible to emerging readers is a key element in encouraging the independent use of the library by young children. If one educational goal is the increasingly independent use of the library and its resources, children need access to age-appropriate material in various formats and languages, including print, digital and online, as well as real objects or artifacts.

Books can be organized in bins for easy browsing, either by theme or the more traditional alphabetical order by author's last name for fiction and the Dewey Decimal system for nonfiction.

Audio books with CDs can be attractively arranged on hanging racks, well labeled and easy for young children and parents to locate.

Provide multiple copies of books that are frequently used in the curriculum so that ELLs can preview and review these materials before and after they encounter them in the classroom or library literacy program.

Searching for quality audio materials with CDs in languages other than English can be quite a challenge, but well worth the effort, particularly when building background knowledge for a topic of study.

Themed boxes or knapsacks for parents to check out might include several books on a topic, a memory game of vocabulary encountered in the topic, a DVD, perhaps puppets for retelling the stories, a suggested website or two if appropriate and some guidelines for parents to make use of the collection of resources to explore language with their child in an enjoyable way.

Working with all teachers

It is essential to work with all teachers in the school – classroom teachers, English language and learning support specialists, as well as the art, music and PE teachers. At the beginning of the school year it is necessary to ascertain the first languages of children new to the school who will be using the library. Knowing which first language a child speaks will help the library staff when guiding those children to books and other resources in that first language. It also makes it much easier to find translators when confusion arises, whether that translator is another student in the same class, an older student, a teacher or parent volunteer. Knowing the countries of origin as well as the language background of young ELLs can help library staff make connections with new students, perhaps offering a book (in English) about their country of origin with high-quality photographs or illustrations, or guiding students to the international collection where the books in the home language are shelved.

Another important reason for close collaboration among all teachers that ESL children will meet is so that all parties are aware of the terminology being used with the children, routines being established, thinking habits being developed and the reading comprehension strategies for both fiction and nonfiction that are being taught. When teachers work together so that children encounter the same vocabulary, the same routines, the same behavioral expectations, the same approaches and strategies for learning in various settings, student learning is supported. Children are more able to concentrate on learning language and content and developing skills and understanding when the structures are similar.

Library personnel should spend time with their ESL colleagues in order to become knowledgeable about basic language acquisition so that they can be better advocates for a multilingual collection. Teachers and administrators must know why it is essential for children to continue to develop the home language(s) while learning the new school language. To establish and develop the team approach, the teacher-librarian should attend grade-level planning meetings at least on a monthly basis to share new materials and to provide copies of articles from journals relating to a topic of interest to teachers, as well as searching for co-teaching, enrichment or language-development opportunities. Such small group work, led by the classroom teacher or by the teacher-librarian, depending on what meets student needs at the moment, ranges from organizing an author study for a small group of competent Grade 1 readers to a group of ELLs in which the vocabulary connected to an upcoming unit of study is introduced and developed.

The library literacy program

It is essential to think very carefully about the texts chosen for reading aloud. In addition to the considerations that one would make when preparing a library lesson for native speakers of English, such as: the age of the children, their natural interests, what special interests this group might have and what opportunities exist for making connections between the literature presented and real-life experiences, one must pay particular attention to the language challenges of the text. The effective teacher-librarian of young ELLs must become skilled at locating titles that engage children with the text in nonverbal or minimal language ways, such as movement responses, the making of animal sounds, counting in a chorus, guessing the missing element and repeating a refrain such as *'Run, run, as fast as you can, you can't catch me, I'm the Gingerbread Man!'*

Thoughtful consideration of the language challenges offered by the text is vital for supporting children's understanding. Does some vocabulary need to be pre-taught? Are visuals needed to support comprehension? Is there a connection between another story, poem or song the students know that will help them make sense of the new text?

There is a wealth of fiction and nonfiction books that use predictable story structures as the framework on which the story is constructed. Have the children had other experiences with a particular framework so that it is recognizable to them or must the structure be taught to enhance enjoyment of the text? Which text structure is used?

Examples

Rhythm and rhyme sequence, such as Tony Mitton's *Down by the Cool of the Pool* and Anna Dewdney's *Llama Llama Red Pajama*

Repetitive sequences, such as *Over in the Meadow* by Paul Galdone or *This is the House that Jack Built* by Simms Taback

Cumulative sequences such as *The Gigantic Turnip* by Aleksei Tolstoy, *Stone Soup* by Jon J. Muth or Ed Young's *Seven Blind Mice*.

A familiar cultural sequence, for example, hours of the day, days of the week, months of the year and seasons of the year, such as can be found in Eric Carle's *The Very Hungry Caterpillar* or Susan Middleton Elya's *Eight Animals Bake A Cake*.

Song-picture books, such as *The Wheels on the Bus – An Adaptation of the Traditional Song* by Maryann Kovalski or *Twinkle, Twinkle Little Star* retold by Iza Trapani or Raffi's *Baby Beluga* are favorites of young language learners whose first expressive language in English is very often in song.

Another feature that can foster learning and enjoyment is an opportunity for acknowledging other languages. Examples include: Lois Ehlert's Moon Rope (bilingual picture book) or Yuyi Morales' *Just in Case: A Trickster Tale* and *Spanish Alphabet Book*. If a story structure offers counting in one language, an easy lesson extension is to have children who speak other languages share counting in their first language. In a matter of minutes, the group has enjoyed a multilingual experience and each child has had a moment of special recognition. The spontaneous learning that occurs is rich, such as when a child observes that 'rojo' in Spanish, 'rouge' in French and 'rosso' in Italian all mean 'red' and all start with the letter 'r'. The Dutch speakers will point out that 'rood' also starts with 'r' and German speakers that 'rot' does as well, and that leads on to other language exchanges. There are multiple opportunities to enrich everyone's vocabulary if a teacher takes just a moment to point out that Americans have 'car trunks' and the British have 'car boots'. A helpful resource for exploring the linguistic origins of words is *Words Borrowed from Other Languages* by Sue Palmer and Eugenia Low in big book format.

An international school library's secondary function: Meeting family needs

After a brief presentation about libraries and young children in international schools at a recent Early Childhood conference, I was asked questions such as

- Do you allow parents to borrow books?
- Do you have books that are specifically aimed at parents?
- Do you have books in languages other than English?
- Why would you have languages other than English in your collection?
- How do you find materials in other languages?
- What do you do with them once you have located them?

As I reflected on these questions, it became very clear to me that I had made a number of assumptions about how other international school libraries operate. Perhaps there are librarians in international schools who have not yet thought about what they would like their libraries to offer. Perhaps they have yet to find their own solutions to the types of questions posed. Or perhaps not all international schools view their libraries as having a responsibility to the families in the school community as well as their children and teachers.

I believe that international schools are in themselves unique communities, comprising students, teachers and families. My commitment to a wholeschool community service might also reflect my training and years of experience teaching young children and students with special learning needs. Perhaps it is also that it is in Early Childhood education that it is most evident that parents and teachers are partners in the education of their children. However, those potential partnerships are often not obvious, certainly not to all parents, and sometimes not to all teachers and librarians. Many families may come from a culture without a school library or from a culture that has an approach to education that is very clearly 'please leave your child at the school door and we will do the rest'. These families need to have us reach out to them, to tell them of the necessity of an inclusive approach. We must make the initial effort.

Some suggestions for involving families via the library program

It is essential that the library staff see students as members of families that can benefit from involvement with library programs and services. Careful consideration of library lending policies and opening hours is required. Do the policies and procedures support families?

Recruit parent volunteers, especially amongst new arrivals

Find tasks that do not demand a high level of English language competence if that best suits the parent volunteer. Attend any Back-to-School events and distribute flyers inviting families to the library. Include some information about your volunteer program in case parents are interested in contributing their time and energy. Communicate through regular newsletters, a library website or a library blog. None of these communications need to be lengthy. It is far better to write briefly and often. Make sure that news about the library is included in newsletters sent home by your divisional Head. Provide reading tips, lists of recommended books for parents and articles about family literacy. Highlight new additions to the international collection and commend and celebrate those individuals or families who have assisted you.

Host Book Fairs in the library, including books written in the host country language. Or, if you have a large population of a particular language group, find out if there is a language specialty shop in your area and invite them to do a book fair at the school.

Invite visiting artists, including authors, illustrators, storytellers and musicians from different cultural and language backgrounds. After the guest artist has been available to the students and teachers during the day, consider hosting an evening event in a language other than English for members of the community who speak that language. Involve parents from that language group in planning the evening with you, in choosing refreshments and music and producing a printed program.

Invite parents from different language groups to help develop an international collection of books following guidelines that you as the professional establish. The value and purpose of an International Collection, as well as the ways one can develop such a collection of materials, could be a chapter in and of itself. For the sake of brevity, an international collection is simply a collection of quality titles written in the various languages represented in a particular international school community. It need not be large, at least not initially, but it must be very prominent in the library. Perhaps the international collection is at the center of the library or just inside the main door. Perhaps a large map is displayed and flags of all the countries represented in the collection are arranged on shelves. Perhaps artifacts from various cultures are displayed as well. When a family helps add titles to a section or translates text summaries for the catalog, consider taking a photo of that family and displaying a *'Thank You to the Yoshida Family'* card on a shelf for a few weeks.

The International Collection is a source of pride for non-English-speaking children when they find books in their home language in the international school library. It is a means of honoring those for whom English has not yet become a working language. In addition, it is hugely educational for English-speaking students to discover that there are scripts other than the Roman script, that in some other scripts the text looks more like pictures than strings of letters, that texts do not always go from left to right and that not all books open from the same side. Wait until your Japanese students and your Israeli students realize that books in their home languages open in the same way (the opposite way in which English books do)! The language learning and literacy learning opportunities are many.

Whenever possible, work with parents of ELLs to locate curriculum support materials in their home languages for the school library. For example, if the second grade has a unit on geology, what might be available on that topic in a language in which the child is already literate? Parents can help you locate these resources if they exist. Student learning is supported, as the English vocabulary will be much easier to learn when the concept has been grasped. Invite parents to create displays and/or to assist you in creating displays that reflect the cultural diversity of your school community.

Some ideas include:

- How birthdays are celebrated around the world.
- What happens when a baby tooth/milk tooth is lost.
- How babies are welcomed into families around the world.
- Special cultural holidays or national days.

Invite parents to be storytellers or readers in their different languages. Encourage older students to read to younger students in their language. Search for similar themes from folktales that can be told in a variety of languages accompanied by visuals. Creation stories and trickster tales are two genres rich in cross-cultural connections.

The library can host special events, such as a Second Grade Fathers and Sons Night with books that especially appeal to boys, including craft books, science experiments

(Who says science experiments cannot be done in the library?), biographies of important people from various cultures; or a First Grade Mother-Daughter Book Club – just once a week for a few weeks, meeting after school. The friendships made in these sessions can last long after the activity has ended.

Survey parents or ask informally about topics they would like to see represented in the professional collection which, in our case, includes books on child rearing, language learning, bilingualism, developmental concerns, special learning needs, coping with transitions, friendships and so on. Although this point has been mentioned earlier, it is a critical one: remember that 'the environment is the third teacher', as the practitioners in the preprimary education programs in Reggio Emilia, Italy, have taught us. Have signs and welcome posters in the library in a variety of languages. Display artifacts from around the world. Let the library environment proclaim positively: 'We are International and proud of it!' Be ever mindful of opportunities to have the library celebrate the cultural, artistic and linguistic diversity that is the essence of an international school community. View parents as partners. Remember that everyone in the community is a learner and that the international school library is well placed to support and celebrate learning.

REFERENCES

Carl, E. (1987) *The Very Hungry Caterpillar*. New York: Philomel Books.
Chin, C. (1993) *China's Bravest Girl – The Legend of Hua My Lan*. San Francisco: Children's Book Press.
Dewdney, A. (2005) *Llama, Llama, Red Pajama*. New York: Viking.
Ehlert, L. (2003) *Moon Rope – Un Lazo a la Luna*. Orlando, FL: Harcourt.
Elya, S. (2002) *Eight Animals Bake a Cake*. New York: G.P. Putnam's Sons.
Galdone, P. (1986) *Over in the Meadow – An Old Nursery Counting Rhyme*. New York: Aladdin.
Gonzalez, M.C. (2007) *My Colors, My World – Mis Colores, Me Mundo*. San Francisco: Children's Book Press.
Haskins, J. and Benson, K. (1996) *Count Your Way Through Japan*. Minneapolis: Carolrhoda Books.
Imoto, Y. (1986) *Best Loved Children's Songs From Japan*. Torrance, CA: Heian International.
Kovalski, M. (1987) *The Wheels of the Bus – An Adaptation of the Traditional Song*. Toronto: Kids Can Press.
Lee, H.V. (2000) *1, 2, 3, Go!* New York: Henry Holt.
Mitton, T. (2001) *Down by the Cool of the Pool*. London: Orchard Books.
Morales, Y. (2008) *Just in Case: A Trickster Tale and Spanish Alphabet Book*. New York: Roaring Brook Press.
Muth, J.J. (2003) *Stone Soup*. New York: Scholastic.
Palmer, S. and Low, E. (1998) *Words Borrowed From Other Languages*. Harlow, Essex: Addison Wesley Longman.
Raffi (1983) *Baby Beluga*. New York: Crown.
Taback, S. (2002) *This is the House that Jack Built*. New York: Putnam's.
Trapani, I. (1994) *Twinkle, Twinkle, Little Star*. Milwaukee: Gareth Stevens.
Tolstoy, A. and Sharkey, N. (1998) *The Gigantic Turnip*. Bath: Barefoot Books.
Young, E. (1992) *Seven Blind Mice*. New York: Philomel Books.

Recommended Print Resources

Freeman, Y.S., Freeman, D.E. and Mercuri, S.P. (2005) *Dual Language Essentials for Teachers and Administrators*. Portsmouth, NH: Heinemann.

Genshi, C. and Goodwin, A.L. (ed.) (2008) *Diversities in Early Childhood Education – Rethinking and Doing*. New York: Routledge.

Ghoting, S.N. and Martin-Diaz, P. (2006) *Early Literacy Storytimes @ Your Library*. Chicago: American Library Association.

Jalongo, M.R. (2008) *Learning to Listen and Listening to Learn – Building Essential Skills in Young Children*. Washington, DC: National Association for the Education of Young Children.

Justice, L.M. and Pence, K.L. (2005) *Scaffolding with Story Books – A Guide for Enhancing Young Children's Language and Literacy Achievement*. Newark, DE: International Reading Association.

Kiefer, B. Z. (1995) *The Potential of Picture Books – From Visual Literacy to Aesthetic Understanding*. Englewood Cliffs, NJ: Prentice-Hall.

Meier, D. R. (2004) *The Young Child's Memory for Words – Developing First and Second Language Literacy*. New York: Teachers College Press.

Tabors, P. O. (1997) *One Child – Two Languages – A Guide for Preschool Educators of Children Learning English as a Second* Language. Baltimore: Paul H. Brookes Publishing Co.

Recommended Websites

http://www.ala.org
The American Library Association offers numerous resources for parents and teachers of English Language Learners.

http://www.reading.org
The International Reading Association is another rich resource of helpful information.

http://www.readingrockets.com
Reading Rockets is a multimedia project offering information and resources on how young children learn to read and how caring adults can help.

http://www.regandlellow.com/
This site has been developed by a teacher of ELLs and includes a number of digital stories for young learners, aged three to six, with a number of pedagogic features included. The stories can be found by clicking the tab entitled 'Stories Here'.

Recommended publishers of bilingual children's books

Alsalwa Books
http://www.alsalwabooks.com/index.php?option=com_frontpage&Itemid=1
Bilingual Books for Kids
http://www.lights.ca/publisher/db/4/8694.html
Children's Book Press
http://www.childrensbookpress.org/
Soma Books
http://www.childrens-books.uk.com/
Tulika Books
http://www.tulikabooks.com/revbilingpicbooks.htm
Word Pool
http://www.wordpool.co.uk/ccb/biling.htm

About the author

Jeffrey Brewster has worked in international education for 25 years. He has been a classroom teacher, learning support specialist and curriculum coordinator before becoming, 14 years ago, Head Teacher-Librarian of the Early Childhood Center/Elementary School Library at the International School of Brussels. Jeffrey served on the ECIS Early Childhood Education Committee and was committee chair in 2000 when the triennial conference was held in Brussels. He is Regional Editor of the Early Childhood Education Journal and is passionate about connecting books and children.

Chapter 15

Breaking the Silence: One School's Solution to a Noncommunicative Class

ANGELA HOLLINGTON

A new International School in Switzerland was the scene of an interesting observation in an Early Childhood class, first by the teacher and then by the Head: that of utter silence throughout the day. This chapter concentrates on the difficulties that all parties experience when no one understands the other's language. It led to certain changes that made things a great deal better.

INTRODUCTION

Three years ago I was in the very fortunate position of being asked to establish a brand new school as part of a very successful international school in Switzerland. I welcomed this exciting challenge. The new school was in an old villa in a wonderful location, had a supportive administration and excellent links with the local community, who in fact, had been instrumental in requesting the start-up of the school. Parents were committed and the staff young and enthusiastic – all happy to be part of this new venture. What could go wrong?

Organizing the classes

The school opened with a total of 20 students from Pre-school to Grade 5 with combination classes throughout the school in all but the Early Years section. We had decided to keep the Pre-school class (3-year-olds) separate from the Pre-K (4-year-olds) as we only had a few Kindergarten children (5-year-olds) and we felt that they combined more easily with those in Pre-K. Consequently in our Early Years section we had a class of five Pre-school children and a class of six Pre-K and Kindergarten children. The teachers for these classes were at an early stage in their careers and were willing, keen and excited to face the challenges that lay before them. As the school was so 'teacher heavy' and the classes were so small, we decided that a specialist ESL teacher was not necessary: the classes were small enough to allow for the individual attention required in an ESL class, and the class teachers felt able to do the job themselves.

As an experiment, and because we had sufficient teacher time in the timetable, we also introduced five periods of German per week into the curriculum from Pre-school upwards. This was an innovation in the school and one that I had been thinking about for a long time. Having seen children seemingly absorb language so quickly, I wanted to see if non-English speakers could learn two new languages without any negative effect on their progress. The other reason for doing this was that I wanted the host country language and culture to be an integral part of the curriculum and the school. Having been in many situations where the school's host language was very much an 'add on' subject that the children did not see a need to learn, I wanted this to be part of the school from the very start. It would help students and parents value the culture in which we all lived at school and also have a positive outlook on our host culture.

How did it work out?

The first day of school went very much the way that most first days of Preschool go – with everyone crying including the parents! This is always an emotional time and such reactions are to be expected. It soon became very clear, however, that these tears would continue throughout the next few weeks unless we did something and did it quickly. Since there were no two speakers of the same language in the room, these young children, not surprisingly, found it extremely distressing to be in an environment where *no-one* understood their language. We did have one teacher who spoke Dutch but for the other language, Swedish, there was no other member of staff who spoke it. There was one other Swedish child, but she was in Kindergarten also trying to settle into a new environment, and clearly it would have been unfair to ask her to be our interpreter.

And so our youngest students were in a situation where they had no 'lifeline' or 'language line' to comfort them or to help them make sense of their new school environment. During these early days, in the staff room, we would joke that the teachers in these two classes would be well on their way to learning Swedish, rather than the children English. However, as the weeks went by, this proved to be not quite so funny. The children got over the emotional stress of leaving their parents and settled down in school. The class teacher had a routine to which the children soon adapted and everything seemed to be working, apart from one worrying development ... the utter silence of the children throughout the day. Obviously, this was more than just good behaviour.

Children of this age are very egocentric and, as we know, often play alone. In a Pre-school class one of the main goals is to develop the child's ability to socialize, and yet these children were not only not socializing, they were not communicating at all. The Swedish child, if she spoke at all, would do so in Swedish. The Dutch child did not make any effort to communicate and remained for many months extremely distressed throughout the day. And the one native English speaker had stopped talking and would only speak when spoken to.

One of Krashen's (2008) five hypotheses of Second Language Acquisition, the Affective Filter hypothesis, states that a number of 'affective variables' play a facilitative, but noncausal, role in second-language acquisition. These variables include: motivation, self-confidence and anxiety. Krashen claims that low motivation, low self-esteem and debilitating anxiety can combine to 'raise' the affective filter and form a mental block, thus preventing the comprehensible input necessary for language acquisition. Clearly in this Preschool class, there was high anxiety and probably low motivation. I would question whether low self-esteem played a role since the children seemed to be perfectly fine when with their parents speaking their own language. However, this lack of language, indeed any spoken communication, was clearly something that had to be addressed.

There was another issue, which also evolved over the first term; it was a side effect that none of us had imagined. This was the isolation of the teacher. She was the only person giving linguistic input into this uncomprehending class and confessed how difficult she was finding her role to be. This was an issue that I as the Principal had foolishly not considered. Having taken the class myself when she was absent, however, I realized how very difficult a situation it was. The teacher was providing a very rich environment that was stimulating and exciting. She was also structuring sessions where she would work individually with the children and give many opportunities for free inquiry and exploratory play and yet there was no real 'feedback' or reaction from the children. It was extremely difficult not to become de-motivated in this situation because, as she said, 'most of the time I am talking to myself!'

Searching for a solution

Having observed this situation firsthand, it was clear that we had to rethink how to develop the language of the children, increase their socialization and also support the teacher more in her teaching. There needed to be a way such that the children were exposed to more language and not only adult language but children's language. As Macaro (2003: 26) states 'We cannot dissociate the progress learners will make with regard to their proficiency in speaking, from the quality of the oral input they are exposed to and the interaction they are invited to engage in.'

In discussion with the other Early Years' teacher it was decided that the Pre-school class would continue with its own routines but would spend part of the day integrated

into the Pre-K/Kg class in order for the children to have more comprehensible linguistic input. We decided that using this type of 'mainstreaming' model, also gave
the Pre-school teacher support, a colleague with whom to plan and scope to develop
the curriculum. It was also an excellent way to pool our resources and to generate
more learning opportunities for both classes.

The new timetable started with the groups mixing between the classes quite freely.
And the Pre-school children, although initially somewhat intimidated by the older
children, were soon tempted by new resources and a different environment. Over a
period of time, the Pre-school children settled into the new routine and looked on the
other teacher as part of their class. In fact this was an added bonus as the teacher of
the Pre-K/K class is male and his way of working with the children was very different from that of his female colleague. The children had the advantage of being taught
by both genders.

The question of assessment

We were not satisfied with the traditional way of measuring achievement (e.g. can
the child name a triangle and colour it in correctly?). This kind of task was a standard
measure of achievement, one to which the parents could relate and which fitted well
into the reporting process. Yet, for us, it did not accurately or fully document our
children's learning. If we valued communication, exploration and discovery, why did
we not assess and report on these? We began looking at the work of Margaret Carr,
who has done much of her work in New Zealand. She writes as follows about developing 'learning dispositions' in children:

> Learning dispositions will be about becoming a participant in learning and
> taking a critical approach to that participation. They won't be fundamentally
> about enhancing numeracy and literacy, a beloved topic of curriculum develop-
> ers, but learning dispositions will contribute to the development of understand-
> ings in a range of school curriculum areas. (Carr, 2001: 22)

She lists the domains of learning disposition as:

- Taking an interest.
- Being involved.
- Persisting with difficulty or uncertainty.
- Communicating with others.
- Taking responsibility.

She then goes on to clarify these dispositions as having three requirements:

- Being ready.
- Being willing.
- Being able.

We decided to look at this type of assessment for our very youngest children to see if
using these new criteria gave us the information about our children's learning that

we wanted, particularly about those children who were unable to communicate in English. We decided to focus on a Unit about Light and completely transformed the two classrooms into inquiry environments. Observation was obviously a very key component of this type of assessment, and an analysis of the observations was also crucial in forming conclusions about the learning that was taking place. We also requested that an au pair join us for part of the session so that she could interpret some of the language that the children were using.

Using this kind of assessment gave us much more information about the children's learning than we had previously garnered and also allowed us to look much more closely at how they learned. I do think that in schools we sometimes tend to rely on language-based assessments that obviously cannot do justice to the students who are only just beginning to learn the language of instruction. This observational assessment gave us a clear indication of the children's thinking and this in turn, informed our teaching. It was not dependent on communication as this was only one of the 'learning dispositions'. As Cummins states, *'The common underlying proficiency (CUP) model holds that what we know in one language is accessible in a second language once we acquire sufficient proficiency in the second language'* (Cummins, 2000: 98). Therefore, if the children were able to inquire and articulate their learning in one language, it would probably be just a matter of time before they would be able to do the same in English. In the meantime we could document their learning process and just refer to communication as part of a bigger assessment, instead of making it the main conduit for our assumptions about learning.

The verdict

How did it all turn out? I am very happy to say that the children's language continued to develop, they all settled into school and by the second term the level of English spoken in the class had risen considerably. Now, two years later, the children are functioning at grade level in English and also have a good vocabulary in German. However, what is more important is that they feel comfortable speaking German and sometimes use it in the playground or, interestingly, to interpret for a classmate. The teachers forged a very good working relationship and we all were made more aware of the needs of the language learners in the school, especially in the Early Years. Unfortunately, none of us picked up much Swedish but maybe that had something to do with the lack of necessity once the children had started to pick up English ... or maybe we were just lazy!

And if I had it to do all over again ...

What would I do differently? I would have intervened earlier and not have assumed that it would somehow all work out in the end. I am sure it would have done had we mixed the classes earlier, providing them with more comprehensible input at an early stage. And more important, perhaps, there also would have been fewer tears ... from all of us! I should also have taken a video of the children's learning and documented the process much more carefully. Photos were taken but obviously having a video of a student's interactions, starting off with native language utterances that develop into English sentences, would have been extremely helpful. We could have analysed the process of language acquisition and also shown it to the parents as part of the child's learning portfolio. It would also have been interesting for the children to see the language level that they had when they started at the school and the stage they are in now. Hindsight is 20/20 but I do think that the documentation of this type of process would have been very helpful in informing further teaching and also would have given us further points at which to start our research.

I certainly learned a great deal during this process, and not only about language acquisition. It really was quite a 'wake up call' for me that I had not taken into account the effect on the teacher of continued lack of feedback from the children and how demoralizing that could be. The experience eventually worked out well for the children, and put the teachers on the right road for the future. So all in all, it was an interesting learning process for everyone. And, I suspect, one of the reasons why we so enjoy working in international schools!

REFERENCES

Carr, M. (2001) *Assessment in Early Childhood Settings*. London: Sage Publications.
Cummins, J. (2000) *Language, Power and Pedagogy: Bilingual Children in the Crossfire*. Clevedon: Multilingual Matters.
Krashen, S.D. (2008) *Principles and Practices in Second Language Acquisition*. New Jersey: Prentice-Hall International.
Macaro, E. (2003) *Teaching and Learning a Second Language: A Guide to Current Research and Its Applications*. London: Continuum.

About the author

Angela Hollington has been a teacher and administrator in international schools in Austria, Belgium, Switzerland and Tanzania. She has given many workshops in all parts of the world, published articles and a book, *Effective Learning Support in International Schools* published by Peridot Press. She was a visiting scholar at Texas A&M University and developed a teacher-training programme for undergraduate students. She is currently in the Middle East where she is heading up a new educational project.

Chapter 16
Library Programming for Young English Language Learners

COLLEEN MACDONELL

International schools, more than other kinds of schools, are liable to have a preponderance of children who upon arrival do not speak the language of instruction. For such a constituency equipping a library can be a complex task. In this chapter a veteran school librarian in Azerbaijan outlines her program for young children, especially those who are just beginning to learn English.

INTRODUCTION

In my pre-school and early elementary libraries, each and every class has children who are learning English as a second or often, a third language. In Azerbaijan local children might speak Russian, Azerbaijani or a combination of both before entering an English language program. Add to this mix the children of foreigners who have come to work in Azerbaijan from all over the world: they speak German, Turkish, French, Hebrew, Spanish, Norwegian, Italian, Arabic, Hindi and more. Many of the children are already bilingual before they begin to learn English. Some enter school with prior exposure to English; some have not a single word. In Lebanon, children attending the international school might speak Arabic and English at home but be placed in a completely French stream at school.

In my pre-school and early elementary library programs, I see every child once a week on a fixed library schedule. Sometimes a teacher or assistant attends to work collaboratively on the lesson; often I run the library program alone. Given these constraints, what can a school librarian in the early childhood years possibly hope to do for ESL learners? The answer – a great deal! In my experience, teacher-training and MLIS (Masters of Library and Information Studies) curricula do not cover the theory and practice of teaching English language learners in the early years. So how do practicing teacher-librarians in international schools ensure that they are supporting them? My strategy is twofold:

(1) Reflect on firsthand experience and observation. What do you *think* has worked with ESL children?
(2) Seek professional development using a current, research-based training guide in the theory and practice of ESL education.

Reflect on what works

Consider moments of obvious success, when a child struggling with English participates in an engaged and self-confident way. Ali jumps up – face red with excitement – and identifies a lion in the boy's garden during a lively reading of *Would You Rather . . .* by John Burningham. Masha slowly raises her hand to answer a question, although she has been speaking English for just two months. Elvi seems tuned out until he hears the words 'abuela' and 'mantilla' in a retelling of the Cuban folktale, 'Martina, the Beautiful Cockroach' by Carmen Agra Deedy. 'You just spoke Spanish!' he exclaims in disbelief.

Leila's puppet asks for 'poulet' when the caterpillar demands: 'Qu'est-ce que tu veux manger?'

Before exploring the research and expert literature about ESL in the early childhood years, I reflected on moments like these. What exactly was it that engaged our ESL students? An initial brainstorm quickly filled with the following words and phrases:

- Rhymes
- Repetition
- Puppets
- Drama
- Singing
- Playing instruments
- Movement and actions to go along with words
- Dialogic Reading strategies
- Patience
- Scaffolding
- Using the mother tongue yourself
- Peer helpers
- Bilingual staff
- Parents
- Humor
- Hyperbole
- Slowly, slowly said the sloth (apologies to Eric Carle)
- Making the library a safe place to share

- Caring
- Listening
- Love

Use a professional development guide to ESL

For a guide, I chose a detailed but practical training document from Australia: *Early Literacy and the ESL Learner: Participants' Manual. For Early Childhood Educators Working with Children from Language Backgrounds Other Than English*. Available online, this document confirmed many of my original ideas about what was good for ESL children. But more than that, it provided me with the language and best practice of current ESL scholarship related to early childhood education. Armed with this training and further professional readings, I offer the following as practical, research-based advice for international school librarians in the early years.

The basic goals of ESL programs

Those unfamiliar with the theory behind ESL teaching may believe that the one and only goal is to teach children to speak English. This is the primary goal, but as Donovan R. Walling points out in his guide to ESL, 'There are secondary goals that cannot be overlooked' (Walling, 1993: 9). ESL programs must also ensure that students maintain and develop their academic skills, so that they can be integrated into the regular classes and society at large as soon as possible. Furthermore, it is clear that, alongside the teaching of English, it is imperative that the teaching 'validates and preserves the students' native language and culture' (Walling, 1993: 9).

This last point is most likely to be misunderstood by teachers who have not had the benefit of ESL training. It is also the most likely to cause consternation. How can educators support a language they do not speak and a culture they may not understand? Teachers will not need the knowledge of native speakers (though it would help) but should try to accumulate a wide variety of mother-tongue and English language materials. The school librarian has a key role to play in providing teachers with the resources they need to support this goal.

By supporting native languages and cultures, the school as a whole ensures that the other two secondary goals of ESL education are achieved. Academic goals are often maintained and developed through the mother tongue because the level of English language is not yet high enough to learn or to express an understanding of new concepts. Thus, to continue to develop skills in math, for example, it is necessary that the skills be learned in the native language, if that is feasible, not English.

As children integrate with English speakers in the school and society, they still need to use and develop their native language. Students who appear to be functioning in English may not be quite ready for learning in English. The kind of language that allows them to make friends on the playground is not always sufficient for learning new concepts and skills. ESL researchers make Cummins' distinction between the survival English of the playground – Basic Interpersonal Communication Skills (BICS) – and the language of learning – Cognitive-Academic Language Proficiency (CALP) (*Language Australia*, 1998: 77).

The learning environment

Early childhood educators must always take into account the social and emotional needs of young children. The development of academic proficiency (building concepts and skills) is only part of the picture. An Early Childhood learning environment must be stress free and nurturing. Indeed, research has shown that a child's natural disposi-tions of curiosity and eagerness to learn can be destroyed by a strictly academic approach (Katzs & Chard, 2000: 36). Not surprisingly, this caring approach toward each individual student is even more important for ESL children. *Language Australia* recommends that the learning environment be as close to the home environment as possible. 'Although it is not possible to reproduce the exact conditions in which the first language is learned, we should work towards a learning environment where stress is minimized, where children are encouraged to take risks in language learning and where they find success, enjoyment and stimulation' (Language Learning, 1998: 79).

One could hardly find a better definition of the ideal Early Learning library! In addition to creating a safe, engaging environment, this approach encourages the development of important nonacademic strengths. As I have written elsewhere, these nonacademic strengths include both intellectual and social dispositions. As educa-tors, we can help 'young children develop many positive habits of mind and behavior: persistence in the face of a difficult problem, curiosity about new concepts, motiva-tion to learn, cooperativeness, and even humor' (MacDonell, 2007: 5). The develop-ment of these traits has been found to be 'strong predictors of academic skills in later grades' (Arizona Department of Education, 2005: 141).

Strategies that work

Strategies help us put theory into practice. Librarians should incorporate specific strategies into their planning. But they must also be open to using strategies as oppor-tunities arise – the so-called 'teachable moments'.

Strategies that support native languages and cultures

There are many ways that teachers, and librarians in particular, can 'validate and preserve' the native languages and cultures of ESL students. A combination of good public relations, collection development know-how, lifelong learning and confidence on the part of the librarian will help the library program become a central support of this important ESL goal.

(1) *Build mother-tongue collections*
Both children and adults need access to materials in their native language. If children are to develop concepts and skills through their native tongue, they

need resources to work with. This means an age-appropriate collection of picture books, easy readers and nonfiction. Because these collections are often much smaller than the English language collection, it is best to put them in their own special section, for easy browsing by children and parents.

(2) *Collect materials in English on other cultures*

Children need to have their own cultures represented in the general collection. This achieves three aims. First, the child is aware that his cultural identity is valued by the English language society at school. Second, the children will grow in their understanding of other cultures. Third, teachers and librarians can integrate age-appropriate stories and nonfiction about other cultures into their unit plans.

(3) *Incorporate mother tongue within English language activities*

There are myriad ways to include mother tongue in regular library sessions. Some can be planned formally with unit planners, others may happen spontaneously as teachable moments. One such moment happened when I introduced a story in English translated from the Dutch – *Benny* by Sieb Posthuma. The children found his name very strange. This generated a discussion about translated books – why they had to be translated, if the pictures were the same in both. Children wondered what the story would sound like in Dutch. Until that moment I had forgotten that this particular class had a Dutch speaker. Femka, a native of Holland, jumped up and volunteered to read a part to us in Dutch. A bubbly girl, with excellent English and bags of confidence, she read the first page with a little help from me and then boldly restated the opening in her first language. It was a magic moment for all of us.

(4) *Use mother-tongue songs and stories*

This sounds daunting at first. However, it could be as easy as telling in English the many Cinderella stories that come from other cultures. Parents and children might share songs and stories on a particular theme. Many English picture books that retell stories from other cultures incorporate the mother tongue into the story itself. One that has worked well as a storytelling book is Judy Sierra's *Tasty Baby Belly Buttons*. She uses traditional Japanese storytelling words throughout the story. More onomatopoeic than anything else, the simple repetitive words can be easily learned by any child. 'Boro-boro' is the sound of babies crying, for instance. This makes a wonderful story for children to help retell. I printed posters with pictures of the characters to sequence each stage, along with the Japanese words in big, bold print. ESL learners eventually worked themselves up to joining in the chorus of the monstrous Onis: 'Belly buttons/Belly buttons/Tasty baby belly buttons', sung in an appropriately scary voice.

(5) *Learn or develop your knowledge of other languages and cultures*

In a school that has children from many different language backgrounds and cultures, this may seem to be an impossible task. However, by collecting age-appropriate stories and nonfiction about other cultures written in English, the school librarian will have provided herself and other staff with the resources to inform themselves about them. They are essential reading for librarians if they are to help teachers integrate such resources into their lesson plans. Learning the languages of all your students is another matter. An achievable goal might be to focus first on whatever foreign languages you already speak. Can you improve them to a level where you can speak clearly and fluently to children? Look for international associations such as a *Centre Culturel Français (CCF)* or the *Goethe-Institut*. If there are enough parents from a particular community, they will often run a special language class if there is enough interest in your community. Schools with strong ESL programs are characterized by 'positive attitudes to bilingualism amongst staff' (*Language Australia* & the Department of Education, Training and Employment, 1998: 29).

Perhaps the most important language to attempt to learn is the mother tongue of the host country. This makes such a lasting impression on both students and parents – and talk about validating their language! Their appreciation alone makes all the hard work worthwhile. But additionally, learning the local language will improve your own quality of life, making shopping and other daily tasks much easier. Learning more about the culture may lead you in surprising directions.

Strategies that build an engaging learning environment

Good teaching engages young children, no matter what language they speak. Not surprisingly, approaches within Early Childhood education are often inherently good for ESL learners as well. Building on a caring, nurturing learning environment, these strategies help children integrate with their peers and participate as equals.

(1) *Draw attention to forms of language*
   As the *Language Australia* document points out, 'there is explicit focus on form inherent in all areas of early childhood language education' (Language Australia & the Department of Education, Training and Employment, 1998: 79). Each time we read a picture book, teach a rhyme, sing or recount a nonfiction narrative, we are exposing children to different forms of language. ESL children will not have as much knowledge or experience of some of these forms. For instance, children may have learned at home that texts are read in a different direction. While this is a skill we explicitly teach native English speakers as well, librarians can raise awareness among all children of the variations among languages. Examples of texts from the library collection could be read by parents to demonstrate the difference. Pairs of students could 'retell' the stories in their own words, following the picture clues.

(2) *Scaffold children's language*
   Another way to draw attention to the forms of language is to scaffold children's language. *Language Australia* describes this as 'recasting children's

utterances to correct and extend the structure, but maintain the meaning' of what the child has attempted to say (Language Australia & the Department of Education, Training and Employment, 1998: 79). This is common practice in the early childhood years, but with English language learners we may require the help of bilingual assistants or peers to understand the initial statement. New elements of the restatement should be spoken slowly and with emphasis. Sometimes this will encourage students to repeat what you have just said.

(3) *Use visual and concrete materials*

Picture clues and cues are important for pre-emergent, emergent and early readers. For ESL children, they are absolutely necessary. Librarians should supplement visuals and seek out tangible items that will bring stories alive for students who cannot follow the language of the text.

(4) *Incorporate music and drama*

Using elements from the fine arts within library sessions will enliven the activity for all. For ESL students, they are readily understood as nonverbal contributions to a story. Movements and exaggerated facial expressions and sounds can have children with little or no language actively joining in the fun. Through drama, all children understand the expression of basic emotions without the need for words. The rhythm and melody of music and song appeal to children, whether they are following the words or not. The advantage here is that children can participate at the level that they are comfortable with: rocking or clapping to the beat, joining in for all or part of the chorus. For instance, within a unit on food, a group of five-year-olds asked again and again to sing along with Jim Arnosky's rollicking *Gobble It Up! A Fun Song about Eating!* Because I thought some of the ESL children might not follow his rendition on the CD, I sang the song myself, using the book to provide picture clues. Presenting songs oneself allows the librarian to monitor how much children are picking up, and slowing the pace, repeating lines or exaggerating sounds in a funny way.

(5) *Ensure that content is age appropriate and relevant*

This basic principle of Early Childhood education applies to every child. Although children in a particular peer group might have a very high interest in certain content (say, a scary monster in their closet), ESL children, depending solely on pictures for information about it, might have trouble commenting on the story. Working with the classroom teachers and assistants can help. If they are studying emotions, you might ask that the vocabulary in class and special ESL instruction expose the children to words that they could later make use of or recognize in their library session. For children with little English, as with native English speakers, knowing their background and personal likes and dislikes can help the librarian to select materials that will appeal to them. For items they borrow to take home, it is important to try to include mother-tongue selections as often as possible.

(6) *Use dialogic readings*

One way of incorporating many of the strategies already listed here is through dialogic readings, an alternative approach to the typical read-aloud style of a traditional story time. Rather than read *to* the children, the librarian uses this method to encourage the children to interpret and *tell* the story themselves. It gives the librarian excellent insights into what children actually understand and what personal connections they have made to the story. The advantage of this approach for English language learners is that there is no single correct answer that the teacher is fishing for. Rather, the librarian wants to hear from each child, prompting responses that are highly personal. Thus, English language learners have a chance to sit back and think while native English speakers share their responses. Encouraged by the responses of their peers, they inevitably join in. Knowing children and their background and interests can help the librarian think of questions that might elicit responses from particular children.

Dialogic readings are conducted by the library using fiction or nonfiction. PEER sequences promote short exchanges between the librarian and the children. PEER stands for *Prompts, Evaluates, Expands and Repeats.* This approach has much in common with the earlier strategy No. 2 – 'Scaffold Children's Language' (above). Prompts fall into five main categories, summed up by the acronym CROWD: Complete a statement, Recall something from the book, Open-ended queries, 5W questions (who, what, why, when and where) and distancing prompts (that ask for connections to their own experiences). For a detailed description of how this works, see my *Project-Based Inquiry Units for Young Children* (MacDonell, 2007: 17–19; 24–26) or visit the website version of Whitehurst's classic 1992 article on dialogic reading.

(7) *Be flexible*

As Donovan R. Walling points out in his guide to ESL, we must not lose sight of the fact that second- or third-language learners are still just learners. Aside from their needs related to ESL, these children, like all children, have preferred learning styles. Some may be more visual learners or more auditory learners, and this is sure to be evident in the new language as well their own. Thus, it is important that teachers make use of all the strategies they usually use with English language speakers. Be flexible: When one strategy does not work, teachers need to try a different strategy (Walling, 1993: 26).

Continuing professional development

Keeping a journal is a good way to reflect on your growing knowledge and improved practice. Teaching techniques develop through reading, practice and reflection. Supporting ESL learners is now an essential part of a teacher's job. In the global village of the 21st century, knowledge of ESL principles and practices are an essential part of every teacher's and librarian's toolkit.

REFERENCES

Arizona Department of Education (September, 2005) *Early Learning Standards*. On WWW at http://209.85.229.132/search?q=cache:g6ynQGLTHf0J:wwww.ade.state.az.us/earlychildhood/ downloads/EarlyLearningStandards.pdf+arizona+early+learning+standards&cd=1&hl= en&ct=clnk. Accessed 20.12.09.

Katz, L.G. and Chard, S.C. (2000) *Engaging Children's Minds: The Project Approach*. Stamford: Ablex Publishing.

Language Australia & the Department of Education, Training and Employment (1998) *Early Literacy and the ESL Learner: Participants' Manual for Early Childhood Educators Working with Children from Language Backgrounds Other than English*. From EBSCO host database. Accessed 9.10.01.

MacDonell, C. (2007) *Project-based Inquiry Units for Young Children: First Steps to Research for Pre-K-2*. Worthington, OH: Linworth.

Walling, D.R. (1993) English as a second language: 25 questions and answers. *Fastback* 347. From EBSCO host database. Accessed 21.11.09.

Whitehurst, G.J. (2008) Dialogic reading: An effective way to read to preschoolers [1992]. *Reading Rockets: Reading Comprehension & Language Arts Teaching Strategies for Kids*. On WWW at http://www.readingrockets.org/article/400. Accessed 20.12.09.

About the author

Colleen MacDonell has been Head Librarian in a school in Lebanon and is now a Library Coordinator at The International School of Azerbaijan. She is the author of two books on Early Childhood education: *Project-Based Inquiry Units for Young Children* (see above) and *Thematic Inquiry Through Fiction and Nonfiction, Pre-K to Grade 6* and another on managing school libraries: *Essential Documents for School Libraries*. She speaks French and Azerbaijani with her ESL students and enjoys playing traditional music on the kamancha.

Section 3

Chapter 17

Listening to Parents: Acknowledging the Range of Linguistic and Cultural Experience in an Early Childhood Classroom

COREEN SEARS

In this chapter the author draws on a small-scale study of a group of parents of diverse linguistic and cultural backgrounds whose children were then being educated in Early Years classrooms in an international school. She sets her findings in the context of her earlier research and experience working with young globally mobile second-language children in international schools. The aim of the chapter is to offer some thoughts about the realities of language usage and aspiration in the families of English language learners.

INTRODUCTION

Experienced educators of young children in international schools know that it is essential to understand and build upon the children's linguistic, cultural and relocation histories. Only by understanding each family's unique story, can we offer the best possible teaching and learning experience. We need to acknowledge the journey that each family has made, both geographically and experientially, if we are to enter successfully into the sort of partnership with parents that we all wish to foster. In particular, we may not realize that parents have thought deeply and made all sorts of conscious choices about their child's present and future linguistic experiences.

Although I have worked in the world of international education for more than 30 years, I received many surprises while interviewing globally mobile parents as part of a three-year research enquiry into the lives of their families. Chiefly, I had not sufficiently appreciated the degree to which parents weigh and assess the choices relating to their children's education during the years of mobility. I found that most parents, often highly educated, make decisions concerning their children after much heart searching and evidence gathering. In particular, for the parents of children whose home language is not English, much of their care and concern centres on issues relating to language and the implications of placing young children in an environment where the language of instruction is new to them.

The choice of an English-medium education appears to be made largely for practical reasons. Parents feel that opting for it will provide their children with some consistency as they move around the globe. They appreciate also that the acquisition of English will be useful for their children in all sorts of ways in the future. Their views relating to the home language and culture are more nuanced. Most parents express a strong attachment to their home language and culture, and for some it is clear that they must plan to make provision to ensure that their children maintain and develop that language or languages to a high level of competence. For other families, however, the role of the various languages in their domestic and social setting is less clear-cut and quite complex. This can be the case where English is already one of the national languages in the home setting, or where parents already speak two or more different languages. For these families, the very concept of a home language may be a subject for discussion.

The aim of this chapter is to present these perspectives in the hope that this information will help teachers to act as more effective advocates for the additive outcome that we all wish for, that children acquire competence and ease in a new language and culture without detriment to their existing competences in those areas. Where an English-medium school is involved, the global status of English as the language of business, diplomacy, the internet and much of the new media tends to overwhelm other languages, diminishing their value and status. This is the reason why schools need to advocate so strongly the maintenance and development of the primary language in a child's repertoire, since competence in this language is essential for an additive outcome. Not only is this language valuable in itself as core to the lives of second-language learners, but research indicates strongly that it provides an effective and necessary basis for learning a second language (Cummins, 2000).

Further source material for the content of this chapter was obtained via a small-scale investigation carried out in one English-medium international school. This investigation took the form of a questionnaire for parents and a focus group discussion. One kind teacher with experience working in Italian international schools with high numbers of Italian speakers has also provided some valuable insights into the linguistic issues in this context. Combining the information from all sources, I have found that it is possible to group the families in useful ways. The aim is certainly not to offer stereotypical comments, or to make blanket assumptions. However, families with similar experiences tend to express some of the same concerns, and in turn their young children present somewhat similar challenges to teachers who work with them. In the sections that follow I shall try to describe some of the linguistic issues that seem to be associated with certain types of family makeup and experience. I hope the discussion that follows will offer new insights into this area so that teachers may be better placed to work effectively with young children and their parents.

UNDERSTANDING THE VARIETY OF FAMILY LANGUAGE USAGE

'Globetrotters': Families that have made multiple moves

Many international schools have been established to serve the families that are the subject of this first section. These are the parents for whom global mobility is a way of life, usually brought about by new career assignments: the parents in the school where my small-scale study was carried out typically fit this lifestyle pattern. Like most of the parents who place their children in all types of international schools, they tend to come from economically well-established and aspirational groups in their home society. They also tend to be highly educated, a fact that teachers should bear in mind when they talk to parents about language or educational matters. Often the parents have read widely, and may have firm views about language learning and education. Among these 'globetrotters' (the name I gave to this group in a recent research project) their life of mobility and change seems normal. Increasingly, in many schools, and certainly among the majority of the parents in my research sample, we find that the parents themselves may have experienced part of their schooling or college-level education in an English-speaking setting. Among these parents also, it now seems to be quite common to find siblings and cousins who also live away from the home country or base.

The adults in these families become 'expert' movers, proficient in rapidly setting up a home with all the necessary support services in the new location. These parents are familiar with the process of identifying possible schools, and have an understanding of the various approaches to education that they may represent. It is clear that the advantages and disadvantages of particular schools are assessed and weighed up against certain criteria that are important to the family. In my small focus group of 15 mothers, and in the 25 questionnaires that were filled in by representative parents, there was universal agreement that English-medium education was a very significant criterion. Indeed among the fathers, so it was suggested, the presence of English had been the primary basis for the eventual choice. The mothers, however, had looked for other features and the most commonly cited reason for choosing the school in question was that it looked the 'most international'. They had liked the inclusive nature of the school where the survey took place and felt their children would be part of the mainstream rather than a minority of nonnative speakers of English.

The role of English among globally mobile families

The acceptance of English as a necessary tool for a global way of life was a defining feature of the thinking of this group of parents. They wanted their children to be part of an international environment and appeared to view English as 'part of the package'. However, alongside this ease with English, all the parents in the group affirmed their regard for their home language and culture, two-thirds of the survey answers citing these areas as 'very important'. For them, English appeared to be a true 'lingua franca', that is, a language that serves as a mutually understood medium for accessing all that the globalized world has to offer. This ease and competence in English seemed not to imply that they had ceased to value and participate in the linguistic and social systems of their home countries. Indeed, among families of this type, there are very practical reasons for maintaining strong links with home. They may return at very short notice, and therefore they understand the need to keep in touch with all aspects of the home society, including the home school system. They invariably have access to the appropriate technology to communicate with their extended families and network of friends, and the financial resources to make home visits on a regular basis.

Views on maintaining the home language

The more uncertain area with the focus-group parents was their view of the practicalities of maintaining the home language. They expressed a strong affinity with their home language or languages, and were evidently eager for their children to maintain a high level of competence in this area. However, several mothers with older children had realized that their children did not now speak a rich form of this language, and much discussion centred on the reasons for this and how such languages might be enriched. Most parents accepted the necessity to arrange formal reading and writing classes, but many were doubtful of placing their young children in the position of learning to read and write in two languages at the same time.

It was noticeable that parents with older children had generally arrived at an acceptance that living and being educated in at least two languages led to children being less expressive and up-to-date in their own language than their peers back home. There was a general chorus of agreement when one Polish mother expressed her feeling in this way: 'His Polish is just not like someone in Poland would speak'. After further discussion, several reasons for this perceived lack of competence were pinned down. Many felt that their older children, despite going to home language classes, had not read or been exposed to many of the stories or advanced literature customary in their home culture and school system. There was agreement also that their children's spoken language was neither as rich nor as colloquial as their contemporaries at home. They spoke of their children not picking up on references to current topics or to the slang that occurred in the talk of their home-based friends. Listening to this conversation, I was struck by how wistfully the mothers described this diminution of familiarity on the part of their children with all the nuance and cultural expressiveness of their family language.

Families who use a local language and English in their home context

In the introduction I mentioned those families for whom English is already a significant language in their home context. In my experience, these parents are representative of many families whose real-life linguistic circumstances make them a 'special case'. Just when teachers new to international schools feel they have gained an understanding of the pattern of family linguistic profiles in their class, a new circumstance makes an appearance. In the case of the parents in my group, an issue for discussion was the role that English played in the home country contexts from which they came.

For historical reasons, English is used to a significant extent alongside one or several other national languages in many countries. The role it plays is subtly different according to the context. In India, for instance, it may be used as an overall medium of communication in a multilingual country. In other countries, such as Malta, English is used as the medium of instruction in much higher education, and for accessing information and data from the wider world. In many countries in Africa, English occupies a variety of language roles within the fields of schooling, higher education, government and for communicating across continental Africa. Within a family, the linguistic divide may be generational: grandparents may still largely or wholly use a national language while parents and children may largely use English. In other circumstances, all socializing and early education takes place in the local language or languages, with English being introduced at a later date. In many cases, the use of English is perceived as having a higher status, or at least, giving access to worldwide higher education and other globalized aspects of society such as the internet.

What does 'maintaining the home language' mean in these contexts?

Families who are accustomed to hearing and using English in those ways in their home countries, may not 'fit' with our standard advice (to maintain and develop the home language and culture) for achieving an additive experience for children in our schools. Their view of an additive experience may indeed be quite different. Even when their child appears to use a national language, say Hindi or Maltese or Xhosa, within the family or for socializing with fellow nationals, parents may disagree when we talk about the maintenance and development of these languages as being essential for full linguistic competence. Among globally mobile families it is often their relocation history that makes them feel this way.

In our focus group, there were several significant expressions of regret among parents that their children did not use their home language spontaneously. Indeed, sometimes the children appeared not to value it. One Indian mother expressed her feelings in this way: 'Me particularly, when I am a little excited, I try to talk to them in my own language. And my son rebukes me: Mama, I don't like the sound of it anymore.' She clearly felt a good deal of pain on hearing her son say this, especially as one set of grandparents spoke only the local language. Other families are more accepting of what they see as reality. One mother from Malta regretted the loss of Maltese, but added: 'After all, I took them away and we have been away for 15 years. They may go back to Malta to university but after that they will be off to see the world'. It appears here, that the reality for some families is that the home language only has meaning for their children as a spoken language. When they socialize with their fellow nationals, within the family and to some extent when they spend time in their home country, the use of the local or national languages is obviously of importance. However, it appears that they can 'get by' by using only English as a written language. It may even be the case that in their home countries they socialize solely with young people who have the same sort of experience themselves, that is, with a group for whom English is the prime medium of expression.

Varieties of English

A further issue that we might mention here in connection with families who use English to a greater or lesser extent as part of their language repertoire in their home contexts is the emergence of new varieties of English. The special features of syntax, vocabulary and pronunciation that make a certain variety distinct and different from, say, American or British English are now well documented.

The issue for teachers in international schools is to deal sensitively when young children from Indian or Singaporean backgrounds, for example, arrive speaking their local variety of English. Probably, as is the case with many children who speak some form of English at home, the students concerned will gradually acquire and use in class a form of English that resembles more closely what is current in the school. Quite likely they will continue to use their local variety at home and, arguably, this is an advantage for them. Many children who attend international schools learn to use several different dialects, accents and varieties of a language according to circumstance.

Allowing the lapse of the home language

In other schools, teachers have told me of families who appear not to value the continuing use of the home language in any context. They seem content with a certain level of the spoken language but otherwise appear relaxed, even positive, about allowing their children's studies in English to dominate. Generally, these families come from countries where the upper echelons live international lives, work in globalized business and service industries and travel extensively. Perhaps they feel that English will increasingly be the sole language in which these activities will be carried out. It is very interesting to talk to parents from these contexts – in my experience, often from countries in East Asia such as Thailand, Malaysia and Indonesia. They maintain strong links with their families and with their national culture and customs, but seem less convinced of the need for their children to maintain and develop their use of the written language. In another context, several teachers in schools in Africa where the student body includes children from many African nations have told me that parents seem happy to set aside an African language. Indeed, it is quite common, it appears, for parents to describe time spent on maintaining the home language as largely 'a waste of time'.

Multilingual families

Increasingly among globally mobile families it is common to find that parents are of different nationalities and speak different languages. Often the parents have met while being educated away from their home context or while working abroad. One of the focus-group parents, for instance, described herself as French speaking with globally mobile English/French parents and a German husband. Very significantly, in answer to the question, 'Please list the sequence of your moves beginning with the place you view as your home base', she wrote: 'We have no home base for the moment. Home is where we live at the time, in reality.' For the children of these marriages, English may be a third language, or perhaps used as the common language within the home. For many of us, being a monolingual is the norm, and we may unconsciously feel that very young children who experience life through several languages are in danger of being overwhelmed, or may live in a state of linguistic confusion.

In fact, in many countries of the world it is usual for the different activities of a child's life to be conducted in different languages. In parts of India and Africa, for instance, it is common for children to experience a home or kinship language, a national Indian or African language, as well as English or another language probably associated with a former colonial presence. It is important that teachers understand the prevalence of a multilingual way of living, and show that they comprehend what is reality for the child. They need to listen carefully to parents in these instances, so that they can understand how the various languages are used at home. It remains the teacher's job to work largely in English, but where there are opportunities for introducing home language(s) in class, they need to show that they are incorporating their understanding of the child's situation, rather than making assumptions that may be incorrect. The parents, for instance, may have 'chosen' one language to be the main home language, or to have committed themselves to raising bilingual children. Or they may have opted to use only a third mutually comprehensible language at home.

The more the teacher talks with the parents and understands the reasons behind the pattern of language use in the family, the more relevant and appropriate can be the discussion between the teacher and parents about language matters. We sometimes talk about 'parent education' in this area. Perhaps we should acknowledge that parents may be more experienced than ourselves in knowing how to live in a multilingual context.

'First-timers': Families moving for the first time

In describing the 'globetrotter' families as I have done, I do not mean to imply that frequent global relocation is easy. It would be more accurate to say that seasoned 'movers' come to understand the likely challenges. They know that they usually have a peer group of similarly mobile people with whom to share problems, and understand that things will settle down eventually. Many educational and linguistic factors present a challenge to families on the move and these are accentuated when the move is a first for the family concerned and particularly if they speak a language other than English at home. There are several recurring issues that worry parents. These include any variations of timing between the start of formal schooling in the home system and that of the international school, differences in pedagogy and approach within the classroom, and the fact that they are placing their young children in an environment where they cannot understand or speak the language. Teachers new to dealing with this situation must be ready to expect anxiety and even guilt among parents. The natural concerns of all parents when their children start school are compounded by the unfamiliarity of so much of the new context. With many parents, their concerns centre on the language issues and here teachers must be ready to talk, at length if necessary, about how language learning may progress in fits and starts, about potential features such as silent periods, language plateaux and so on. (See book list at the end of the chapter for helpful reading in this area.) In many cases, this is the time when teachers should first mention the value of maintaining and developing the home language, although parents' anxieties are liable to be centred on English.

Classes with a majority of host country children

Many teachers reading this book will work in international schools where the linguistic profile of the students is quite different. This next section addresses the challenges in classes containing a large number of host country nationals all speaking the local community language. As with students in other international schools, the parents tend to be well educated and come from the higher socio-economic groups in the community. Similarly, they view an English-medium school as the means to equip their children with the valuable tool of English, perhaps with a view to English-speaking higher education, certainly for the purpose of opening up wider career opportunities. In the experience of my teacher informant, such parents are rarely attracted to the idea of an international education as such, indeed in many schools with high numbers of host country students, the parents are also committed to keeping their children in touch with the requirements of the local school system. In fact, it is common for parents to transfer their children at some point into the local system so that they can participate in the national school-leaving examinations. Such parents, typically in locations such as Italy, Spain and South America where such international schools abound, appear to value their culture and language highly. These parents may be vocal in questioning some of the curriculum content and this can be very challenging for teachers working with young children in such a classroom.

From the point of view of achieving an additive outcome, it might seem that these children are ideally placed. Their parents are in a position to ensure continuing access to the home language and culture, while they learn English at school. However, many teachers in this situation find that the reality in the classroom is extremely challenging. On some occasions, the teacher may be the sole English language model; the children continue to speak the home language among themselves and the result, as many teachers have told me, is that children rarely acquire high-quality English. In addition, it is interesting to note that children often fail to reach an age-appropriate level in their home language as well, particularly in the areas of reading and writing. Teachers feel uneasy about banning the home language from the classroom absolutely, and indeed the latest bilingual methodology advocates the use of both languages in the room alongside one another. Parents, on the other hand, may insist on an English-only experience in school, feeling, perhaps, that this is most effective way for their children to learn English, and in any case this is what they paid for! A further interesting circumstance was described by my teacher informant: children who speak neither language at home, frequently learn both languages well because they are motivated to be part of the social life of the class.

Perhaps the challenge in these classrooms arises out of the artificiality of the linguistic circumstances. These children have been placed in an environment where the language is different from that of their parents and the wider community, not out of immediate need, but for the sake of a longer-term objective. Very young children, of course, understand none of this. They find themselves in a classroom often consisting mainly of fellow speakers of the local language, but being addressed by a teacher who speaks another language. For teachers who are monolingual speakers of English, this is a very difficult situation and clearly the first strategy for new teachers is to take steps to learn the local language. However, certain strategies appear to be effective in introducing young children to English is this circumstance. The layout and visual aspect of the class should be welcoming and attractive, and should contain, if at all possible, a variety of English-based games, activities and play and learning centres. The methodology of the classroom should be similarly appealing and child centred and include active and participatory materials to teach English. The introduction of IT at an early age is undoubtedly an effective purveyor of English-based activities in the classroom and offers something uniquely in English that perhaps children do not find in their own language. (Further chapters in this book address this area in greater detail.)

Alongside the work of the classroom, however, the essential element is to persuade parents that they have a primary role in ensuring that their children become effective bilinguals. They should promote the home language by means of attractive and engaging social opportunities, including the normal after-school activities of that age group. At an appropriate time, if the school does not do so, they need to introduce formal literacy classes in the home language, since this is the area where children in this situation frequently show limited levels of proficiency. In general, very little research has been carried out in schools with this type of student profile, although, in my experience, this situation causes teachers a great deal of anxiety.

Maintaining the home language: What should teachers say to parents?

In the face of this variety of language use among families in one class, what should teachers advocate as the best path for parents to follow? The first course for teachers to follow with new families is to listen. How the parents describe the family history and the individual experience of each of their children will offer valuable insights into a child's use of language. Often, siblings in one family may have different repertoires of language at their disposal, these perhaps varying according to the timing and location of their moves. Sometimes care-workers in a family have had an influence on children's language experience, and of course, where they have attended preschool or school previously. All experienced teachers have their favourite stories about children who have been exposed to multiple languages when they arrive in an Early Childhood classroom. For many of these children, that is the inbuilt norm in their lives.

In many cases, the appropriate stance is to recommend to parents that they continue to speak a rich form of the home language in their family setting and ensure that their children continue to mix in enjoyable situations outside school with speakers of that language. Learning to read and write in the home language will require formal lessons. Some families, where such classes are available, may choose to continue their children's full home language maintenance and development alongside the learning of English. In some major cities there are schools offering complete national curricula. Very often, for instance, Japanese parents who have opted for an English-medium school, will send their children to the Japanese school on Saturday morning to keep in touch with the traditional systematic progression involved in learning that language. In any case, the school and individual teachers should make it a consistent policy to offer written information relating to the language offerings available both in the school, if any, and the surrounding community.

What about the 'special cases'?

As to 'special cases', where a child's language repertoire may consist of multiple languages used for different purposes, and may already include English, the discussion and advice cannot be so straightforward. It is certainly unwise for teachers to suppose that parents have not thought through the linguistic issues that relate to their child or that they as teachers should advocate a one-size-fits-all policy. We are united in our aim for children to acquire further languages without detriment to their existing linguistic heritage, and indeed there are few countries where knowledge of a local spoken and written language is not an asset. We as teachers need to appear ready to learn about the situation for each family and be ready to advance the reasons why maintenance of the base language is so valuable. The only way to act as effective advocates for an additive linguistic outcome is by listening and dialogue.

CONCLUSION

The aim of this chapter has been to set out the varied and complex nature of many families' language usage, bearing in mind that for each family this pattern of usage is normal. Indeed, as many experienced teachers in international schools will affirm, it appears that more and more new young children in international schools have been exposed to a range of languages during their short lives. In the light of this diversity, we as teachers need to be circumspect about laying down what course of action will lead to an additive linguistic outcome. In the case of a monolingual speaker of a language other than English entering an English-medium school, it may be relatively straightforward to advocate how this desirable outcome should be achieved. In order to engage effectively with many parents however, teachers need to adopt a more collaborative and open approach, and base their advocacy on the realities of the situation. Only by following this course of action will teachers be able to bring about the best possible linguistic result for the young children in their care.

REFERENCE

Cummins, J. (2000) *Language, Power and Pedagogy*. Clevedon: Multilingual Matters.

About the author

Coreen Sears has taught in international schools in Brussels and London for more than 20 years. She was awarded an ECIS Fellowship enabling her to write a book, published by Multilingual Matters in 1998, titled: *Second Language Students in Mainstream Classrooms – A Handbook for Teachers in International Schools.* She has since continued to research, present and write about the issues associated with educating bilingual children in international schools. Her work has appeared in the *Journal of Research in International Education.* Her most recent assignment has been to work with Cambridge International Examinations in setting up bilingual schools in the Middle East.

Chapter 18

Writing and Implementing a Language Policy in the Primary Section of a Linguistically Diverse School

JANE SCOTT

This chapter describes how a Language Policy was put in place by a whole-school committee, and how the Primary School followed it up. The clear step-by-step description of the process lays out useful guidelines for those considering a Language Policy revision for their school.

INTRODUCTION

School Language policies are viewed by many in education as an integral and necessary part of the administration and the curriculum practice of schools, especially those operating in settings of linguistic and cultural diversity (Corson, 2008).

Bangkok Patana School (BPS) opened in 1957 as an overseas school for 28 expatriate children whose parents wanted them to continue their schooling in the English language. Today BPS is a thriving international school providing an education for a population of 2200 students largely made up of second-language learners, aged between two and 18 years, from 57 countries. For admission to the school, children must be fluent in English or be at a stage where they can achieve fluency given specialist support. When an application is made to enrol a child whose first language is not English, a member of the English as a Second Language (ESL) staff will meet the child to assess language competence before admission.

Starting the process

In 2008, a group of volunteer teachers from across the school was selected to represent their different language departments in the task of writing a whole school-language policy. A Primary subgroup was also formed. One unplanned but additional bonus of this process was that it acted as a catalyst for forming links, drawing together staff from the different language departments of the school. These are ties that we are now actively seeking to maintain.

The first step was to inform our understanding of what a language policy looked like (Corson, 2008; International Baccalaureate, 2010). We read and discussed existing language policies from six other international schools. The critical analyses of these existing policies helped us to clarify our own vision, not only of the elements of a strong and clear policy but also those of a weak policy.

As with all school policies, the group felt strongly that decisions made by the group should be informed by the thoughts and perspectives of all members of the school community and also be agreed by them. Opinions of the community were gathered by members of the group liaising directly with their teams, by articles in the school weekly newsletter informing and inviting feedback, and also through the use of a Wiki for direct feedback on draft aspects of the policy.

The group set about writing the school's language philosophy. According to International Baccalaureate (IB) guidelines, 'A statement outlining the school's language philosophy should be the starting point of the language policy itself. It should be written clearly and unequivocally so that the whole school community can attain a common understanding of what is stated' (IB, 2008: 2).

After lengthy deliberation and discussion the group produced and agreed upon the following philosophy for the school:

> Language is central to all learning and teaching at Bangkok Patana School and is both a tool for further learning and an outcome in itself. Multilingualism is a shared responsibility of all members of our school community. English is the school-wide language of instruction and communication, and the language through which students realise their academic potential. The importance of the home language is recognized as a foundation for all subsequent learning. We value the role all languages play in personal, social and cultural development as well as in promoting, maintaining and celebrating internationalism within our community. (Bangkok Patana School Language Policy, page 1)

Having this philosophy to refer back to when writing the remainder of the policy proved invaluable in keeping the team focused. In many ways the philosophy statement became the criterion of our success; that against which all our work would be measured.

Each of the language departments across the school was examined, focusing on strengths, weaknesses and areas for development, with each member of the group bringing the details of his or her own specific area to share. This certainly highlighted how little we really knew of the organization and teaching outside our specific language area and how much we could benefit from meeting more frequently. Details about language teaching gathered from visits to four other international schools in Bangkok were also discussed. These discussions along with our philosophy statement highlighted school-wide strengths as well as the areas within the school where the most work was yet to be done. Most significant was the area of recognizing and valuing mother tongue and to some degree supporting the development of children's first languages within the classroom.

> The complexities of a student's language profile may make the process of determining a mother tongue difficult. For the purposes of the PYP, the mother tongue describes the language most frequently spoken at home, but there may, of course, be more than one language that a child uses comfortably at home. (*Primary Years Programme: Language Scope and Sequence.* IB, 2009)

The language of school communications to parents was also highlighted as an area lagging behind other schools and flagged for further development.

Writing a draft

The next stage was to write a draft document of the language policy, which we broke down to include 11 objectives with corresponding outcomes and implementation strategies. We were fortunate at this stage to have the internationally known expert in the area of language learning, Virginia Rojas, visit the school for a day and work with the language review group to discuss our work so far and to edit the draft document. A fresh set of eyes from someone outside the school certainly gave the group and the policy an injection of energy and vigor. We also invited Virginia to revisit the school in a year's time to help launch and raise the profile of the language policy. She is scheduled to work not just with the teaching community of the school but also with the parent body and the children as well, the message of the week being that 'All teachers are language teachers'. Meanwhile the next step in the process was to share the policy documentation with the school community.

Sharing the policy

Feedback of the policy to staff was given through year-team meetings with each of the Grades in the Primary School and through faculties in Secondary; having small groups allowed for plenty of discussion during the feedback process. Although positively received, it became apparent during these discussions that more training was needed to arm staff with practical teaching strategies that actually utilized and did not simply recognize the multicultural makeup of their classes. The first step for many class teachers was to actively find out the different languages that were spoken by the children. At parent consultations Year 3 (7–8-year-olds) staff completed a language profile of all the children. This proved a very simple and accurate way of collecting the data with all of the teachers being surprised by a number of profiles within their classes. This has also highlighted the need for a centralized online database that would store data and allow easy access to the information. Speaking to new staff who joined the school direct from the United Kingdom there was little recollection of relevant training to prepare them for teaching a multicultural class. This was another area flagged for further development, that is:

> ... to build linguistic and cultural awareness training into the ongoing professional development of teachers and administrators. (Cummins in Carder, 2007)

How the primary section followed up with ESL parents

Primary parents were invited in for a morning presentation about the new policy. We combined this presentation with some small practical workshops, including truths about reading with ESL children and looking at transferable skills when reading in different languages. There was an unusually high turnout with more than 100 families represented; in itself a very strong indicator of the importance of the policy to the parent body. Interestingly, this group was distinctly different from the normal Austro-Anglo high-profile group that attends and dominates many parent gatherings at the school. There was an excited buzz in the air that this group of ESL parents had a collective voice and that the school was listening to it. It was recognized then that there needed to be someone responsible for listening to and coordinating this dialogue.

Furthermore, at this meeting parents were invited to come into the classrooms and share stories in their mother tongue with all the children. Training emphasizing practical tips in sharing a book with a class was also offered and parents were invited in again to observe best practice demonstrated by a Modern Foreign Language (MFL) teacher sharing stories with a class. This also provided a forum for the sharing of anecdotes that reinforced the need we had highlighted of doing more to support the home language. Many families spoke about how, when their children started school, they had retrospectively focused too much on English at the expense of their mother tongue, supporting their children with the acquisition of English to help them do well at school.

Like the children in the classroom learning from their peers, the parents learned as much from each other at this session as they did from the actual presentation: sharing successes, resources and common difficulties. Most powerful was the sharing of experiences with parents of Year 6 (10–11-year-olds) children with parents of younger children. There were lessons learned here that were valuable to new parents unsure of the possibilities ahead. Many of the Year 6 parents were finding, as their children were growing up, that English had become their stronger literate language and many children had become increasingly resistant to making the necessary effort to pick up their mother tongue in any depth. Subtractive bilingualism had taken place with possibly lasting negative consequences (Lightbrown & Spada, 2006). One parent pondered the future with her elder daughter, who always chose to converse in English and was now at university in England. She wondered if her grandchildren would be able to communicate with her in time to come. She regretted not doing more early on to maintain their mother tongue in the home. Another lesson learned was that more opportunities were needed for parents to come together in order to learn from one another. The possibility of creating a link person for each language was noted for future action.

One mother reported how her son had given her an ultimatum – she could only come to school as a parent helper if she promised to speak only in English and not in her mother tongue, Croatian, in front of his friends. This child is obviously receiving the message that it is not 'cool' to be bilingual, reinforced in some schools where parents are charged for extra ESL support as if their children had deficiencies which needed to be remedied, and that they were less valued than their fluent-speaking monolingual English-speaking peers. In fact a message coming through from ex-Patana children now actively seeking postgraduate jobs is that English is not enough and many companies are listing bilingualism as a requirement.

Parents became increasingly aware of the importance of keeping the home language literacy skills strong to support their child's English language acquisition. But many were still operating on the mistaken idea that they should focus on English for the first few years of joining an English-medium school. There is also the need to inform parents of current thinking on the importance of maintaining mother tongue both orally and in the areas of reading and writing. Overall though, the message that came through at this forum was that the parents wanted their children to maintain their mother tongue, but that this was proving very difficult and more support from the school was needed. It was not something that could be left as a private matter for parents to deal with outside of school. Clearly for the school language policy to be most effective parents were going to be needed to play a key role in its implementation. As Baker (2007: 193–194) points out in his discussion of effective bilingual education 'plenty of parent involvement, with home-school collaboration that is reciprocal is typically a major dimension of school effectivenessess'.

Implementation: The management

The next step for the Language Review Group was to discuss responsibility for and also the management of the policy. The idea of a whole-school Language and Learning Coordinator; a position akin to an assistant principal, was raised. Such a Coordinator should be able to implement the language policy but have the responsibility also to maintain its profile, and link the whole community together in the pursuit of its goals. Very few schools have such a post and, although we agreed the idea would be the most effective way to implement the policy, it proved to be too great a leap from the school's current, more modest, development plan. A more realistic proposal from a budgetary point of view was to appoint two home language coordinators for the school; one Primary and one Secondary. These posts already exist in many schools, such as the Vienna International School, which has an after-school program supporting more than 15 different languages. Certainly something to aspire to.

In the library

We have now invested in building up a stock of quality bilingual books in the Primary school library. There are signs that the market for such books is currently expanding both in availability of texts and in the range of languages available. This purchase has been an instant success with parents and something we are asking year teams to promote to encourage the children themselves to borrow them. Library records also make this an easy resource to monitor and to provide data to inform future investment and promotion in this area. It is also hoped that the new home language coordinators will forge links with parents who, as their children grow up, will be in a position to donate unwanted quality books to the school.

In the classrooms and the lunchroom

A range of initiatives to extend our mother tongue support has been blossoming through the Primary school as a result of the new language policy. These have proved much easier to initiate lower down the years and are therefore concentrated mainly in Key Stage 1 (KS1, 3–7-year-olds) and lower KS2 (7–9-year-olds). In the Foundation Stage (FS, 3–5-year-olds), when nursery rhymes in a range of languages were played, the look of delight and pride on the children's faces when they heard 'their' language is clearly sending a message that speaking languages other than English is something of which they should be proud, not embarrassed. During free play slots, children have been able to opt to listen to stories read by volunteer parents in a variety of languages. We have found that books that work well for this type of activity need to have pictures that clearly match the story, familiar story lines and repeating language structures throughout the story. Similar initiatives up to Year 2 (6–7-year-olds) have been started by parents and are working successfully, with success being measured by observing children during the sessions and verbal feedback from them, their teachers and parents. Everyone agrees that this type of activity is helping to promote the message that the teachers are interested in and value the children's other languages.

Simple strategies such as asking the children to answer the register in a different language each day, to having a 'language of the week' chosen and taught by a group of children within the class, have proved very powerful. One mother reported how her son who has ESL support came home so excited, being for once the expert in class and for once in the position of teaching his friends, had boosted his self-esteem and consequently pride in his own culture and language. Another teacher decided that he would use his numeracy lessons to explore the languages of his class. He himself thoroughly enjoyed the conversations that resulted in the classroom, but more significantly he gained an insight into another dimension of the children's lives previously closed to him. Furthermore, having taken an active interest in the children's languages, he was better placed to teach them.

In Year 3 (7–8-year-olds) parents have been invited to school to take a weekly Golden Time slot; sharing their language and their culture through activities such as

French *boules*, Japanese food tasting and German Christmas songs and stories. We are fortunate that two members of the MFL department lead two of our school choirs; and consequently we are increasingly treated to songs in a variety of languages celebrating cultures from across the world.

One parent-teacher set up a lunchtime language club that brings together children from different year groups having the same first language to have lunch and talk together in their mother tongue and then continue afterwards with games. The advantage of this type of activity is that it allows very natural conversation. 'The child will use her language in the context of natural communication when she has a real purpose for talking and when she can communicate a message efficiently in that language' (Gallagher, 2008).

Early signs encouraging

These are small steps on the path of making the language policy a reality in the day-to-day operation of the school. But they are all encouraging the children to take pride in and share their mother tongue in the school setting. A next step would be to look at ways of facilitating actual and practical instruction in the first language. As we create an atmosphere in the school community that 'it is cool to be bilingual' we hope the children will bring more of themselves to the learning process in the classrooms. 'When students have to leave their primary language at the school gates, they also leave a part of their cultural identity behind' (Agirdag, 2009: 23).

We have already started to see a change in the climate in our Primary classrooms with many examples not just of celebrating cultural and linguistic differences within our school but also utilizing these differences as a valuable resource. The practical guidelines we have generated in the policy now need to be integrated into all aspects of the school and the policy allowed to evolve with constant dialogue and reflection among all members of our school community. 'By supporting students' mother tongue(s) and English or other language of instruction in a hand-in-hand partnership throughout their schooling, children will benefit greatly in academic and cognitive ways, and especially as regards that innermost and most valuable area of all, their identity and self-esteem' (Carder, 2007: 99).

REFERENCES

Agirdag, O. (2009) All languages welcomed here. *Educational Leadership* 66, 23.
Baker, C. (2007) *Foundations of Bilingual Education and Bilingualism.* Clevedon: Multilingual Matters.
Bangkok Patana School. Language Policy, 1. On WWW at http://www.patana.ac.th/Go/?To=188.
Carder, M. (2007) *Bilingualism in International Schools.* Clevedon: Multilingual Matters.
Corson, D. (2008) *Language Policy in Schools.* New York; London: Routledge.
Cummins, J. (2007) Foreword. In *Bilingualism in International Schools.* Clevedon: Multilingual Matters.

Gallagher, E. (2008) *Equal Rights to the Curriculum*. Clevedon: Multilingual Matters.
International Baccalaureate (IB) (2008) Guidelines for developing a school language policy. On WWW at http:/www.ibo.org/
International Baccalaureate (IB) (2009) Primary Years Programme: Language Scope and Sequence. From www.ibo.org.
Lightbrown, P. and Nina, S. (2006) *How Languages are Learned*. Oxford: Oxford University Press.

About the author

Jane Scott after qualifying as a teacher from Oxford University, began her career as a Secondary science teacher in the United Kingdom. Four years later she moved to her first overseas teaching post in Kuwait and there, exposed to an international student body for the first time, an interest in language development was stimulated. After a short break to re-qualify and have two children she returned to work as an ESL teacher, this time in Bangkok. She is currently the Primary Home Language Coordinator at Bangkok Patana School.

Chapter 19

Maintaining Mother Tongue and Home Culture in a Child's School Experience

SALLY FLANAGAN and SARAH FORD

As an answer to the challenges of maintaining and supporting every child's native language and culture in school, two educators put forward a convincing argument for the creation of a new post in international schools.

INTRODUCTION

Language acquisition is a complex and highly personal thing; children, each in a different way, develop an understanding of the sounds around them. The process begins at birth when a baby's ear becomes accustomed to the most frequent language heard, most often that of the mother or primary caregiver, and begins to attempt to imitate it.

All children will therefore enter a school setting with diverse early experiences on which to base their further language acquisition. Increasingly in international schools, the children entering have little or no knowledge of the language of instruction, and schools recognize their obligation to make the transition from Mother Tongue to English as gently and effectively as possible.

Parents as partners

When exposed to a language other than their mother tongue, many children will become 'receptive bilingual learners' very quickly. They will take in, understand and comply with many instructions, directions and learning experiences, conceptualizing and acting on information they process while responding initially only in their mother tongue. The penalties of abandoning the development of the first language, or abandoning it altogether, have been widely bruited and educators in international schools need to be very aware of them. The purpose of learning in the early years is to excite and stimulate children in their learning, while providing safe environments for them to develop the necessary skills to go forward. For many, the biggest single challenge is in the area of language learning. It is vital therefore that parents become partners with educators in their children's learning. In this way they can jointly support the learning in the child's first language and become an essential link between the child's family and the school.

The role of Mother Tongue Coordinator

In international schools, and increasingly in many national schools, there are often many different nationalities, languages and cultures represented in one class. The challenge therefore is to be able to support all students and families in authentic and useful ways. In response to this challenge our school created the post of 'Mother Tongue Coordinator'. It is a relatively new role, but in a short space of time it has become an essential link between the school, teachers and parents in promoting the importance of maintaining children's native culture and language.

It was initially created to be in line with the International Baccalaureate Primary Years Programme (IB PYP) standards and expectations, and the person who took on the role would be expected to promote throughout the whole school community the importance of maintaining learning (with its promotion of cognitive development) in each child's mother tongue. As the role developed over the past three years many other important aspects have emerged which make this particular coordinator's job specific for young children and their parents.

A job description was finally put together as the role became clearer:

> The Mother Tongue Coordinator is expected to keep up to date with current research relating to language acquisition, bilingualism and other areas relevant to students' learning in a language other than their mother tongue. The Coordinator will be responsible for promoting awareness and understanding throughout the primary school community of the importance of maintaining cognitive development and learning in students' mother tongues, in line with IBPYP standards and expectations. The Coordinator will be responsible for encouraging and supporting the integration and involvement of families within the school community.

This job description is brief and succinct but it outlines a very complex role. For the purpose of this essay we have therefore broken it down into a number of individual aspects in order to give further insights and personal examples of how this is being put into practice in a large primary school.

Some background statistics of the school will be helpful to understand the makeup of the community in which it is set. The Primary School has approximately 550 children from over 30 countries. A huge 95% are ESL students with little or no knowledge of English, of whom 30% are learning English as a third, fourth or sometimes even fifth language. More than 80% of our students have exposure to the host country language, Italian, at home; so although English is our language of instruction, it is not unusual to hear the children speaking Italian amongst themselves both in school and even more so, outside on the playground.

To address the younger population of the Primary School, the statistics are very similar and within our Early Years Section (up to the age of 5 years) we have 180 students. Eighty percent of them speak Italian at home with both parents while of the remaining 20% many of them have one parent who speaks Italian as mother tongue and only 12 students have one or more parents with English as their mother tongue in this section of the school.

Although there are aspects of the role that may appear as surface-level information, there are essential conditions behind the scenes for making them work. To take the role of Coordinator point by point:

> The Mother Tongue Coordinator is expected to keep up to date with current research relating to language acquisition, bilingualism and other issues relevant to students learning in a language other than their mother tongue.

In order to do this, the school will need to provide some teachers with the specific opportunities for the professional development that is widely available at international conferences. Post-conference feedback could then be given to all staff on inset training days or twilight sessions. Teachers with more experience of working in a multicultural setting could share their experiences in order to create an internationally minded environment all around the school – at the entrance, along the corridors and in every classroom. School libraries would need to provide literature and access to professional reading for the Coordinator who would then encourage other members of staff to use them.

> *The Coordinator should have a budget for creating a supply of dual language children's books for young children in the different languages and cultures present in the school. These books should be available for classroom use by the teacher and children and also by parents.*

> *The Coordinator will be responsible for promoting awareness and understanding throughout the school community of the importance of maintaining cognitive development and learning in students' mother tongues, in line with IBPYP standards and expectations.*

There are many pieces of research that give a clear direction and guidance in the handling of children's cognitive development and how to enhance or reduce it.

> Any credible educator will agree that schools should build on the experience and knowledge that children bring to the classroom, and instruction should

also promote children's abilities and talents. Whether we do it intentionally or not, when we destroy children's language … we are contradicting the very essence of education. (Cummins, 2004)

The way we respond to children's tentative use of language, whether in mother tongue or a second or subsequent language, has a huge impact on their confidence and willingness to develop as communicators. This is particularly true for younger learners who need to be encouraged and nurtured in all aspects of their learning. As Stephen Krashen has said:

> Students' self-confidence and cultural identity are intrinsically linked to their mother tongue. To admonish students for speaking their mother tongue promotes an atmosphere antithetical to a positive educational experience – one in which students' backgrounds are utilized to further their knowledge and understanding.
>
> … Education of second-language English speakers is made more effective if they are provided with a foundation in their mother tongue, and the knowledge that children get through their first language helps make the English they hear and read more comprehensible. (Krashen, 2009: 4)

Our school keeps this and other similar research clearly in mind when dealing with students and their parents. This important background knowledge is clearly imparted to prospective parents as early as their first approaches to Early Years education with us.

The Coordinator will be responsible for encouraging and supporting the integration and involvement of families in the school community.

The 'Mind Map' (see Figure 19.1) of parental partnerships at our school demonstrates how we support and involve the parents in school life on a daily basis. It is important to remember that this role is to be a coordinator for all mother-tongue languages including the host language (Italian in this case), English and the many other languages represented in the school. This is particularly important in terms of keeping an appropriate balance of experiences and activities for all the children and an involvement with all parents.

In order to support teachers who are helping parents maintain mother tongue language and culture in their children's school experience, the school should provide some concrete but practical strategies that can be used in class. If these strategies are shared at parent meetings and evidence of this support can be seen throughout the whole school, then this will show parents how both their home language and culture are being supported. By communicating with parents, teachers can provide them with some practical examples of ways in which they can help maintain their native language at home, making connections with the way this is carried out at school.

Research indicates that students who are learning in a language other than their mother tongue develop proficiency in the language of instruction more quickly and effectively if they maintain and develop proficiency in their first language. Supporting

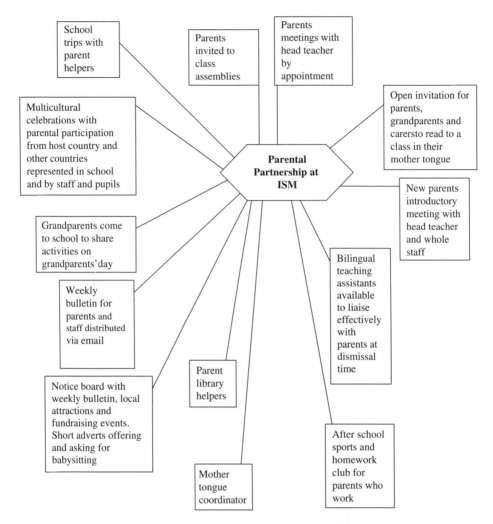

Figure 19.1 Mind Map of parental partnership activities

its development and using it as a resource in terms of background knowledge, is therefore a key element in supporting these children in their learning.

Bearing that in mind, listed below are some tips to teachers for supporting a first language other than English, in the classroom.

Create a multilingual classroom

• Take the register in a different language; allow the children to teach each other how to answer in their own languages.

- Give the child a buddy who speaks the same language.
- Use every human resource that the school has (classroom assistants, teachers, nonteaching staff or parents who can speak other languages) to translate when problems arise.
- Help the children to create dual-language books.
- Invite a parent or sibling to read in their first language and create a taped version for the book corner.
- Display different languages around the school and in the classroom.

Ideas that can be used to by teachers to create and maintain a communicative relationship with parents:

- Involve families: keep in regular contact with parents, for example regular brief meetings or a communication book. Share ideas, discuss problems, search for solutions together and celebrate achievements.
- Introduce parents to each other, including across classes and grade levels to provide additional support for students and their families.
- Ask families to send in picture books which can be shared with the children in school. Use to develop vocabulary in English and to allow the children to share their own language, for example what is the word in your language for dog?
- Ask parents to send in a list of key words and useful phrases in mother tongue.
- Planning and ongoing communication are key to the success of all students. It is our shared responsibility to support every student. It is particularly important to establish good one-to-one rapport with ESL students, making regular contact with them and giving assistance as much as possible.
- An Early Years setting is the perfect place for young students to become comfortable and confident learners, without all the pressures of a more structured classroom. The classroom environment is crucial to any learning for young students and careful consideration should be given to the resources, books and games provided.

Practical strategies for supporting young ESL learners

- Seat each ESL learner with a more advanced student who speaks the same language (if possible). This will build up the confidence of the buddy, as well as assisting the beginner in following the lessons.
- Seat them near the front of the class or as near as possible to you, so that they can easily see your facial expressions and body language. This will help them in listening and speaking, as well as comprehension.
- Speak slowly and clearly, especially when introducing new concepts or vocabulary.
- Give explanations of key vocabulary in more than one way (verbal, visual, physical); use gestures and facial expressions to aid meaning.
- Demonstrate, mime and use fingers to list/point.

- Use short sentences and simple vocabulary.
- Use visual aids such as flash cards to aid understanding for:
  - Daily routines
  - Child-friendly time tables
  - Permission to have a drink or go to the toilet
- Use visuals, real-life artefacts, pictures, objects, practical demonstrations and activities. This is beneficial to all students for clarifying concepts and promoting learning, but is especially effective for English language learners.
- List multisensory activities in writing and have the students repeat them orally. Multisensory activities are important to suit the learning styles of all students. For example, when giving instructions, walk around the classroom and ask English language learners questions about what they are working on. This gives them the opportunity to use their developing vocabulary, practise pronunciation and ensures that they understand the process of completing their assignment.
- Modify assessment tasks according to the skills of the students, especially beginners. For example, an oral presentation may be accompanied by a visual/drawing, allowing students a wider possibility for demonstrating their knowledge and understanding.
- Continually repeat stories/phrases/songs supported by visual aids/body language and action.
- Ensure a balance between formal and informal language instruction.
- Provide time and opportunities for children to make connections to their own mother tongue.
- Provide time and opportunities for students to communicate in meaningful situations, to have their mistakes corrected, and to have correct language use reinforced.
- Make use of available resources, for example sets of books that are related to units in small group reading sessions, in order to develop and reinforce language and vocabulary appropriate to the area of research/discussion.
- Set appropriately differentiated activities.
- Give short instructions, not multistage or lengthy.
- Provide instructions in oral, written, visual form.
- Demonstrate activities, showing example of desired end product.
- Break tasks down into small, individual parts.
- Use flexible grouping to allow peer support.

And use scaffolding

Scaffolding is a temporary strategy which enables learners to accomplish a task that would otherwise be much more difficult or even impossible to accomplish. One important means of scaffolding for students learning in a language other than their mother tongue is to allow them to use their first language to carry out research or other tasks that would be too difficult or even impossible in another language.

Other examples of scaffolding:

- Visual aids.
- Graphic organizers.
- Demonstrations.
- Dramatization.
- Small, structured collaborative groups.
- Teacher language.

Through scaffolding, students will gain increased independence in developing their own strategies for learning.

Another key aspect of the role of the Mother Tongue Coordinator

Sharing the celebrations and festivals represented by our school community in an authentic and meaningful way is part of the role of the Mother Tongue Coordinator, allowing us all to both share and learn in an environment that is welcoming and receptive. This can move from the simplest everyday experience shared by a nursery child to a large national or cultural festival acknowledged by many.

Our coordinator puts together a calendar of celebrations for the school year, which differs from year to year and is made relevant to our current community. It is carefully constructed to include some festivals and events that transcend cultures or nationalities to emphasize the commonalities of our human experiences as well as celebrating our diversity. Examples of these include World Peace Day and the UN Children's Day and also our own 'Cultural Roots Day' looking at our own personal backgrounds and family trees to identify our individual cultural journeys.

Some celebrations, such as Christmas and Easter, take place in our school at the same time every year in recognition of our host country's culture. Other celebrations can be chosen from international calendars or from specific cultural celebrations websites and we try to maintain a rhythm of one age-appropriate and internationally significant celebration per month. At our school we carried out a survey of our families to find out more about the individual cultures of the school community. By communicating with teachers and parents in this way, we learned more about particular celebrations popular in their countries of origin.

By encouraging parents, grandparents or carers to come to school and share aspects of one or more of their cultural celebrations we enrich the whole school environment. Children benefit from this positive recognition of their culture and language and are always delighted to see someone from their own family at school reading a story or sharing a poem or a skill in their first language. Almost all schools have a wealth of human resources that can be used to help parents maintain native language and culture in their children's school experience.

Particular celebrations which have taken place in our school

In *September,* to celebrate linguistic diversity and promote language learning, we celebrate the European Day of Languages (EDL). Launched by the Council of Europe

(45 member states – http://www.coe.int) during the European Year of Languages 2001, the EDL has since built up a momentum and thousands of activities are organized throughout Europe to mark the Day. It is a great opportunity for teachers to discover, if they have not already, which languages their children and parents speak and to use these parents to help turn their classroom into a multilingual learning environment. By involving parents early on in the year, the children will feel that their language and culture have been immediately recognized and accepted in the school.

In *October* we were searching for an alternative to our usual Halloween celebration when a Brazilian member of staff suggested Children's Day in Brazil. Children's Day is celebrated in many countries of the world but on different dates. It was first celebrated in October 1953, under the sponsorship of the International Union for Child Welfare in Geneva. It was adapted by the United Nations General Assembly in 1954, and since then the UN and UNESCO have observed 20 December as Universal Children's day. The General Assembly recommended that all countries institute a Universal Children's Day, to be observed as a day of worldwide fraternity and understanding among children. It is a day of fun devoted to promoting the ideals and objectives of the charter and the welfare of the children of the world.

What did we do in school?

In Brazil, Children's day is celebrated on 12 October. So for that day we made an Amazon forest at the entrance to school. We learned about Brazilian music, carnivals, artists, food and, of course, football. We all wore yellow or green t-shirts. Mums made *brigaderos* (little cakes) and brought pineapple for us to eat. And they brought their amazing carnival costumes to show us. At the end of the day we attached messages for other children around the world to hundreds of yellow and green balloons, and we let them go up into the sky. Although our Brazilian families seem to be outgoing, confident people, they must sometimes feel marginalized because they do not speak the host country language. So this celebration was a real 'ice-breaker' for everyone and we learned how to say a few words in Portuguese as well.

In *November* last year we celebrated a special Japanese day. Our second-largest community at school is Japanese, but unlike the Brazilian families, we rarely see Japanese fathers at school and the mothers are generally very reserved. The special day was called *Shichi-Go-San* which means seven-five-three in English. It is a traditional Japanese rite of passage and celebration day for three- and seven-year-old girls, and three- and five-year-old boys. It is said to have originated in the Heian Period to celebrate the passage of children into middle childhood. The ages three, five and seven are consistent with Japanese numerology which dictates that odd numbers are lucky. The sum total of 3 + 5 + 7 is 15, and that is why it is celebrated on 15 November.

What did we learn?

- We learned how to greet each other in Japanese.
- Some Japanese mums came to school to read stories and to share their origami skills with us.
- We wrote messages to each other on red paper, for luck, and stuck them on classroom doors.
- We learned to write our names in Japanese.
- We made bags for 100-year-old candy (Chetosan).
- Some of the Japanese children shared their judo and karate skills.

These are only a few examples; there are many more. The important thing to remember is that any celebration needs to be age appropriate for young children and above all something authentic to celebrate with the community. Young children are the best judges of this; they are always very keen to share experiences that are real and meaningful and should be encouraged to do so.

And finally, change ...

The role of the Mother Tongue Coordinator is one that is constantly developing and changing as our school population changes. In essence, the coordinator must be an internationally minded person who speaks, at the least, both the host country language and the language of instruction fluently. Being able to communicate with parents, grandparents and carers is a way of providing security and comfort for families who have chosen an international school for their children.

The coordinator should be the 'friendly face' or link person that the children and parents see on corridor duty every morning when they arrive at school, and again every afternoon outside on the playground at dismissal time. On these occasions they would be available to help where they can in translating conversations between parents and teachers. They should in fact be considered approachable by everyone in the school community. They should learn early on which languages are spoken as first languages at home by the children, and as far as possible be able to greet everyone in the school in their own language. The Mother Tongue Coordinator is the one person who knows all the linguistic resources in the school at any given time.

This is a demanding job and there have been successes and failures, trials and errors along the way to developing this role in our school. But the overriding feeling of community and 'family' that can be created by the bonding together of student, parent and teacher in a common, multilingual, positive experience, makes it all worthwhile.

REFERENCES

Cummins, J. (2004) *Bilingual Children's Mother Tongue: Why Is It Important for Education?* Toronto: University of Toronto.
Krashen, S. (2009) In *The Bilingual Family Newsletter*. Channel View Publications Ltd.

About the authors

Sally Flanagan is Mother Tongue Coordinator and Learning Support Assistant. She has worked in both Early Years and Elementary sections of the International School of Milan, guaranteeing a familiar face for children, parents and staff in both sections. She has made Italy her home and lives just outside Milan with her two bilingual sons.

Sarah Ford is director of the Early Years Section at the International School of Milan. She has taught both in the United Kingdom and in International Primary Schools, specializing in Music and Early Years education. She has twins, now grown up and speaking four languages fluently, and has lived in Italy for the past nine years.

Chapter 20

Joining the Mother-Tongue Conversation from an Administrator's Perspective

ELAINE WHELEN

An experienced Head adds her voice to those who would like to see first-language teaching in every international school classroom. She has overseen such a curriculum successfully for many years and well knows its benefits.

INTRODUCTION

Children in internationally mobile families need to maintain and develop their mother tongue; it is not enough to speak the language at home. If we make provision to sustain and develop a child's first language throughout his/her formal education we are providing the scaffolding for that child's emotional well-being. In addition, we are providing the foundations of a language-rich environment enabling the child to access his/her culture, history and literature. Moreover, we are providing the increased likelihood of better academic progress in all subjects and all future learning. Psychologically, sociologically and educationally students need to have their mother tongue sustained and developed at school.

It is axiomatic that the best medium for teaching a child is his mother tongue. Psychologically, it is a system of meaningful signs that in his mind works automatically for expression and understanding. Sociologically, it is a means of identification among the members of the community to which he belongs.

Educationally, he learns more quickly through it than through an unfamiliar linguistic medium. (UNESCO: 1)

The role of the administrator

As international school educators, particularly administrators, we leave discussion of mother tongue out of the significant conversations, despite decades of academic research and endorsement from global organizations. Mother tongue languages are marginalized by educators. From my experience as a head of three international schools, all offering mother-tongue programs, I have noticed that unless the head of school is supportive, initiatives from individuals or groups of teachers remain undeveloped. Administrators need to take this issue seriously, overcome the obstacles and develop mother-tongue programs in their schools.

The case for mother-tongue teaching

Mother tongue represents more than a language; it is the child's connection with his/her family, extended family, country, culture and self-identity. Mother-tongue programs provide an opportunity for students to relate to teachers and other students from their cultural background. They build a bond with other students from their cultural or linguistic background and relate affectionately with a teacher who becomes a significant adult for the transmission of language and culture.

A child's sense of identity as a multicultural, multilingual individual is enhanced when his or her mother tongue is sustained and developed. A mother-tongue program provides the cultural cohesion necessary for a student to develop into a secure young person, with a strong sense of cultural identity. As one Italian mother-tongue teacher describes it: 'Children moving countries find their identity again in their mother tongue classes.'[1] Parents often feel guilty that they have taken their children away from their culture, extended family and national education system. With a quality mother-tongue program students learn to thrive, not just survive, in the internationally mobile community. Parents replace feelings of guilt with a sense of accomplishment that they are enabling their children to feel 'at home' wherever they may go in the future. Teachers replace conceptions of static identities and cultural stereotypes with a view of their students' identities and literacies as transnational and transcultural (Taylor, 2008). A Dutch mother-tongue teacher describes it as enabling students 'to go in and out of cultures, but to return to his or her first language to make sense of the other cultures'.

Written and oral language are about communicating ideas and expressing feelings. That is our motivation for learning to read and write. How many frustrated young children have teachers seen trying to function without the language of the school? Jae Yun,[1] a six-year-old Korean boy lets out a tirade of Korean sentences when asked to sit in his chair in a busy classroom. The three adults who witness this emotional outburst do not understand one word of what he says, but they all understand his sense of frustration. Jae Yun has a well-developed vocabulary in his first language and cannot function in the new English-speaking environment. Similarly with Nadia, a five-year-old girl who does not know how to ask for something so she just takes it. How can she explain that the pencil is broken and she needs the sharpener to sharpen it? Nicholas, a four-year-old boy, used to run to the German mother-tongue teacher's classroom throughout the school day desperate for her help to explain his problem to the class teacher. Eventually he learns not to run out of class and waits until his mother tongue lesson to explain the problem to the only teacher who speaks his language.

The litmus test of whether a mother-tongue class is right for a child is whether they feel and look relaxed in the lessons. Students have described it as a feeling of 'being at home' or 'being released from prison' to enter the mother-tongue classroom. Nicholas visits his mother-tongue teacher regularly during play time. Her room is a place where Nicholas can relax and feel safe. Children learning to speak English as a second language often experience extreme fatigue. One mother said the mother-tongue lessons are a 'lifeline' for her child. A German mother-tongue teacher sits in the Early Childhood playground to be with her two-year-old son, but all the other German-speaking children gravitate to her like a magnet. She sees this as a very positive relationship and one we should try to replicate. She also notices that over 80% of the students who go to the Chinese teachers on duty to seek help for conflicts during morning and lunch breaks are Chinese-speaking children.

We can ensure there is a mix of language speakers on duty in the playground. The problems arising during playtime need to be resolved or children return to class emotionally upset and not ready to learn.

Some things can only be said in your first language

We often find that jokes are inappropriate in international schools because of the many cultural differences regarding humour. In contrast, in the mother-tongue classes a teacher can joke with children. There is a common understanding of jokes. They can express finer points. Understanding is achieved without any feelings being hurt. Similarly, a teacher uses familiar gestures and body language to make a child feel at ease. Japanese parents and teachers speak to children in culturally different ways from German, Arabic or Kenyan parents and teachers. The differences are often subtle, but they have the effect of making a child feel at ease. One mother-tongue teacher had to persuade a small child to leave a room and she used an approach similar to what his mother would have done. For small children lost in a foreign world, where everybody speaks English, adults can appear to be aliens. The provision of a mother-tongue buffer each day alleviates that problem while the child gradually grows accustomed to his or her new world.

And sometimes forgetting can be a problem

As children become acculturated to their new language environment the tendency is to speak English at home as well as at school. An Italian mother said in despair that she is the only person who speaks their mother tongue at home. Her poignant description of what is at stake is noteworthy: 'It is surprising how quickly children can pick up a new language. At the same time, they can lose the richness of their own language'. Some mother-tongue teachers find children are functioning in English for most of their daily life and forget high-frequency words and simple words, such as colours or animal names in their own language. When asked to describe a picture in a mother-tongue lesson a child fills in the vocabulary gaps with English words.

And the benefits?

The academic benefits of a mother-tongue program are well documented. Bilingualism becomes a positive force when the school supports and develops the students' first language; this is known as 'additive bilingualism'. This is in contrast to the negative effects when the first language is neglected and replaced by a dominant and more prestigious additional language, which is known as 'subtractive bilingualism'. Cummins (1979) argues that 'a cognitively and academically' beneficial form of bilingualism can be achieved only on the basis of adequately developed first-language skills. He argues (Cummins, 1996) against spending more time on the mastery of English and predicted that more time on the development of first language would transfer to proficiency in English as a second language. Thomas and Collier's (1997) seminal research undertaken on several hundred thousand second-language students over 20 years in the United States revealed that students who developed their mother tongue alongside a well-planned ESL program outperformed their monolingual peers in high-school grades.

Mother-tongue teachers

Program coordinators can encourage mother-tongue teachers to develop higher-order thinking skills and enquiry-based learning in the child's first language. It is imperative that mother-tongue teachers are included in all school-based training and sent to outside professional development (PD) to ensure they are up to date with pedagogical changes. Administrators often restrict PD funds to mainstream and full-time teachers, leaving mother-tongue teachers out of the provision. Specialist language teachers need to be part of the collaborative planning sessions with mainstream classroom teachers. Too often teachers are released to do their collaborative planning in teams when the students attend specialist classes. There are other permutations possible. However, It needs a commitment from senior administrators who create the timetable and meeting schedules to make it possible.

Teaching in mainstream classes

Teachers should make use of the languages in their classrooms, not limit the discussion to 'English only'. Ask children to explain something to a non-English speaker in his or her mother tongue and then push the boundaries further with encouragement to talk about prior learning and ask questions. A secondary school physics teacher tried this method one day. He asked a Japanese boy to explain a difficult concept to a newcomer in Japanese. The student obliged and explained. The new student responded in Japanese at length and the helpful buddy turned to the teacher and said: 'Oh, now I get it!' Children, not able to express their ideas fully in English, relish the opportunity to show what they know in their mother tongue.

Children functioning in their first language in Early Year classes begin to appreciate that there is a complex structure to their mother tongue. They learn about letters that correlate to sounds they know well. They hear words and can picture objects or scenes in their mind. They recognize the sense of words, phrases and sentences. When a child unfamiliar with English has to learn to read and write in a second language, he does not have the same depth of understanding and learns through repetition. These children often look lost because they are alienated from the language being used in the classroom. In schools where a mother-tongue program is in place children begin to see the difference in languages; they understand that sounds for letters vary, spelling rules vary, scripts vary and cultural contexts vary. Sustaining and developing the mother tongue of a young child is of prime importance in an international school. Some teachers think it is more important to develop mother tongue as a child's first language for reading and writing than English. They believe learning to read and write English should be delayed until it has been developed in the first language. However, most children in international schools do not have the opportunity to learn their mother tongue during the school day. Where mother-tongue lessons are available, most teachers of L1 and L2 agree that children can learn the two languages in tandem, contrary to the myth that there will be brain overload.

The importance of school-wide agreement on the program

Resistance to mother-tongue provision comes from many corners. Senior administrators and middle-management faculty members usually see the curriculum as full and varied. Unless they are multilingual and/or recognize the importance of languages for a student's academic, social and emotional progress, they often perceive the inclusion of mother tongue and additional languages as desirable, but not possible. As a senior administrator in international schools, I have often sat in meetings as the sole defender of a mother-tongue program. In contrast, when I talk to students and parents about mother-tongue provision, they are always supportive. Can it be that administrators are preventing students from reaching their potential and failing to meet the best interests of their families because they have a myopic or mono-cultural view on the importance of languages? The evidence is compelling; why is it ignored?

The International Baccalaureate Organization (IBO) weighs in on this debate and urges schools to incorporate mother-tongue programs into the curriculum.

> The role of language, one's mother tongue, and the study of other languages in this context has a special place in any programme's design. It is through language that we access our own and others' culture. The role of language acquisition and development from early childhood in order to foster bi- and

multi-lingualism is fundamental to any sequence of programmes. (Helen Drennen, former director of academic affairs at IBCA. IBO, 2004)

At IB Diploma level over 80 languages are offered as Language A1. Bilingual diplomas are possible. The IB is constantly evolving and moving towards a better articulation of all three programs. Its full support for a continuum of mother-tongue provision is inevitable. IB schools need to be aligned with this change and investigating how to provide a continuum of mother-tongue programs from the Early Years through to high-school graduation.

There are many ways to recover costs for a mother-tongue program. Some schools have a system where parents pay a proportion of the cost, depending on the number of students in the class. Other schools cover all costs, even when the classes are small, knowing that the class will attract new enrolments from each language group.

In international schools it is possible to timetable mother-tongue lessons as an alternative to the host country language or as an additional language to the host country language. It is possible to offer two or three language options in a curriculum. It is also possible to run a full mother-tongue program after school. The best scenario is to offer mother-tongue lessons during the school day, fully integrated in the curriculum, alongside host country and additional languages.

Quality in MT courses essential

The quality of mother-tongue programs is critical. They must be appropriate for the age and stage of development, consist of enough lessons to provide a rigorous program and be taught by qualified teachers who are native speakers. Children under seven years need frequent and short lessons. A trained kindergarten teacher, who volunteered to teach mother tongue in an international school, argued successfully for daily 30-minute lessons, rather than one or two lessons per week. Her lessons were structured with greetings and open discussion, followed by a main teaching point delivered through a variety of learning activities followed by a song at the end of the lesson.

Almost all mother-tongue teachers describe the same need for a consistent approach to language learning. Perhaps, with so many other factors in flux in an internationally mobile community, the need for regular patterns and structure within the school is comforting. Maria is a six-year-old girl whose father is from Germany and her mother from the Philippines. Although her father speaks German to her at home she is not confident enough to speak in the mother-tongue class at school. The mother-tongue teacher also noticed that Maria was afraid to speak. When the frequency of lessons was changed to daily, Maria's relationship with the teacher became more trusting and her fear disappeared. Since then, her language acquisition has grown rapidly. As children advance in their mother tongue, however, it becomes increasingly difficult to place a non-mother-tongue speaker in a class with fluent speakers.

As an administrator, I have been called to sort out problems for mother-tongue teachers when parents insist on placing a child in a mother-tongue class, but the language is not being spoken at home. We see this when parents have previously placed their children in bilingual schools and when a parent, usually the father, has one language and the mother another language. If the child is not speaking the language at home they are lost in a mother-tongue class with fluent speakers. The teachers often have to revert to English for the sake of the non-mother-tongue students. It does not work: these are the children who look tired and overloaded by the end of the school day. There is often a social and political dimension to this problem. We need to encourage mothers from developing countries, who marry men from the developed world, to use their first language when they raise their children. There is sometimes an imbalance of power in these relationships and advice from teachers could support the mother's need to use her language as the primary one in the home. A fully developed, enriched language is the best foundation for additional languages.

From our experience we have learned that the lesson should be in the same place: in a well-decorated room that feels like a familiar cultural space. At my previous school in London we offered 17 mother-tongue languages. Lessons used to be held all over the school: in a variety of classrooms, in the library, in the corridors and in prefabricated sheds. Then we created the languages floor by dividing large classrooms into 2/3 and 1/3 with a corridor in between. Try it. From every large room you can create two small rooms for up to five students on one side and approximately 15 students on the other. Another option is to convert a residential house into a hive of small- and medium-sized language classrooms. In my current school I inherited an almost complete new secondary school building with large classrooms on each of the six floors. I was able to change the internal walls and create 12 language rooms instead of five large general-purpose rooms. Now we have a 'languages floor' and each room is decorated according to the language group's national identity or identities. This becomes a place where students feel at home once the place is established and children get used to daily lessons with a person they feel is more a family friend than a teacher. Language acquisition needs to be connected to a person, place and time. It becomes an oasis in the day for the children; a time to recharge their batteries.

Reaping the rewards

If we make provision to sustain and develop a child's first language, we provide the foundation and scaffolding for his or her cultural identity, emotional well-being and all future learning. Maurice Carder, a prolific writer and advocate for ESL and mother-tongue provision believes that: '… with good guidance and ethical leadership, international schools can serve as role models (to national systems) in the area of providing successful language programmes for second-language students' (Carder, 2008). Administrators can continue to say the barriers are insurmountable and retain the status quo, where dominant languages are valued over mother-tongue languages to the detriment of their multilingual students, or they can start experimenting with the addition of mother-tongue lessons in their schools. It is a challenge to all 21st century administrators.

Note

1. All references to, or quotes from, parents and teachers are anonymous. They were gathered from families and faculty at the International School of London (2001–2005) and Utahloy International School (2007–2010). Similarly, anecdotes about students have fictitious names to protect the children concerned.

REFERENCES

Carder, M. (2008) The development of ESL provision in Australia, Canada, the USA and England with conclusions for second language models in international schools. *Journal of Research in International Education* 7, 205–232. On WWW at http://jri.sagepub.com. Accessed 26.10.09.

Cummins, J. (1979) Linguistic interdependence and the educational development of bilingual children. *Review of Educational Research* 49, 222.

Cummins, J. (1996) Bilingual education: What does the research say? In J. Cummins (ed.) *Negotiating Identities: Education for Empowerment in a Diverse Society* (pp. 97–133). Los Angeles, CA: California Association for Bilingual Education.

International Baccalaureate Organization (IBO) (2004) *Second Language Acquisition and Mother Tongue Development: Guide for Schools*. Geneva: IBO.

Taylor, L.K. (2008) Of mother tongues and other tongues: The stakes of linguistically inclusive pedagogy in minority contexts. Special Issue: Multilingual Literacies, *Canadian Language Review* 64.

Thomas, W.P. and Collier, V.P. (1997) *School Effectiveness for Language Minority Students*. Washington, DC: National Clearinghouse for English Language Acquisition.

UNESCO (1953) The use of vernacular languages in education. In *Monographs on Fundamental Education*. UNESCO.

About the author

Elaine Whelen studied at the University of Melbourne and completed her BA and MA at the University of Canterbury. This was followed by a year at Christchurch Teachers' College in New Zealand. Her career in education spans over 30 years, including three headships of international schools in Europe, Africa and Asia. Elaine has written articles and presented at numerous conferences to promote inclusion of mother-tongue programs in international schools.

Chapter 21

Native Languages and the International Baccalaureate

LAURA BRIDGESTOCK

Language learning reaches beyond the use of words to impact on culture, identity and international mindedness. This article relates how the global International Baccalaureate community is responding to the challenges of a changing linguistic landscape.

INTRODUCTION

Languages and the International Baccalaureate (IB)

As the school day bursts into life at the American British Academy (ABA) in Muscat, Oman, students file into classes and the corridors are filled with boisterous chatter and enthusiastic greetings. The scene is identical to those played out daily in every corner of the globe, with one crucial difference: the sheer number of languages being spoken would leave almost any visitor, a little ironically, lost for words.

From English and French to Arabic and Chinese, plans are made and schoolwork is dissected in almost every recognizable language on the face of the planet. It resembles a United Nations conference where the delegates all wear school uniform.

Languages have always been at the heart of the IB. You cannot build an international organization without embracing them, and you cannot nurture international mindedness without enabling students to do the same. Beyond that, language is an issue no educator can afford to ignore: studies show that a firm grounding in a first language is essential for academic development, and learning additional languages enhances the learning of the 'mother tongue' as well as broadening a student's worldview.

Much of this is second nature to teachers. After all, as the IB continues to grow and extend access to its programs to students from an ever more diverse range of backgrounds, languages will naturally have a vital part to play. But their impact is further reaching than many realize. For areas ravaged by war, genocide or natural disaster, indigenous languages can be one of the few links left to a dying culture. If systems of education fail to encourage the learning of native languages, they can fall out of use and ultimately exist only as relics.

Tove Skutnabb-Kangas and Robert Phillipson use the emotive term 'linguistic genocide' to describe the effect of ignoring such needs, and believe that the right to a native language and culture should be enshrined as an inviolable human right. The IB's special request languages scheme, and its emphasis on mother-tongue entitlement, attempts to make progress in this direction, but the problem, as any linguist will tell you, is as complex as the myriad languages themselves.

Celebrating linguistic diversity

At ABA in Oman the school's 940 students represent more than 60 nationalities and speak more than 50 languages. Once, this made ABA 'a place where everyone came from somewhere else', but now, says Primary Years Programme ESL teacher Nancy Stauft, it has become a truly international community.

This transformation dates to 21 February 2004, when the school decided to celebrate International Mother Language Day. Since then it has become an annual week-long event including film screenings in a variety of languages, daily multilingual news broadcasts from the school's radio studio, lessons given by teachers in their own native languages and even some where English is banned, forcing students to pool together their collective language skills to act as translators for each other.

Banning English may seem like a step backwards. But Nancy believes encouraging students to use their mother tongue gets them interested in their native language and heritage:

> As teachers we're generally excited by all the different languages our students speak. It's always a surprise to find they're often too shy to use their language. They seem to lack pride in their own culture.

Mother Language Week has changed that – and not just for the week. Placing language centre stage has made teachers aware of different learning styles and backgrounds, and encouraging students to use their mother tongue alongside English has become second nature. In a PYP class creating story books, every second page will be left blank so that students can translate the English, with the help of their families. In chemistry, Middle Years Programme (MYP) and Diploma Programme students create multilingual periodic tables, and in maths translate functions.

There are posters on the walls in every language, with tongue twisters, proverbs, greetings and even animal sounds – as Nancy points out, a cow does not say 'moo' in every language!

'It's completely transformed the way we approach students, and the way students and their families approach the school' she says. 'We have students and parents who are proud to be from Nigeria, for instance, and to speak a special dialect. They feel valued – part of a community.'

The power of words

Around half the students at United World College-USA (UWC-USA) in Montezuma, New Mexico, are not native speakers of English, the school's teaching language. Until recently, the task of improving these students' language skills was left to ESL teachers. Many students felt cut off from a system that seemed to favour native English speakers. 'It's a strong political issue', says English A1 teacher Hannah Tyson. 'Language is power and the second-language students have always felt the first-language students had more power'. Teachers are now running a series of seminars looking at ways of integrating language development into all lessons.

UWC-USA is just one step ahead of an initiative that could soon be IB-wide. Language and learning manager Carol Inugai-Dixon is heading the development of a course that will be open to all IB teachers and will provide guidance for schools coordinating language teaching across the curriculum, with a particular focus on improving support for students learning in a language other than their mother tongue. This initiative reflects the IB's aim of increasing access, to 'enable more students to experience and benefit from an IB education regardless of personal circumstances'. This means viewing growth not just in terms of numbers of schools and students, but social and geographical diversity too.

The IB is also extending the support it provides for students and teachers in languages other than English, French and Spanish. In 2007, the IB Board of Governors increased the number of languages in which resources and services are available to schools, and IB students can take the Language A1 examination in more than 80 different languages, many of which are not available in any other examination system.

English is not enough

It is generally acknowledged that English is more widely studied as a second language than any other, and demand is still growing. But as UK-based linguist David Graddol argues, the growth of English as a 'near-universal skill' has, in fact, increased the importance of speaking other languages. Where once English gave students a competitive edge in the employment market, it has now become a new 'baseline', and it is the extra languages you speak that makes you stand out.

There are other reasons for supporting both mother tongue and second languages. Tell a child to leave their native language at the door, says Mike Bostwick of Katoh

Gakuen Gyoshu High School in Numazu, Japan, and you send a clear message: an important part of me is not valued.

Students who are cut off from their mother tongue are also alienated from a culture, heritage and sometimes even a family. But equally, students who are shut out from other languages are denied a valuable point of access to other cultures and ways of thinking. And as Katoh Gakuen Gyoshu shows, gaining a second language and culture does not have to mean losing another; the two can strengthen each other.

Mike is head of the school's bilingual program, in which students – who are almost all Japanese – are taught in English most of the time, and the majority gain the bilingual IB diploma. When the program was launched in 2001, parents expressed concerns that immersion would alienate students from their own language and culture, but a study carried out in the same year showed the reverse to be true. Compared to students at three nonbilingual Japanese schools, the bilingual students had a more positive attitude towards the English language and English-speaking cultures, and also had a greater awareness of, and identity with, Japan and its culture.

It does not surprise Mike. The school teaches the full national Japanese language syllabus and also runs an additional course in Japanese culture. This gives students a vital route to understand and appreciate a second language and culture. He believes: 'If you don't see or experience a culture other than your own, you can't compare it to anything. Encountering another culture doesn't just broaden perspectives, it sharpens distinctions – even the ones we didn't know were there.'

Reviving culture

This philosophy has proved even more revolutionary for Murray Bridge High School in Murray Bridge, Australia. The school works closely with the local Ngarrindjeri Aboriginal community to teach its language and culture in MYP classes, from specific classes in grammar, vocabulary and sentence construction to Ngarrindjeri units in art, science and English. Local primary schools are running similar initiatives, with the aim of reviving a language falling out of use as English becomes increasingly prevalent among Ngarrindjeri students in Australian schools.

Not all schools run bilingual programs, but the concept of language as a tool for inquiry, rather than an end in itself, is at the very heart of the IB approach. The new PYP language scope and sequence document, due in February 2009, is aimed at all PYP teachers. 'Language underlies all learning', says Sandy Paton, PYP curriculum manager. 'It provides a vehicle for inquiry and, in turn, language skills are best developed in the both structured and informal inquiries.'

When the University Laboratory School in Baton Rouge, Louisiana, USA, introduced the PYP in 2005, PYP coordinator Christelle Thompson rethought the way she approached languages. 'I went from teaching my French curriculum in isolation, to an approach that takes into account all the different units of inquiry', she says.

When her second-grade class study animals, they learn how to describe and talk about them in French. When the fourth grade start a unit on measuring and analyzing change, French lessons may focus on weather variation. 'Interaction is essential', she says, 'as is making issues significant to students and relating them to a global perspective'. The final criterion, languages should be fun – something every teacher and student can certainly relate to.

Increasing access

Extending access to IB programs to the greatest possible number of students is not always simply a case of nurturing minority languages. In Ecuador, a government-led initiative to gain IB authorization for a state school in each of the country's 22 provinces has led to the development of a beginner-level English course.

IB language courses were already offered in 11 other languages, but no demand for English at this level had existed. The scarcity of second-language teaching in Ecuador's state sector meant schools lacked teachers of the required level to offer the English B course.

To meet the language Group 2 requirements, Simon Roberts, subject area manager for languages Groups 1 and 2, travelled to Quito to run workshops training teachers for the new beginner-level course.

'There's a perception that English is taught everywhere in the world and that it's just not needed at this level', he said. 'But as we've found, that's not true.'

About the author

Laura Bridgestock is a journalist who has written extensively for the IB World Magazine, among other titles, and is currently studying for an MA at University College London. This article first appeared in the January 2009 edition of the IB World Magazine, and is reprinted here with the kind permission of its author and the IBO.

Chapter 22

If You Ask a Silly Question You Sometimes Get a Serious Answer

EMILY MUENI MUNYOKI

This light-hearted account of language learning downplays the efforts the author made to master each language as the opportunity presented itself. Most of the world is bilingual or multilingual; and this is the story of how one young Kenyan girl learned five languages. (And we are told she is working on her sixth.)

THE QUESTION

'So … do you speak African?' Seriously, I must say that this question really made me wonder if I missed a very important history lesson on the origin of the 'African' language! This thought was soon followed by a feeling of annoyance at the ignorance of the unfortunate individual who obviously thought that Africa was one big country and the local language was called African.

Well, I patiently explained that I came from East Africa, Kenya actually, and I spoke Kamba, which is one of about 40 different languages spoken there. 'Oh, I know a Kenyan word', my questioner hastened to say, 'It is hakunamatata!' (It is amazing how many people have been to Mombasa.) Well … hakuna matata (two words not one, thank you very much) is Swahili, a language we Kenyans use to communicate with one another because if we all spoke our home language, we would not understand one another, I continued to explain. 'Really?' Yes really. It would be like you speaking German and your companion, Greek! I do not think you would get very far.

'So … how come you speak English?' was the next logical question. Because, and I do not mean this in a negative sense, we were brainwashed by the British! 'So … how many languages *do* you speak?' Ummm … 1,2,3,4,5. 'Wow … you are really multilingual. How lucky!' After a while I started to appreciate that many people spoke only one language and it really is a wonderful thing to be able to speak more than one language, to be multilingual. 'So … how did this happen?'

THE RESPONSE

Mother tongues: Kamba and English

Kamba was spoken mainly when we visited our relatives up country during the school holidays three times a year. My mother also spoke Kamba with us children at home in Nairobi, but my father, who had studied abroad for a while in Manchester, England, preferred speaking English with us. I know he thought he was doing us a favour. As both of my parents worked full time, we had a nanny (actually we had quite a few!) who was of our tribe and spoke Kamba with us. One of them, I remember, was a wonderful nanny who scared us half to death with the most terrifying bedtime stories ever told. But we loved them! Looking back, I can say that I learned most of my Kamba from our nannies.

Doing homework with my mother was interesting and frightening too, because, since Kenya was a former British colony, all education, including text books, were in English, not my mother's first language. We came home from school and, after a tea-time break, we had to sit at the table and do our homework in both Kamba and English under the supervision of my mother. There was a lot of explaining to do, and an equal amount of frustration going on in both languages. My mother stuck to Kamba unless there were terms that came across more clearly in English, which had already become the dominant language for us children as we were obliged to speak, read and write it all day at school. I have always enjoyed reading for pleasure and as a child I read a great deal, always in English. Through this I built up my vocabulary, improved my grammar and English became the language I am now most comfortable with. I grew up speaking English for the simple reason that it was the most popular language spoken in my environment: at home with my siblings, in school with the teachers and school mates, and during play with the children in the neighbourhood. I was further helped by all the exciting children's programs imported from the United States (I loved Kermit the frog) and Britain. This was not at all a unique situation; it was the same for a whole generation of Kenyans and continues to be so.

National language: Swahili

Swahili was different. It took real effort to learn, unlike English and Kamba. We never spoke it at home or when playing with the children in the neighbourhood;

there we spoke in English. Although there were some programs on TV and radio in Swahili, we seldom watched them or listened to the Swahili radio station, because we had a choice. Of course, I picked up words and expressions, and when I was sent to the shops for things like milk, bread, sugar and other daily necessities, I spoke Swahili to the shopkeeper. It was also considered polite to do so because not everyone in Kenya has a formal education in English, and everybody is exposed to Swahili through the media to some extent and it is the language of many small businesses, especially traders. So as not to embarrass anyone by assuming that they have been to school and learned English, we speak Swahili.

I was confronted with Swahili formally when I started school in the Standard One class at the age of six. We had a textbook with pictures and English words, so we started with vocabulary building and continued with grammar exercises, group reading and the writing of compositions. This system carried on until Standard Six. It was very formal and no real effort was made, as far as I remember, to make it interesting or exciting, but I did learn enough to be an effective communicator. Unfortunately, Swahili was not included in the final exams, which I thought was a big mistake.

Two years later in secondary school I was confronted with Swahili again. This time around the lessons were more formal and extremely boring (the fear of detention for being caught sleeping while the lesson was going on kept me awake!), with grammar exercises, reading and so on, without any effort on the teacher's part to make the language interesting for those of us who had lost touch with it. I dropped it as a subject in my second year. Today, I can communicate in Swahili and even read texts if they are not too complicated, but there is certainly room for growth.

Sign language: The fun begins

When I was in my early 20s, a good friend of mine was very interested in learning languages. She tried to get me interested, but at the time I thought three was enough. When she became involved in learning sign language, however, and because it was completely different from any language I had ever come across (e.g. French at school and Italian from my first boyfriend), I could not resist. She was a wonderful teacher and our friendship made it easy for me to keep the interest going.

She taught me the alphabet that in Kenyan sign language is done with one hand. I practised as often as possible to get the speed that is necessary if you come across a word that you do not know and have to spell it, for example, while translating a program for a deaf person. She also gave me copies every week with new words to practise at home, after which she tested me before giving me the next worksheets. Practice at home also meant standing in front of a mirror to make sure that the signs looked clear and correct. It also helped me to overcome any shyness in using the facial expressions, gestures and body language that came along with some words, such as 'a pregnant woman', 'a fat child' and the phrase 'What a horrible thing to do!' To gain speed, I would listen to a song on the radio or listen to the news and translate simultaneously as best I could.

My friend also took me along to visit some people she had become acquainted with, members of the deaf community in Nairobi. After four months of practice at home and communicating with these new acquaintances, my friend and teacher decided that I was ready to translate a 40-minute lecture for our deaf friends. First, I had another lesson to learn, namely that you need to wear the right clothes, which meant clothes that would not distract or draw attention away from the signing: one colour only and no flowery or printed background for your hands. I was nervous and apprehensive and surprised how fast the time went by when I was signing! I guess it was a success because after that, I was on an unofficial list of translators for our new friends. Learning sign language was very interesting and fun because of the teacher I had and because of the unusual method, if I may call it that, of learning a language. So now I had language number four!

Welcome to Germany

In December 1995, I moved to Germany for personal reasons. Arriving in winter was a bad idea because I was suddenly confronted with too many things to deal with, from extreme winter conditions to a very different culture and a language that sounded strange to me. Pronunciation was a big problem because it required the use of different parts of the mouth, the words often coming from the back of the mouth close to the throat. It was not a very nice-sounding language to me, I often thought, as I struggled not to spit or sound like I was gargling when practising my vocabulary. After about two years I joined a language school. This was another mistake: there I found that I had in the previous years picked up some words and expressions that were not grammatically correct, and my pronunciation was not always good either. This sometimes led to embarrassing situations. We had three different teachers – two for grammar and the third for everyday language use. We went through a lot of grammar exercises, role play, games and even singing and I did manage to unlearn most of my 'bad' German and discover muscles in my mouth and tongue to use for proper pronunciation of this now not very strange-sounding language. I also watched TV programs, mostly German soap operas as one of my teachers had advised me to do, and I was pleased when I started to understand whole sentences without having to look in the dictionary. My biggest problem was finding someone to practise with, as strange as that sounds, because all my German friends preferred to practise their *English* with me.

However, three years ago I went back to working in my profession as a preschool teacher in an international/bilingual school where 50% of the children are from German-speaking families. For the first time I was forced to use my German language skills with the children as well as with those parents who did not speak English. I always made sure, especially before parent–teacher conferences, to check the dictionary and to ask my German colleagues if I was getting across the important information in a clear, an understandable and accurate manner. This experience has helped me to be even more emphatic when working with children who come to the pre-school with absolutely no English and no understanding of why on earth their parents were 'doing this to them!' At an ECIS language forum in February of 2008, I learned what has become a very special expression to me, and that is 'responsible code switching'. So I do not hesitate to speak German to those lovely children when I find it necessary to do so, no matter what their well-meaning parents think or say to me. But I make sure I speak English as well. In September 2008, I took a German language test for the first time and I did quite well. The test involved listening, reading, writing and speaking. It finally convinced me that I had done the right thing in trying to become proficient in this language too – language number five. I am ashamed to admit that my German language skills are now better than my Kamba (please do not tell my mom I said this), and my Swahili and sign language skills.

Or, to be brief ...

No, I do not speak African (not to be confused with Afrikaans, derived from Dutch and spoken in South Africa) because no such language exists. I am a Mkamba and Kamba is my mother tongue, the first of my five languages.

About the author

Emily Mueni Munyoki was born in Nairobi, Kenya. After graduating from the Kenya High School in Nairobi, she attended the Kindergarten Headmistresses Association, a private college and obtained a Diploma in Early Childhood Education in 1990. After working at Kestrel Manor School in Nairobi in 1995 she moved to Germany where she worked as an English Language Teacher for Studio Mondiale, a Language School before returning to her Profession. She taught at The International Preschool Seeheim in Germany from September 2005 and a year later was appointed Deputy Principal until December 2009.